The Complete Idiot's Guide Marriage Reference

Five Qualities of a GREAT Marriage

G for **Good** communication

R for **Real** partnership

E for **Effort**

A for **Adaptability**

T for **Total** commitment

Ten Steps to Clear Communication

1. Figure out what you want to say. Before you talk with your spouse, make sure you know what you want to tell him or her to minimize possible misunderstandings.

2. Decide what you need from your spouse. You're more likely to get your need met, whether it be a hug or an answer to a question, if you know what you want.

3. Use good judgment in timing. Is your spouse sick or preparing for a big meeting at work? Consider your partner's state of mind when choosing a time to talk.

4. Make eye contact. Your spouse will be more likely to listen and hear you if the two of you are looking right at each other.

5. Get your spouse's undivided attention. You will not be heard if your spouse is thinking about something else when you're trying to talk with him or her.

6. Be a good listener. By being attentive to your spouse, you will have a more productive discussion.

7. Confirm that you were heard. Ask your spouse if he or she understands fully what you just said. Then, and only then, will your spouse be able to respond properly.

8. Rephrase what your spouse has told you. This will let him or her know for sure that you've heard what was said.

9. Schedule a better discussion time if necessary. Sometimes it's just not possible to get your spouse's attention at the exact moment that you want it.

10. Remember that communication is a two-way street. If you both agree to follow these steps, you will both benefit and strengthen your relationship.

alpha
books

tear here

Ground Rules for Resolving Conflict

1. Set aside enough time to work through a conflict.
2. Have a clear goal.
3. Don't use the accusatory word "You," such as "You did…" or "You made me feel…."
4. Use the word "I" to describe how you feel.
5. Stay on target and only discuss the issue at hand.
6. Avoid using one-liners, such as "You're impossible" or "I'm leaving you."
7. Remember that you are really both on the same side—your marriage.

How to Make Your Daily Reunions Special

1. Greet each other warmly. Stop whatever activity you're doing and walk to the door to greet your spouse. It might seem trite, but the effort will make both of you feel special and taken care of.
2. Take a few minutes to find out how your spouse's day was. We are all extremely busy, but this small effort can make a huge difference. Instead of two strangers trying to get things done, you will be partners working together to create a warm family environment.
3. Reconnect to your spouse after a day apart. Share a warm hug, deliver a kiss, or pour a refreshing glass of ice water for him or her.

Forgiveness Box

Which box best describes you?

Quick to anger and slow to forgive	Quick to anger and quick to forgive
Slow to anger and slow to forgive	Slow to anger and quick to forgive

Your goal is to be slow to anger and quick to forgive.

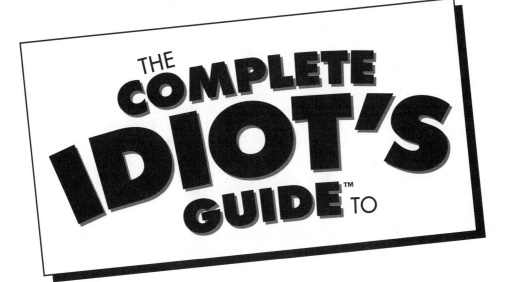

THE COMPLETE IDIOT'S GUIDE™ TO

the Perfect Marriage

by Hilary Rich
and Helaina Laks Kravitz, M.D.

alpha books

A Division of Macmillan Reference USA
A Simon & Schuster Macmillan Company
1633 Broadway, New York, NY 10019-6785

Copyright © 1997 Hilary Rich and Helaina Laks Kravitz, M.D.

All rights reserved. No part of this book shall be reproduced, stored in a retrieval system, or transmitted by any means, electronic, mechanical, photocopying, recording, or otherwise, without written permission from the publisher. No patent liability is assumed with respect to the use of the information contained herein. Although every precaution has been taken in the preparation of this book, the publisher and author assume no responsibility for errors or omissions. Neither is any liability assumed for damages resulting from the use of information contained herein. For information, address Alpha Books, 1633 Broadway, 7th Floor, New York, NY 10019-6785.

International Standard Book Number: 0-02-861729-0
Library of Congress Catalog Card Number: 97-071173

99 98 97   8 7 6 5 4 3 2 1

Interpretation of the printing code: the rightmost number of the first series of numbers is the year of the book's printing; the rightmost number of the second series of numbers is the number of the book's printing. For example, a printing code of 97-1 shows that the first printing occurred in 1997.

Printed in the United States of America

Publisher
Theresa Murtha

Editorial Manager
Gretchen Henderson

Editor
Nancy Warner

Production Editor
Laura Uebelhor

Cover Designer
Mike Freeland

Illustrator
Judd Winick

Designer
Glenn Larsen

Indexer
Sandy Henselmeier

Production Team
Angela Calvert
Cindy Fields
Daniella Raderstorf
Laure Robinson

Contents at a Glance

Contents

Foreword

Throughout the life cycle, from birth to death, relationships mold and define who we are. For many of us, our most important relationships can have a far-reaching impact on our personal happiness and success in life. As we mature, it usually becomes clear that there is no single, flawless, perfect individual who can meet our every need. Ultimately, our desire for love and companionship leads to a new understanding whereby our strengths and weaknesses find those of another and, through work, can form a nurturing relationship.

A good marriage can be the foundation of a happy, content life. Unfortunately, the opposite is also true; a troubled marriage may be a significant source of stress and hardship. In fact, problems with relationships are frequent reasons why individuals seek help from mental health professionals.

With such high stakes resting on the health and well-being of our most important relationship, it is surprising that most of us do not do more to understand and plan for the challenges and rewards of marriage. Many of us spend far more time on more trivial areas of our lives, such as hobbies or managing finances, than we do trying to understand the process of sharing life with another person. This may be due in part to the huge complexity of this task. Fully understanding the challenges and dynamics of marriage is a lifelong education that, as this book describes, can be a joyfully shared journey.

Hillary Rich and Dr. Helaina Kravitz offer us a comprehensive travel guide for making the most out of this adventure called marriage. Like a good travel manual, this step-by-step guide to marriage will help readers make the most out of the familiar and prepare for the unexpected. Moreover, this book offers individuals the chance to take marriage into their own hands, teaching common sense and insightful techniques for controlling some obvious and not-so-obvious aspects of coexisting with a mate.

On this journey, we move through all of the major areas of long-term relationships, including getting started, understanding and developing expectations, improving communications, identifying and managing conflicts, dealing with shared finances and chores, and parenthood. Later in the text, we confront some of the potential problems that can have devastating effects, including adapting together to life's stresses such as unemployment, illness, alcoholism, and infidelity, and how to get help from others when necessary. Each section reinforces the major points, presenting useful skills and offering pointed advice. Going beyond a set of lessons, this book will also serve as a useful reference that we can call on from time to time.

Since marriage represents one of our most significant undertakings and responsibilities, it seems to be a worthwhile investment to take some time to consider its many facets and challenges. In fact, not doing so may be ill advised. Many may feel that once married, the outcome is predetermined and out of our control. As this book clearly describes, marriage is a work in progress in which each partner can have an active role in its success. Within these chapters are many of the secrets to that success.

Scott M. Fishman, M.D.

Assistant Professor of Psychiatry, Harvard Medical School
Assistant Professor of Anesthesia, Harvard Medical School
Medical Director, MGH Pain Center, Massachusetts General Hospital, Boston, MA

Dr. Scott Fishman is a subspecialist in pain management, having been residency trained in internal medicine and psychiatry as well as having completed subspecialty anethesia fellowship training in pain management. He is the Medical Director of the MGH Pain Center at Massachusetts General Hospital in Boston and serves on the faculty of the Harvard Medical School as Assistant Professor of Anesthesia and Assistant Professor of Psychiatry.

Introduction

Welcome to the start of a whole new life! As you read along, you'll learn many secrets for having the marriage of your dreams. At first you may not notice the differences, but soon you'll start solving problems more easily and handling conflicts more productively. As a result, you'll have a more satisfying relationship than you ever thought possible. If you're determined to have an extraordinary marriage, you've come to the right place. We'll give you all the tools you need.

How to Use This Book

In **Part 1: You Can Have the Marriage You Want** we show you how to give yourself a relationship makeover. We tell you the necessary qualities for a great marriage. We show you how to make the most out of every day with your spouse. And we show you how to keep the passion alive in your marriage.

In **Part 2: Tools for Success** we discuss communication. We also show you how to make the most of your time with your spouse. We show you how to identify conflicts before they become blow-ups and give you ground rules for resolving those conflicts. And finally, we discuss the role of ongoing forgiveness in your relationship.

In **Part 3: Daily Hurdles** we talk about the challenges that you and your spouse face daily. We show you why money is such an emotional issue and how to organize a budget. We show you ways for creating sexual compatibility. We also discuss housework and how to divide it up in a fair way. And we give you strategies for dealing with your family and your in-laws.

In **Part 4: We're a Family Now** we discuss how children affect your marriage. First, we provide guidelines that will help you decide whether to have children. We show you how a child will change your relationship and also share techniques to make that change a positive one. And we discuss ways to create a happy family.

In **Part 5: Transitions** we discuss changes in your life and how to make them as smooth as possible. We discuss how your job affects your marriage and show you how work and marriage *can* mix. We give you guidelines to help you decide whether to move, and we show you ways to make the move as easy as possible. We discuss caring for aging parents and the importance of supporting each other during this time. And we talk about the special challenges of second marriages and how to make the most out of your past experiences.

In **Part 6: Bridge Over Troubled Waters** we discuss difficult situations that some couples face. We explore how an illness affects a marriage. We explain what an addiction is and tell you where to turn for help. We discuss infidelity, including deciding whether the relationship is over and how to move beyond the pain. And we help you understand what therapy can do to help you work on your relationship.

In **Part 7: Planning Your Future Together** we show you how to create a vision for the future and give you a goal planner to help you reach your goals. We review the qualities of a wonderful marriage, and we show you how to make the most out of your past, present, and future together. By the end of this book, you'll have the marriage of your dreams!

Extras

To help you get the most out of this book, you'll see the following special information boxes scattered throughout the book:

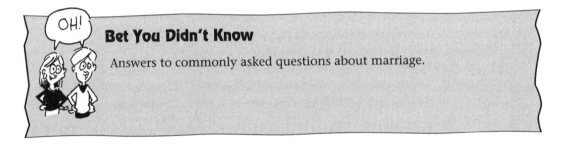

Bet You Didn't Know

Answers to commonly asked questions about marriage.

Think Twice
Pitfalls to avoid in your marriage.

The Spice Rack
Intimacy tips to spice up your relationship.

Soul Mates
Team building and communication tips.

Acknowledgments

We would like to express our appreciation to the many couples who have shared their stories with us through the years. We changed all of the names and details to protect their anonymity. We each counsel couples independently, but for your ease of reading, we have written as if we see the couples together.

We would also like to thank Valerie Herman, M.D., and Todd Berliner, Ph.D., for their assistance on the manuscript. And a special thank-you to our husbands for their love and support.

Special Thanks from the Publisher to the Technical Editor

The Complete Idiot's Guide to the Perfect Marriage was reviewed by an expert who not only checked the technical accuracy of what you'll learn in this book, but also provided invaluable insight and suggestions. Our special thanks are extended to Cheryl A. Spurlock.

Cheryl A. Spurlock, LCSW, DCSW, received her Bachelor of Science in Psychology from Purdue University in 1971, and her Master of Social Work from San Diego State University in 1980. From 1981 to 1988 she was employed at El Centro Community Mental Health Center in Los Angeles as a psychotherapist with a focus on the Hispanic patient.

In 1984, she received her License in Clinical Social Work; in 1985, she received her Certification from the national Association of Social Workers' Academy of Certified Social Workers.

Ms. Spurlock was hired in 1988 by UCLA's Neuropsychiatric Institute & Hospital in the Adult Psychiatry Inpatient Service to perform psychosocial assessments, discharge planning, and crisis family and couples counseling. In 1993, she was asked to develop UCLA NPI&H's Adult Partial Hospitalization Program. She currently is their Program Director for Ambulatory Services, which include both partial hospital and outpatient programs.

Ms. Spurlock successfully sat for the Diplomat in Clinical Social Work in 1994. In addition, she is a Faculty Field Advisor for Smith College School of Social Work in Massachusetts. She has maintained a private psychotherapy practice for adults since 1984. Besides specializing in the treatment of adult survivors of child abuse through individual and group psychotherapy, Ms. Spurlock works with numerous couples with relationship issues.

Part 1
You Can Have the Marriage You Want

In the following section, we begin by giving you new ways to think about your marriage. We'll talk about what a "perfect" marriage is—and isn't. We'll help you identify and overcome obstacles to a "perfect" marriage. We'll point out ways to make the most of your day-to-day life with your spouse. And, you'll learn how to create passion on a regular basis.

Chapter 1

Profile of the Perfect Marriage

A great marriage can make your life extraordinary. A marriage is a nurturing partnership in which both people feel cared for and supported. You develop shared memories and have a lifelong companion who knows you better than anyone else. It may seem like it should come effortlessly. In fact, having a thoroughly satisfying relationship takes time and effort—but the rewards are priceless. Nothing can make your life as spectacular as a wonderful marriage. This chapter will show you how to invest in your marriage to make it better than you ever dreamed possible. We will point out the five essential qualities of a great marriage so that you can start making your marriage better today.

What's So Great About Marriage Anyway?

Being married has many advantages over not being married. Marriage can give you many things that you can't get anywhere else: a constant companion, a good friend, and someone you can really be yourself around. Your spouse knows you better than anyone else. He or she has the potential to really comfort you when times are hard. He or she has seen you in your worst mood. There is stability in marriage that allows us to fulfill our potential as human beings.

The Best Investment You'll Ever Make

All marriages, no matter how good, can be made better. A good marriage has some basic qualities. Both partners are totally committed to the relationship and are willing to invest time and energy. They communicate effectively with each other and know how to resolve their differences. And they have learned to be flexible. There is no right way to be married. Many kinds of partnerships can work out great. However, there is a wrong way to be married—by not investing in the relationship.

Think Twice

Don't get lazy about your relationship. If you stopped investing in your savings account, you wouldn't be very surprised when you had very little money in it. Relationships need a regular investment of time and effort to grow as well.

If you consulted a good financial planner about investing in your future, here's what he or she would tell you: Invest money regularly. The types of financial investments you make will change at different times in your life. When you are younger, you might have more money invested in riskier growth stocks. As you reach retirement age, you might switch your assets to more secure investments. How you invest will change with your life circumstances, but you must continually invest in some way in order to ensure a secure financial future.

These same principles hold true in marriage. Both partners must invest regularly in the relationship to make it flourish. There might be times when it's easy to have a great partnership (like when the stock market is soaring and you're making money without even trying). And there will be times when, even though you are putting forth a lot of effort, things feel like they're going downhill (like when the stock market dips). But hanging in for the long haul will virtually guarantee success.

Bet You Didn't Know

OH!

Q: If my relationship doesn't come easily, does that mean I'm with the wrong partner?

A: Many people think a relationship is only good if it comes easily. In fact, most good relationships require a lot of work. It takes a daily investment of time, communication, and being there when your partner needs you to have a great marriage.

You can make your marriage great if you are willing to invest regularly in the relationship. As you are reading this book, keep in mind that a GREAT marriage depends on good communication, real partnership, effort, adaptability, and total commitment.

Which Marriage Would You Rather Be in?

In this section, we will show you how two couples deal with the same situations. Both couples have been married for 11 years, have a similar household income, have two children, and live down the street from each other. Yet, their marriages could not be more different from each other.

Car Crash

Margaret was nervous while driving home because she had been in a car accident. She wasn't hurt, but she knew that Pete was going to be furious. The rear end of her car had been badly damaged. The other driver had been driving too fast in a residential neighborhood, but she had this bad feeling that Pete would blame her for it. While she was driving home, she tried to figure out what to say so that Pete would be less angry.

Margaret got home, badly shaken, but more worried about what her husband would say. She walked in the door and said, "Hi, I'm home." Pete mumbled, "You're late," without looking away from the TV set. Margaret blurted out, "The car was hit by a speeding driver."

Now Pete looked up. "What do you mean, you got in a car accident?" Margaret nodded, almost in tears. "I can't believe you! Why didn't you watch where you were going? You're coming up with the extra money if our insurance rates go up!" Margaret burst into tears, ran into the bedroom, and slammed the door. They didn't talk all night, and both went to bed furious with each other.

Think Twice
Don't get so caught up in your own emotions that you forget about how your spouse might be feeling. When you're angry, take the time and energy to change your perspective and consider his or her needs.

Kate's experience went differently. She was really nervous while driving home because she had been in a car accident. She wasn't hurt, but the rear end of her car had been badly damaged. She felt terrible that she had contributed somewhat to the accident. She hadn't stopped completely at the intersection. But, then again, the other driver shouldn't have been going so fast in a residential neighborhood.

She got home, looking pale, and Daniel was immediately concerned. He asked her what was wrong. She told him she was in a car accident. He immediately interrupted, asked if she was alright, and gave her a big hug. Then she told him how it might have been partly her fault and described what happened, but Daniel told her not to worry about it. Kate then started fretting about how much it would cost and when and where they would get the car fixed. Daniel stopped her mid-sentence and suggested they order in pizza for dinner. He wanted her to have a chance to relax before thinking about the logistics of their damaged automobile. Kate felt a lot better after dinner, and they tackled the details of the problem together.

Daniel and Kate are real partners. When Kate was in a car accident, Daniel thought about her, not about the car. He was really there for her and put aside any of his own concerns about how they would pay for the damages. On the other hand, if Pete felt any concern toward Margaret, he was unable to show it effectively. He treated her like she was an enemy who had done something wrong. It's clear that Pete and Margaret don't feel they are on the same team.

Bad Day at Work

Pete came home after a horrible day at work. He had been called into his boss' office and had been chewed out. All he wanted to do when he got home was have some peace and quiet. When he got home, Margaret started asking him if he could come home early the next Wednesday because she had a meeting. Pete snapped at her, "Stop making demands on me. I can't possibly commit to that." Margaret was frustrated and started whining that she really needed to go to this meeting and it wasn't fair that he wouldn't come home early. Pete exploded and told her he didn't want to hear about her problems—he had his own problems. He stormed out of the house, slamming the door behind him. Pete came home after midnight, drunk, and stumbled into bed. Both he and Margaret slept terribly and felt even worse in the morning.

Soul Mates
One of the most powerful things that marriage gives you is shared memory. A memory can be funny, like the time one of you wore mismatched shoes to an important event, or very serious, such as when you struggled through a serious illness. Every memory you share with your spouse and every new one you create has the potential to bring the two of you closer than ever before!

When Daniel came home after a horrible day at work, he had a very different experience. Kate greeted him warmly on his arrival and asked how his day was. He told her that it was horrible and he was in a terrible mood. Kate asked if he wanted to talk about it. He said no, it would pass, but in fact, he just wanted some quiet time to himself. Kate suggested that he see a movie to get his mind off of things at work. Daniel thought it was a good idea and did so. When he came back, he was in a better mood. He went to sleep early, and by the next morning he felt fine. Kate needed to ask him about coming home early next Wednesday night, but she knew they would have a chance to talk about it another time when he wasn't in such a bad mood.

Daniel and Kate are excellent communicators. Daniel knew how to tell Kate what was bothering him and also to ask for time to himself. Kate knew she needed to wait until the next day to ask him a question. Timing is important in good communication. On the other hand, Pete did not know how to ask for what he needed, and Margaret just added to the problem. Things escalated, when all Pete probably wanted was a little sympathy and some quiet time. Learning how to communicate effectively is vital in a great marriage.

Fighting the Flu

On the day before they were supposed to leave for their annual vacation, Margaret came down with a horrible case of the flu. She had a fever, chills, and severe muscle aches. She left work early, hoping that she would be able to sleep off her symptoms and still go on the trip, but the symptoms only got worse. She was really ill and had no energy to pack, let alone get on an airplane. Pete was furious. "How could you do this? I've been looking forward to this vacation. Our airline tickets are non-refundable! You always ruin everything." Now Margaret felt terrible, not only physically but emotionally. For months afterward, Pete talked about how disappointed he was.

Kate also came down with the flu the day before she and Daniel were supposed to take their annual vacation. When she saw that she had a high fever, she called Daniel at work. Daniel told her to rest and not to worry about the vacation; he also said he would come home early that evening. When Daniel got home, he realized just how sick Kate was. He went to the grocery store to stock up on canned soup and fun magazines. The next day, Daniel called his travel agent to see what they could do about canceling or rescheduling their vacation. He wrote down the alternatives so that he could discuss them with Kate when she was feeling better. It took Kate five days to recover, and then Daniel developed symptoms. They felt lucky that Kate had developed symptoms before they left for their vacation, or they would have spent all of their time in a hotel room.

Kate and Daniel are flexible. They were unhappy that they missed their planned vacation, but they were able to handle the disappointment and look at the bright side. Pete, on the other hand, couldn't control his own feelings of disappointment. Margaret had certainly not planned to be sick, and everything he said just made her feel worse.

Soul Mates
When your spouse isn't feeling well, think of it as an opportunity to take care of him or her. Your efforts will be greatly appreciated.

Qualities in a Great Marriage

It's likely that you would rather have a marriage like Daniel and Kate's than Pete and Margaret's. Daniel and Kate are true partners. They care about each other and are supportive in difficult situations. What exactly is their secret? And what can you learn from them that will help you in your own marriage? Here are the five qualities that are absolutely necessary for a marriage to be GREAT:

G for Good communication

R for Real partnership

E for Effort

A for Adaptability

T for Total commitment

Good Communication

All good marriages have one thing in common: good communication. And, without exception, all bad marriages have communication problems. Communicating involves being available to talk, really listen to the other person, and say what you need to as kindly as you can. In the previous examples, Kate and Daniel demonstrated excellent communication skills. They were available for each other and were able to express themselves. When Daniel had a bad day at work, he was able to tell Kate that he wanted some time alone, instead of being grouchy or argumentative. On the other hand, Pete took out his frustrations with work on Margaret because he was unable to let her know how he felt and tell her what he needed.

Think Twice
Don't assume that good communication always means you have to talk about something right at the moment it's happening. Sometimes good communication means you won't talk about something now, but will talk about it at a time when you can really have a meaningful conversation.

Communicating effectively is such an important tool in a great marriage that we devote all of Chapter 5 to the topic. For now, remember that the core of communication consists of three things:

1. Be available to talk to your spouse. Both of you need to be engaged in the conversation to communicate effectively.

2. Really listen to the other person. Let your spouse know if it's not a good time to talk.

3. Express yourself as kindly as you can. By speaking kindly, you create an atmosphere of warmth and closeness. This will make it easier for your spouse to really hear what you have to say.

If you start right away doing these three things, you will give yourself a head start in becoming a communication expert.

Real Partnership

The core of a wonderful marriage is creating a real partnership. Both people are equally valuable to the relationship. The two individuals are part of a team. Both people share everything that happens to one person, whether it's good or bad. Each person doesn't look to blame each other when something goes wrong, but instead looks for ways to make it better.

Imagine that you wanted to play on your company baseball team. You would need to commit to making all of the team practices and to working hard. In short, you would need to be a team player. Being a valuable player on a team means caring about the success of the team above all else. If you score a home run but the team loses, you still lose and need to work with the team to do better next time. Similarly in a marriage, you need to do what makes you both happy. Say you get a great job opportunity in San Francisco, but your spouse works in New York. If you're single, it might be a great opportunity. If you're married, you need to think about what's best for you as a couple.

Soul Mates
Always remember: In the middle of an argument, you are both on the same side—your relationship!

Kate and Daniel's marriage seems so attractive because they are clearly teammates. When Kate was in a car accident, Daniel, although concerned about the financial implications of the crash, made it clear that he was worried about Kate first and foremost. Pete, on the other hand, undermined the sense of partnership by treating Margaret like an enemy. In a great marriage, as part of a team, you need to take care of your partner as much as you take of yourself.

Effort

Many people put a great deal of effort into their hobbies, their exercise schedule, even in making sure their car is running right. But they expect their marriage (the single most important determining factor in their own happiness) to simply run by itself!

You need to invest time and energy into your relationship to make it great. Daniel immediately looked into alternative vacations plans when Kate was sick. He didn't put this off because he knew how important having time with Kate was. Daniel also helped her figure out the best solution to getting the car fixed. Pete didn't invest time or energy into helping Margaret or their relationship. But he probably spent just as much time, if not more, being angry and self-absorbed. The effort you put into your marriage is the best investment you can make in your own life. You will get tenfold back in return.

Think Twice
Don't forget about your spouse when scheduling your time. If your evenings are fully booked with committees, workouts, and meetings, how much time will you actually spend with your spouse this week? Remember to put your spouse on the schedule, too!

Soul Mates

When you're feeling disappointed about something not working out the way you planned, try to think about the larger goal of having a great relationship. Recognize that just because things didn't go as planned doesn't mean there aren't positive aspects to look for!

Adaptability

People who are flexible are generally happier than people who aren't flexible. Kate and Daniel did not plan for an automobile accident, or for Kate to have the flu the day before a planned vacation. But they were flexible enough to handle their disappointment and continue to focus on their relationship and caring for each other. Pete, on the other hand, was completely inflexible and only thought about how his plans were being ruined. Unexpected events are part of life. Learning how to absorb disappointment and be flexible are very valuable life skills that will enhance your marriage.

Total Commitment

You need to be thoroughly committed to your marriage. You are choosing to be with your partner forever. It means sticking with this person through good times and bad. If either of you is less than 100 percent committed, the strength of your relationship will be undermined.

It's easy to feel committed to your spouse when things are going well. You feel like you are part of a winning team and that you are getting a lot out of the relationship. It's much more of a challenge to feel totally committed to your marriage when things aren't going so well and you feel despair about your partnership. It's common to feel angry and overwhelmed. In a desperate moment, some people even think that it might be best to just walk away from the marriage. Focusing on the solution, rather than the problem, shows your spouse that you are committed to the relationship.

Soul Mates

When you and your spouse are going through a difficult time, let him or her know that you are committed to the relationship. It will remind both of you that your marriage is long-term and the current problem is short-term.

Imagine if you were grumpy all the time because you weren't quite sure if you should have joined your company baseball team. Surely, your teammates would notice. You would drag everybody down. Your teammates might even resent you because of your bad attitude, and eventually they might want you to leave the team. Maybe they wouldn't say so directly, but you would know. They wouldn't go out of their way to help you. You wouldn't get invited for burgers after the games. They would be less enthusiastic about helping you out in a pinch. In short, you would feel very alone.

A lack of total commitment could mean the same thing in your marriage. Your spouse would notice your uncertainty and might end up resenting you. He or she would stop going out of the way to help you. Both of you would feel alone, even though you were supposed to be partners. Never forget how important your commitment to your marriage is. Anything less than 100 percent commitment can undermine your partnership.

Does GREAT Equal Perfect?

There is really no such thing as a "perfect marriage." The word "perfect" implies there is one right way to be married. All marriages are unique, and there are many different kinds of marriages that are wonderful. But, there is such a thing as a "great" marriage. To remember what qualities are necessary for a great marriage, you just need to remember how to spell the word "great" (good communication, real partnership, effort, adaptability, and total commitment).

The Least You Need to Know

➤ Your marriage can and should be the most important relationship in your life.

➤ Good communication is a key part of all good marriages.

➤ Remember that you and your spouse are partners. You must commit 100 percent to your marriage to be part of a winning team.

➤ Investing in your marriage will bring you a great return. The time and energy you put into your relationship will be well worth it.

➤ Marriage, as well as life in general, is full of unplanned events. If you are flexible, you will be better able to deal with them.

➤ There is no such thing as a perfect marriage…but there is such a thing as a great marriage.

Chapter 2

Obstacles to a Perfect Marriage

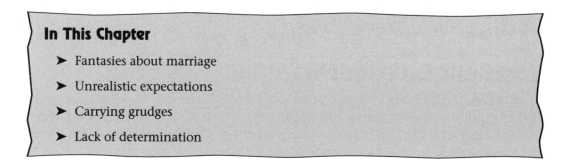

In This Chapter

➤ Fantasies about marriage

➤ Unrealistic expectations

➤ Carrying grudges

➤ Lack of determination

In this chapter, we will discuss many things that can get in the way of a successful marriage. We will show you how fantasies and unrealistic expectations will prevent you from appreciating your spouse. We will talk about the importance of forgiveness in your relationship. And, we will discuss the importance of determination.

Throw Away Your Fantasies

What is your idea of the perfect marriage? Do you envision a young couple walking along the beach at sunset holding hands? Do you picture your two favorite movie stars relaxing on a yacht in the Mediterranean? Do you picture a mom and a dad standing by the barbecue laughing together with a bunch of kids running around? Or do you imagine an older couple whose eyes still sparkle when they look at each other?

Think Twice
Don't try to compare your mate to a character in a Hollywood movie. Those people aren't real! When the film's over, you have to cook dinner, pay the bills, and maybe put the kids to bed—movie characters never have to face life's daily challenges.

You may have a picture in your mind of what a relationship should be like. This image might be based on Hollywood movies, which can make your relationship seem dull by comparison. Or, perhaps you read a book about a fiery romance and see your own partner as inadequate. You may also use other couples as role models, even though you know nothing about their private lives. You might aspire to these fantasy relationships, only to be disappointed when your partner doesn't measure up to your picture of the perfect relationship.

So what is a perfect marriage if it's not the fantasy image you've always thought it was? There *are* answers to that question, which we will provide throughout this book. But you can start creating a perfect marriage *right now* by forgetting about your fantasies of the ideal relationship. You will be taking the first step toward becoming closer to your partner. These fantasies keep you stuck in the trap of pining away for a dreamlike partner who does not exist. It's very important to understand that a perfect marriage is not like the Hollywood image you see paraded in front of you every day.

Unrealistic Expectations

Unrealistic expectations of your spouse can keep you from fully appreciating your partner. If you're always thinking about what your spouse is not, how will you find the time and energy to notice his or her wonderful qualities? Unrealistic expectations are a less extreme version of the movie fantasies that we talked about above.

Soul Mates
The sooner you accept the fact that your spouse isn't perfect, the sooner you will be able to have an extraordinary marriage. Remember, you don't want your spouse to expect perfection from you either.

The following are some common statements from people who have unrealistic expectations for their spouse:

"I wish my spouse were more handsome or beautiful."

"I wish my spouse were wealthy."

"I wish my spouse had unlimited time to spend with me."

"I wish my spouse liked the same things that I do."

"I wish my spouse agreed with me about everything."

If you want to have a fulfilling relationship, you must give up your unrealistic expectations of your partner. A spouse is usually not as handsome or beautiful as a movie star, or as wealthy. A realistic marriage involves two people with different opinions and different tastes, as well as different obligations outside of the relationship. Your differences will add to the richness of your partnership if you let them.

One of the best ways to get beyond your unrealistic expectations of your spouse is to focus on his or her good qualities. The following questions will help you bring out the best in your relationship.

Think Positive! Quiz

1. List your spouse's three greatest qualities.

   a) _____

   b) _____

   c) _____

2. What most attracted you to your spouse when you first met him or her?

   _____

   _____

   _____

3. What do you like most about your spouse's sense of humor?

   _____

   _____

   _____

4. Write down a description of the most romantic evening you ever spent with your spouse.

   _____

   _____

   _____

5. What are some positive things people say about your spouse?

   _____

   _____

   _____

Hold onto these wonderful images of your spouse. If your mind starts wandering to negative thoughts, turn back to this quiz and reread what you wrote.

Getting Over Grudges

Unresolved grudges against your spouse are another obstacle to a perfect marriage. They are a barrier between the two of you. If you are able to forgive your spouse for a past mistake, you will improve your marriage.

Think Twice
Don't spend all your time looking for perfection in your mate. Instead, spend time becoming a better mate yourself.

The Spice Rack
If you have a hard time saying you're sorry, why not leave a note saying "I'm sorry" on the bathroom mirror at night? Your spouse will find it right before he or she goes to bed, and it will probably get the two of you talking.

Mindy was frustrated with her husband, Jack, because he forgot their anniversary. He had done everything he could to make it up to her. He brought her flowers, took her on a surprise weekend away, and even did her chores for a week. But nothing satisfied her. Mindy still felt angry and sad. Now Jack was getting frustrated. He knew that he had made a big mistake by forgetting their anniversary, but he had tried to make up for it. Over time, he become angry with Mindy for not forgiving him.

Even though Jack made the original mistake by forgetting their anniversary, Mindy compounded the error. She is carrying around a grudge that has interfered with her marriage. All Mindy had to do was forgive Jack for forgetting their anniversary. Then they would have been able to move on.

Forgiveness

Are you walking around with grudges against your spouse? This is probably creating a barrier between the two of you. If you are able to, forgive your spouse for something he or she did in the past. Forgiveness is an important part of a good relationship and will improve your marriage.

The following are five steps to forgiveness:

1. Set aside time to discuss the issue.

2. Explain to your spouse why you are upset.

3. Tell your spouse directly that you forgive him or her.

4. Do your best to not bring up the issue again.

5. Remind yourself that you have already forgiven your spouse if you find yourself thinking about the issue.

By forgiving your spouse you will be taking a step to becoming closer to each other.

Overcoming Your Obstacles

The first step to overcoming obstacles in your relationship is to know what they are. To help you identify the obstacles in your relationship, answer the following questions.

Obstacles Quiz

1. Which of the following reasons best describe your reason(s) for buying this book?

   ✓ You are having problems in your relationship and want to learn how to overcome them.

   ✓ You have no role models of a good marriage and you want guidance.

   ✓ You want to avoid divorce.

   ✓ You want to have a better marriage.

   ✓ You want to maximize the potential of your relationship to be the best it can be.

2. Describe your fantasy of a perfect marriage.

   _____

   _____

   _____

3. Name three unrealistic expectations you have of your partner:

   a) _____

   b) _____

   c) _____

   continues

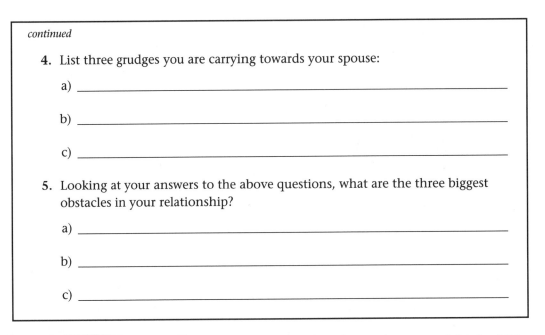

continued

4. List three grudges you are carrying towards your spouse:

a) _____

b) _____

c) _____

5. Looking at your answers to the above questions, what are the three biggest obstacles in your relationship?

a) _____

b) _____

c) _____

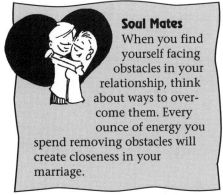

Soul Mates
When you find yourself facing obstacles in your relationship, think about ways to overcome them. Every ounce of energy you spend removing obstacles will create closeness in your marriage.

Go through your obstacles one by one and think of things that you can do to eliminate them. For instance, if you have unrealistic expectations of your spouse, you might do best by focusing on his or her positive qualities. If you have grudges against your spouse, you should probably forgive your spouse and move on.

Don't Give up Easily

When you are going through a difficult time in your marriage, it's very easy to just give up. But this is exactly the time you need to face the challenge. You need to be determined to make your marriage succeed. *The single most important thing you can do for your relationship is to really work at it.* Don't give up easily.

Imagine if you didn't tend to a garden for six months. It would look weedy and uncared for. But that doesn't mean beautiful flowers can't grow there! When things are difficult in your marriage, think about the great times you've had and all that you've shared. Make the effort to get your relationship back to where it was and then some!

OH!

Bet You Didn't Know

Q: If I am always fighting with my spouse, should I think about getting a divorce?

A: Getting a divorce is not necessarily the answer to a conflicted marriage. Many people who divorce one person for another end up with the same problems, probably because they bring the same unresolved issues into their next relationship. We encourage people to stay in their marriage and work through their issues together.

Be Determined

We will give you many tools and techniques to help you create a wonderful marriage. But there is one thing we cannot give you: determination to succeed. That is something you need to bring to your relationship.

What is so important about determination? Determination allows you to see past a tough situation and focus on the long-term goals in your marriage. You might have a difficult goal such as putting aside money every month to buy a house. But knowing that you will own a home in the future helps you budget your money carefully.

The same is true for your marriage. You have the long-term goal to have a fantastic relationship with your spouse. But you will still face situations that are difficult. There are times you will need to compromise. At those times, stay focused by remembering your larger goal—a great marriage.

Think Twice
Don't make the mistake of learning all of the tools in this book without having the determination to use them! The best tools in the world are useless if they aren't used.

★6*@

Go For It!

You owe it to yourself and your spouse to make every effort to have an extraordinary relationship. If you have unrealistic expectations of your partner or are carrying past grudges, you will always be disappointed. You will never be able to see your marriage as wonderful.

On the other hand, if you are able to get over past disappointments, forgive your spouse, and be realistic with your expectations, you will be on your way to having a great marriage.

So many people are looking elsewhere that they don't realize the perfect mate is standing right beside them. Don't let this happen to you!

The Least You Need to Know

➤ Forgetting your Hollywood fantasies will help you get closer to your mate.

➤ Unrealistic expectations can keep you from fully appreciating your partner. Instead, focus on his or her wonderful qualities.

➤ Carrying around unresolved grudges toward your spouse will interfere with your marriage. Forgiving your partner will allow you to move on.

➤ Go through this book, step-by-step. Follow as much of the advice, tips, and techniques as possible. Do not give up easily. Give it time to work.

Chapter 3

Making the Ordinary Extraordinary

Life is humming along. Your marriage is okay, not too bad, but nothing special either. Days, weeks, even months slip by without you even noticing. And somehow, your marriage is slipping by too. You want to take hold of it, shake it, and make it more *there*. Read on.

This chapter will give you ideas you can use immediately to improve your marriage. You can start right now, today, to transform your relationship from ordinary to extraordinary.

Don't Take Your Spouse for Granted

Most couples let a lot of time go by without letting each other know how much they care about each other. They treat their relationship like one more ordinary thing in their lives. Their obligations all run together: projects at work, catching up on bills, getting dinner on the table, and being in a marriage.

Don't take your most important relationship for granted. If you want your relationship to be extraordinary, you can't throw it in with all of the ordinary things that you have to do every day. You want your marriage to be much more than just another daily obligation.

Soul Mates

It's so easy to put all of your daily obligations before your marriage. Don't let that happen to you. Start putting your relationship ahead of other things. By setting it apart, you will be making it more special.

Don't wait around for your spouse to give more; in order to get more, you need to give more. Take action right away. Pay more attention to your spouse. Listen to your spouse. Be there for your spouse when he or she needs you. Take care of your spouse's needs whenever you have the chance.

You'll be surprised how big a return you can get on a small investment. If you are always thinking of your spouse and doing things for him or her, it's impossible to take your relationship for granted. And you'll be keeping it fresh and exciting at the same time.

Be My Guest

If you asked most people whom they treated more politely at the dinner table, a guest or their spouse, they would laugh and say a dinner guest, of course. The reason people laugh when they are asked that question is that they recognize the irony of their answer. We are all taught from a young age to be particularly polite in front of company. Why don't we automatically give the same courtesy to our spouse?

Guests in your home would be given comfortable chairs and asked if they wanted something to drink as soon as they came into your home. You would try to say "please" and "thank you." And you would certainly not yell at your guests if they frustrated or angered you. In other words, you would be considerate of your guests at all times. Imagine what a wonderful time you would have with your spouse if you treated each other so well.

The Spice Rack

When your spouse walks in the door, take his or her coat and ask if he or she would like something to drink. Tell your spouse to have a seat while you get it. Ask about his or her day and really listen to the answer. You may be surprised by the results.

The following is a list of things you would automatically do for a guest. Try to remember to do them with each other:

➤ Remember to say "please" and "thank you."

➤ Do not interrupt his or her sentences.

➤ Do not raise your voice or shout.

➤ Speak kindly to each other.

➤ Think about his or her needs.

Rate Yourself

On a scale from 1 (never) to 5 (always), how do you rate yourself on the following issues?

1. Do you thank your partner for doing little things like pouring your coffee or picking up your dry cleaning?

   1　　　2　　　3　　　4　　　5

2. Do you routinely ask your partner how his or her day was and actually listen to the answer?

   1　　　2　　　3　　　4　　　5

3. Do you ask your spouse if he or she would like another helping of food before emptying the serving bowl onto your own plate?

   1　　　2　　　3　　　4　　　5

4. When your spouse has had a difficult day at work, do you make an effort to be especially attentive to him or her that evening?

   1　　　2　　　3　　　4　　　5

5. Do you show your spouse appreciation when he or she has gone out of the way for you?

   1　　　2　　　3　　　4　　　5

6. Do you stop what you are doing when your spouse comes home and greet him or her warmly?

   1　　　2　　　3　　　4　　　5

7. Are you willing to try a new activity that your spouse wants to do that you have little interest in?

   1　　　2　　　3　　　4　　　5

8. Just to be nice, do you ever do a chore that is usually your spouse's responsibility?

   1　　　2　　　3　　　4　　　5

continues

continued

9. Do you help make your spouse's relatives feel at home when they visit?

        1   2   3   4   5

10. Do you keep your commitment to arrive home at a certain time?

        1   2   3   4   5

Add up you score. How did you do?

10–20	You need to start thinking more about your spouse.
20–30	You're on the right track.
30–40	Keep up the good work.
40–50	Great job!

Small Things Do Count

Lily and Tim came to see us because they felt that something was missing in their relationship. Overall, they had a good marriage. They both knew they would be there for each other when things were really rough. If Tim had a big project due at work, Lily didn't grumble when he came home late. When Lily broke her leg, Tim slept overnight at the hospital to be with her. When she went home, he did the grocery shopping and cooked all the meals. Lily and Tim really came through for each other. When times were hard, they knew they could count on each other.

But, then they told us that something felt wrong. In between disasters, Lily and Tim would get so preoccupied with their own daily concerns that they would go for weeks without having a good conversation. They often didn't even have dinner together. Somehow their marriage seemed to be stale. Lily once commented to Tim she noticed that when things were going well in their lives she felt more distant from him and didn't know why. She told him she even missed the difficult times because she felt so close to him then.

We told them they needed to use that understanding to take action. We pointed out that they should take the thoughtfulness they showed each other when things were rough and use it when things were going well. They needed to realize that the caring they were capable of showing during difficult times was as important during good times. Their marriage would instantly be stronger for it. Lily and Tom needed to expand on the strengths they already had in their marriage.

Do One Nice Thing a Day

The advice we suggested for Lily and Tom—and a sure-fire way to keep the spark in your relationship—is to do one nice thing a day for your spouse. It's not enough to think about your spouse just when it happens to be convenient or when adversity demands it. And even if you did think about your spouse every single day, how is he or she supposed to know that? Actions speak much louder than words. By getting in the habit of doing something special daily, you will keep your relationship fresh!

Think Twice
Don't think that if you do something nice for someone, it's enough for a whole month. The truth is you shouldn't let one day go by without doing an act of kindness for the most important person in your life.

You might argue that you don't have time to do a nice thing every day for your spouse. But there are so many things you can do that take very little time and make a good relationship great. Once you build this giving habit into your relationship, you'll be amazed at how good both of you will feel.

What Kind of Things Can I Do?

There are many wonderful things you can do for your spouse. It doesn't matter if they are small things that only take a minute, or particularly special things that take a lot of planning. You might do your spouse's chore, like taking out the garbage or doing the weekly grocery shopping. You might leave a note in his pocket or call him at work in the middle of the afternoon to let him know how much you love him. You could turn on her favorite music so it's playing when she gets home from work. You might take his clothes to the dry cleaners or buy his favorite ice cream. You could do something more traditional like order flowers or prepare a special meal. Maybe even make pancakes for breakfast. Or do something silly like put toothpaste on her toothbrush ahead of time. The sky is the limit!

The important thing is to try not to let a single day go by without doing one nice thing for your spouse. It doesn't have to be elaborate or romantic, but it does have to be done regularly. You'll be surprised how quickly your relationship will change for the better. Making three lists can help you accomplish this goal. The first list should include small things you can do (these are easy—like pouring his coffee or picking up her dry cleaning), the second one includes medium-sized things you can do (buying a birthday present for his mother or making dinner for her boss), and the third one includes the really big things (these things are really a stretch for you—maybe inviting his parents to

Soul Mates
The deed shapes the heart. Doing kind things for each other will bring the two of you closer together.

come for an extended visit). Refer to the list regularly (put it in your personal organizer, if you use one), and make sure you do one of the things on the first list every day. Those on the second list maybe once a week, those on the third list at least once a year.

Closer Every Day

To continue our example, Lily and Tim realized they missed the closeness they felt when circumstances were more challenging. They came to us to help them figure out how to feel closer to each other all the time. We pointed out that they had a tendency to take each other for granted when their lives were going well. We showed them how their actions affected the relationship. They didn't regularly do things for each other that showed they cared for each other. Deep down they didn't doubt that the other person really loved them. We helped them understand that they needed to take the time and effort to show each other how important they were to each other.

OH!

Bet You Didn't Know

Q: My spouse is on the road a lot and we don't get a chance to see each other every day. What can we do to stay close?

A: Make sure you talk each day and discuss what you did and how you felt about it.

We suggested they make sure to do one nice thing for each other every day. After a few weeks, their marriage began to feel like a courtship all over again. One day Tim would buy Lily flowers and another he would cook her dinner. Lily surprised Tim at work and they had lunch together. Many of the things they do for each other now were things they had done when Lily had broken her leg and Tim had a big project at work. But by doing them during the good times, they have a much happier and more satisfying relationship than ever before.

Make the End of Each Day Special

Many people underestimate how valuable it is to reconnect with their spouse when they have been apart from each other all day. Every evening when you first see your spouse is a chance for an extraordinary moment. The majority of couples spend their weekdays, and some of their weekend days, apart from each other.

You have spent many hours doing activities without each other's company. By the end of most days, you and your spouse have probably been apart for more hours than you have spent awake together. When you see each other at the end of the day, it really is a re-union. Make sure you treat it like one.

There are many things you can do to make the moment you walk through the door at the end of the day a special one:

1. Greet each other warmly. Stop whatever activity you are doing and walk to the door to greet your spouse. It might seem trite, but the effort will make both of you feel special and taken care of.

2. Take a few minutes to find out how your spouse's day was. We are all extremely busy, but this small effort can make a huge difference. Instead of two strangers trying to get things done, you will be partners working together to create a warm family environment.

3. Reconnect to your spouse after a day apart. Share a warm hug, deliver a kiss, or pour a refreshing glass of ice water for him or her.

> **Think Twice**
> Don't head straight for the refrigerator or to the bedroom to change into comfortable loungewear the moment you get home. When you walk in the door go right to your spouse and tell him or her how glad you are to see him or her. This will create a loving atmosphere for the entire evening.

An extraordinary marriage is filled with countless meaningful moments. Every encounter with your spouse that you make special will enhance your marriage. Don't overlook the small chances to create closeness in your relationship.

The Least You Need to Know

➤ Don't take your spouse for granted. Show him or her your appreciation.

➤ Treat your spouse like a guest. The most important person in your life deserves to be treated nicely by you.

➤ Do one nice thing a day for your spouse. It is a sure-fire way to instantly feel closer to him or her.

➤ Make the most of every reunion with your spouse. You will be making a fresh start every time.

Chapter 4

Keeping the Passion Alive

One of the biggest mistakes couples make when they get married is to get so caught up in the *doing* of being married that they forget about just *being* with each other. In the process, they often forget the fun and spontaneity they had before they were married.

How sad. You should have fun with your spouse. Enjoying each other's company is part of what brought you together in the first place. This chapter is about how to have a great time with your chosen life partner. You'll learn why most couples stop creating special times together. And finally we'll give you tips for dating your spouse.

Reigniting Passion

Would you want to settle for a ho-hum life of working, watching TV, paying the bills, eating, and going to sleep? Probably not. Life just wouldn't be satisfying if we were to just get by. What we want, what we crave, is passion. Passion for our work, for activities in our down time, and, most importantly, passion for our spouse. Many people describe their relationship by saying, "I think I still love him, but the passion is gone." Fortunately, this is usually not true, even when it seems to be. The passion is not gone; it just needs to be drawn out.

Many people who say they have passion problems find that they do. It's amazing how something can become a self-fulfilling prophecy. Instead, if you think about the issue in terms of passion obstacles to overcome, it's much easier to see the light at the end of the tunnel. With a little determination and a lot of practice, you can have more passion in your relationship than you ever thought possible.

Passion is not like a butterfly landing on you if you're lucky and fleeing at the slightest breeze. How wonderful that this simply isn't true. In fact, passion is one area in which you can make a difference right away. You don't need to wait for a special love potion or some external stimulus to ignite your passion. You can make it happen in an instant.

It Wasn't Always Like This

Many people get married because they say they have fun together. After they are married for a while, they realize they got married for more valuable reasons: shared values and shared commitment.

It's very common for married couples to get caught up in the day-to-day grind. There are bills to pay, schedules to arrange, and chores to do. It seems like a waste of energy to plan fun activities with your spouse. It's easy to assume he or she will be around to grab a bite to eat or to see a movie with you. Creating special "date time" together makes us feel like we're just adding one more thing to our never ending to-do list.

Think Twice
Don't be passive! You have the power to bring passion into your relationship. It's not something that happens to you; it's something that you do.

There are many reasons to make a date with your spouse. First of all, because it's fun. Everyone deserves to have fun and a break from routines. Second, doing enjoyable things together gives you energy to tackle your responsibilities. And last, every time you do something fun with your spouse, you strengthen your relationship.

Memories

Close your eyes and think back to your first date with your spouse. Were you excited? Did you have butterflies in your stomach? What were you wearing? What was your spouse wearing? Did you go to a nice dinner and get to know each other? At the end of the evening, did you make plans to get together again? Did you talk about the date with any of your friends?

Once you think about it, you can remember really enjoying going out with your spouse. You looked forward to seeing him or her and talking on the telephone together. Where did all of that fun and excitement go? You can get back the excitement of your first date. How? Read on.

Soul Mates
Every once in a while be sure to take out your photo albums and review them together. You'll have a great evening ahead of you. This is valuable for reinforcing the bonds you have.

Good Fun Takes Good Planning

What made those first months of dating so much fun? Both of you put a lot of time and energy into the date. You chose an outfit with special care. Sometimes you bought tickets to a special event or ate dinner in a romantic restaurant. You were thoughtful of the other person and presented yourself at your best. You practiced good dating etiquette.

Bring back those skills. All of these things are important even after being married. The forethought as well as the adoring attitude you brought to your dates then can be re-created. The atmosphere of specialness and excitement made them so much fun!

Let's Do Lunch

Tammy and Jason had been married for two years and were thinking of starting a family. But they were afraid to have children because they felt their marriage was fizzling out. They never had much fun together and had lost most of the passion that they had had while they dated and for the first few months of their marriage. Tammy was even worried they might end up getting divorced. She didn't know what to do.

Tammy finally got up the nerve to talk to us about the problem. At first, Tammy didn't know what to say, because generally her marriage was going well. She loved Jason and he loved her. After much probing, we couldn't find a significant problem facing Tammy and Jason. It seemed like they might divorce just for the lack of interest. Finally we asked, "What do the two of you do for fun?"

Tammy was surprised by the question. She had never really thought about it before. "Well, we see a movie sometimes, and every now and then we go out to eat. We're trying to save money for a house and we've been cutting down on our entertainment expenses."

Then we asked Tammy what it was like in the beginning of their relationship when she first dated Jason. Tammy's eyes sparkled. She talked about how attracted she had been to Jason and how she used to look forward to seeing him. They often went out for dinner and would take walks for their evening entertainment that really gave them the opportunity to have long talks about life and what was important to them.

As she was talking, Tammy smiled. Then we asked, "What is different about how you used to date and what you are doing now?"

Tammy went on to describe how they used to go out every Saturday night. They would often plan the next date a week ahead of time. Tammy would often dress casually, but she always used to spend a lot of time deciding what she wore. She would make sure to match her earrings and necklace to her outfit. She would wash and blow-dry her hair. Sometimes she would even have her nails manicured.

OH!

Bet You Didn't Know

Q: What do most people want from their spouse when they go out together?

A: To have fun and feel close. Do your best to provide this for your mate.

Think Twice

Don't forget to make time for talking with each other on your dates. If you enjoy movies or sporting events, make sure that afterward you stop for coffee or walk home together so you can talk!

Now she and Jason went out rarely. When they did go out, they never planned ahead of time what they would do. They usually wore jeans and T-shirts wherever they went. Sometimes they would even spend 30 minutes deciding what movie to see but would give up when they couldn't agree.

Tammy and Jason were depriving themselves of passion. At first, Tammy assumed that not wanting to spend a lot of money was the reason their dates were not very exciting. But when she thought about it, she and Jason had never spent much money before they were married either. What made their dates so exciting before was taking the time to get ready to go out with each other and looking forward to the dates all week. If you make yourself attractive, you'll feel more attractive and your spouse will be more attracted to you. By planning your evening out ahead of time and getting dressed nicely, you can turn a simple movie into a wonderful, romantic evening together.

We suggested that Tammy and Jason set aside every Saturday night to go out together. We advised them to plan ahead so they wouldn't waste time on the actual evening deciding what to do. Both of them should change into new clothes before they go out, just like they always did before they were married. Their dates began to feel much more special, and they grew closer to each other than ever before. Tammy has stopped worrying about divorce and feels great about starting a family. Dating really strengthened their marriage and brought back the passion!

Does this scenario sound familiar to you? If so, why not try the advice we gave Tammy and Jason. Set a date night with your spouse and stick to it. Even if it's something simple, like a walk in the park or a stop for a cappuccino, make it special. And don't forget to freshen up before you go. Remember, passion is not going to just land on you—you have to make it happen!

Rate Your Date with Your Mate

We're going to ask you questions about you and your spouse's dating habits. Take your time and circle your answers on a scale ranging from 1 (never) to 5 (always). By answering these questions thoughtfully and honestly, you'll have taken the first step to bringing passion and excitement into your married dating life.

Rate Your Date

1. How often do you and your spouse go out alone?

   1   2   3   4   5

2. Do you do things that are fun for both of you?

   1   2   3   4   5

3. Do you spend time getting ready to go out for the date?

   1   2   3   4   5

continues

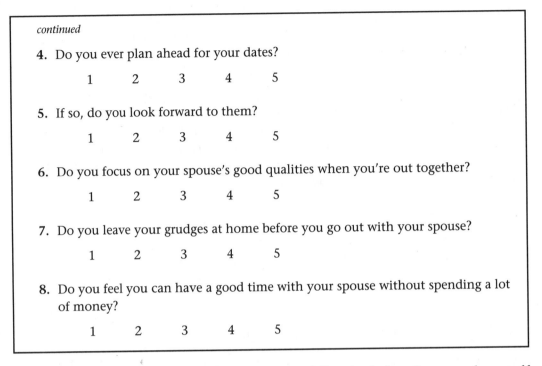

continued

4. Do you ever plan ahead for your dates?

     1   2   3   4   5

5. If so, do you look forward to them?

     1   2   3   4   5

6. Do you focus on your spouse's good qualities when you're out together?

     1   2   3   4   5

7. Do you leave your grudges at home before you go out with your spouse?

     1   2   3   4   5

8. Do you feel you can have a good time with your spouse without spending a lot of money?

     1   2   3   4   5

Go through your answers. If any of your answers fell in the 1, 2, or 3 range, ask yourself what you would need to do so that you could answer 4 or 5. If you answered 4 or 5 on *all* the questions, congratulations! You're already having a great time going out with your spouse.

Put Aside Differences

When you first dated your spouse, you probably weren't thinking about whether he had washed the dinner dishes before you left or if you would meet the monthly budget. And you certainly didn't think about his overflowing laundry basket or his forgetting to buy milk at the grocery store. You were probably thinking about the cute dimple on his left cheek and how much you liked the flowers he gave you. Which of those thoughts are more likely to result in an enjoyable evening?

If you carry grudges with you on a date with your spouse, you will guarantee yourself a bad time. Marriage is complicated. The person that you have a lot of fun with is the same person you need to negotiate with for your day-to-day needs. You need to temporarily put these issues aside to be able to have a good time with your spouse. Discussing your monthly budget while waiting in line to see a movie is not a wise idea. You probably won't resolve anything about the budget, and you'll have a rotten time at the movie. But agreeing to put your differences aside for the evening will let you recharge your relationship battery. Then you'll be able to tackle the budget and other decisions with much greater enthusiasm and a sense of togetherness.

Soul Mates
If something is bothering you before you go out with your spouse, write it down on a piece of paper and resolve to discuss it in the next day or two. That will help you leave the issue at home, and you'll have a better time on your date.

Be Spontaneous Too

While it's very important to have regular time together with your spouse, it can also be fun to be completely spontaneous. Just remember that the spontaneous outing together doesn't substitute for the reliable date. Instead, it's a wonderful addition to it. That way, marriage can give you the best of both worlds. You can have the reliability of regular dates and the chance to be spontaneous too.

One night after a long day at work, you might come home and say, "We're not cooking—I want to take you out to dinner!" Or the two of you might be sitting around reading the Sunday paper and read about a nature hike that looks fun. Don't just say, "That looks fun!" Actually grab your calendar and write it in! Even when you do very small activities spontaneously, such as going out to a Sunday breakfast together, you will benefit from breaking the routine.

The Spice Rack
Think of ways to surprise your mate. It seems cliché to stick a love note in your spouse's pocket, but if you've ever received one, you know how they make you smile.

Hot Date Ideas

Some great dates are free, and others cost more than your weekly dating budget. If there is something the two of you want to do that exceeds your budget, all you have to do is plan for it. Let's say that you have a budget of $25 a week for your dates and there is a beautiful romantic restaurant you have always wanted to try that will probably cost $100 for the meal. You've always pushed aside the idea of going there. But you can get there and stay within your budget. All you have to do is be creative and go on three dates without spending any money, and then you will have your $100.

The Free Date

Use your imagination. There are so many things you can do that are fun and cost no money. Maybe you can drive somewhere special to watch a sunset. Depending on where you live, that could be the ocean, a lake, the mountains, the top of a tall building, or the middle of an open field. In the summer, you can pack a picnic dinner. Spread out a large blanket under a tree in a local park and sit and eat and talk. You can also invite some friends over for dessert and coffee and have the chance to catch up with people you haven't seen in a while. Or you could stay home, turn down the lights in your living room, and dance to music you enjoy. You can have a great time while saving for that very special expensive date.

Remember that some of the best things in life are free:

➤ Watching the sunrise

➤ Taking a walk

➤ Eating lunch under a tree

➤ Talking with each other

➤ Dancing to music in your home

➤ Smiling at each other

➤ Telling jokes

➤ Playing a card game

➤ Spending the evening with friends

➤ Watching the sunset

The Medium-Price Date

Most of your weekly dates with your spouse will cost some money. You'll probably go to a movie or out to dinner. But there are ways to jazz up even your average evening. Maybe instead of going out to dinner at a moderately priced restaurant, you could have dessert at a romantic, expensive restaurant. It would give you the chance to get dressed up and have a quiet, romantic evening without putting a big dent in your pocketbook. You could see a matinee instead of an evening movie, and with the money you saved you could have an inexpensive dinner. Or put the money aside to add to a future date.

The Spice Rack
A great way to make your partner feel completely taken care of is to plan an entire evening out for a special occasion. Take care of all the details and surprise him or her.

The Expensive Date

Plan way ahead. You should relish every moment of this special experience. Anticipation is half the fun! Make sure you have reservations for a busy restaurant or special event. It would be a shame to save money for a play or concert and not be able to get tickets for it. By planning ahead, you won't be disappointed. And you will have more time to re-budget your dating money.

Try to make the evening as special as possible. Take extra care when choosing the outfit you will wear. Give yourselves plenty of time to arrive promptly. It would be a shame to feel rushed and stressed wondering if you will arrive on time. Do everything you can to ensure that the evening will go as smoothly as possible.

But, even though you should do your best to create a wonderful evening, don't put pressure on yourselves to have the perfect date when you are spending a lot of money. You might end up being disappointed. An expensive restaurant might not have the greatest food. Or one of you might have a bad cold on the night you had theater tickets. You just have to roll with the punches and hope things will work out better next time.

Romantic Getaways

One of the nicest ways to renew your relationship is to spend time together away from the day-to-day routine. It's easier to focus on each other when you're in a new place that doesn't remind you of the chores that need doing or the bills that need paying. Going away together will also create good memories the two of you will always have.

The Spice Rack
Want a real *dream* vacation? Fantasize about your perfect vacation, and write down a detailed description of it. What will you wear? What will you eat? What will you and your spouse do together? Now share this with your spouse.

The type of vacation you plan together will vary depending on money and time constraints. You might have some wonderful ideas for expensive vacations that you would like to take with your spouse. It's possible that with careful planning you will be able to go on that trip.

But don't let the fact that you can't spend a month at a villa in Greece keep you from going away with your spouse. You can have great fun on a "free date" with each other, and you can have a memorable getaway for very little money too. Remember, even one night away can be refreshing. Go away for a shorter time to stay within your budget. Or prepare some of your meals instead of eating out for breakfast, lunch, and dinner. If you can't afford a hotel at all, find out when out-of-town friends are going on vacation and offer to house-sit for them.

Plan on going away overnight at least twice a year with your spouse. It will be one of the most enjoyable ways to keep passion in your marriage.

Take the fun date list of ideas and start planning. Mark dates and times on your calendar right away to make sure time doesn't slip by. Remember, your goal is to keep the passion alive in your relationship. As we said, good fun takes good planning, so get started now. Have fun!

The Least You Need to Know

➤ You can create passion by planning fun things ahead of time.

➤ Make yourself attractive to your mate when you go out together. Spend the same amount of time and energy that you did when you were dating.

➤ Leave domestic issues where they belong—at home.

➤ It's important to set aside both time and money for dates with your spouse.

➤ Being in a new place can be romantic. Be sure to go away overnight at least twice a year.

Part 2
Tools for Success

You and your spouse are doing great. You've read Part 1 and are doing all of your homework. The two of you have put aside fantasies about your relationship and feel like a team. You're doing special things for each other on a regular basis and planning fun activities together.

But your marriage is not perfect yet. You have frequent misunderstandings with your spouse and never seem to have time to talk about them. The two of you are getting into arguments and aren't able to come up with solutions. You know you will have your differences, but you were hoping to resolve your differences more easily.

Read on! Part 2 will give you simple, straightforward tools for success. You'll learn how to improve your communication skills to avoid misunderstandings. We'll show you ways to make sure you have the time you need to plan and problem-solve. We'll discuss how to identify problems and discuss them before they get out of hand. We'll explain the ground rules for effective conflict resolution. And we'll discuss the importance of forgiveness.

Two-Way Communication

> **In This Chapter**
>
> ➤ The importance of good communication
>
> ➤ Learning how to be a better listener
>
> ➤ Determining your needs
>
> ➤ Developing effective communication skills

Great marriages start with great communication. And in bad marriages, we can almost guarantee you'll see poor communication. In this chapter, we'll give you pointers for clear, effective communication. You'll learn how to identify what you need and how to make sure your spouse hears you. And even if you feel that you communicate well enough with your spouse, read on. Everyone can learn to communicate better. The better the communication in your marriage, the better your relationship.

What Exactly Is Communication?

Communication is the cornerstone of every relationship. It's letting another person know what you are thinking and feeling, and making sure you are understood. It involves listening attentively and letting your spouse know you've heard him or her. It's knowing what you want and asking for it. There are many things that communication isn't. It's not talking to somebody when that person is not fully listening. It's not nodding your head in agreement when you have not heard what somebody has said. And it's not second-guessing what someone is about to say.

Think Twice

Don't think you can have a good relationship with your spouse without having good communication. Communication IS the relationship.

Topics of communication with a spouse often include:

➤ Sharing ideas with one another.

➤ Answering questions you both have.

➤ Letting your spouse know how you are feeling.

➤ Asking for help with a specific task.

➤ Discussing something that is bothering you.

If you learn to communicate effectively, you will more often than not get what you need from your spouse, whether it's a simple acknowledgment of your idea or a thoughtful answer to your question.

Ten Steps to Clear Communication

Communicating effectively isn't so hard, if you break it down into pieces. Follow these 10 steps, and you'll be on the road to better communication with your spouse:

1. Figure out what you want to say. Before you talk with your spouse about something, make sure you know what you want to tell him or her to minimize possible misunderstandings.

2. Decide what you need from your spouse. You are more likely to get your needs met, whether it be a hug or an answer to a question, if you know what you want.

Think Twice

Don't get into heated arguments with your spouse when you are talking on the telephone. Conflicts are much better resolved in person.

3. Use good judgment in timing. Is your spouse sick or preparing for a big meeting at work? Consider your partner's state of mind when choosing a time to talk.

4. Make eye contact. Your spouse will be more likely to listen and hear you if you are looking right at each other.

5. Get your spouse's undivided attention. You will not be heard if your spouse is thinking about something else when you are trying to talk with him or her.

6. Be a good listener. By being attentive to your spouse, you will have a more productive discussion.

7. Confirm that you were heard. Ask your spouse if he or she fully understands what you just said. Then, and only then, will your spouse be able to respond properly.

8. After your spouse has told you something, rephrase what he or she has said. This will let your spouse know for sure that you've heard what he or she is saying.

9. Schedule a better discussion time if necessary. Sometimes it's just not possible to get your spouse's attention at the exact moment that you want it.

10. Remember that communication is a two-way street. If both of you follow these steps, you will both benefit and strengthen your relationship.

Bet You Didn't Know

Q: Why were we given two ears and one mouth?

A: Because we are meant to do twice as much listening as talking!

The Art of Listening

Now think about communicating with your partner when he or she really needs you to listen carefully and thoughtfully. When your spouse is trying to tell you something, make sure that you can give your spouse your full and undivided attention. If it's not a good time, tell him or her (politely) that another time would be better. Be specific—in 10 minutes, after dinner, tomorrow morning. Just make sure to talk about it when you said you would, even if he or she forgets (or is reluctant) to bring it up again.

When you are listening to your spouse, always ask yourself the following three questions:

1. Are you giving your spouse your full and undivided attention?

2. Do you understand what your spouse is saying to you?

3. Do you know what your spouse wants from you?

Think Twice
Don't put off a conversation for an indefinite period of time. Chances are you'll never get to it, and the issue will only fester. Plan a specific time and stick to it!

To be a good listener, you need to answer "yes" to all of these questions. If you are distracted, suggest a better time to talk. If you don't understand what your spouse is saying, ask him or her to explain again. It's also important to know exactly what your spouse wants from you. If your spouse tells you that he or she has invited people over for dinner on Friday evening at 6:30 P.M., you should do several things. You should clarify what he or she wants from you. Approval for the dinner party? That you should be home by 5:30 to help set up? That you need to help with the food preparation? Maybe you are just being asked to be home by 6:30 on Friday, but you should clear that up now before misunderstandings develop. By having your spouse tell you specifically what he or she wants from you, you will be facilitating good communication and preventing a future argument.

What's Wrong with This Picture?

A young couple came to see us who had communication problems. Susie told us she always felt frustrated with Frank. He never seemed to be there for her when she needed him the most. After she had a long, difficult day with their two children, she would always look forward to when he was coming home. But when he did, she was disappointed. She wasn't quite sure why. He would read the newspaper, play with the children, help put them to bed, and watch an hour of television. But she wanted something more from him.

OH!

Bet You Didn't Know

Q: Everything seems okay in my marriage, but I'm feeling unhappy with my spouse. What can I do?

A: It's likely that some of your needs aren't getting met even though you don't know what they are. Try writing down the times when you are feeling frustrated and see if there is a pattern to them. Identifying your needs is the first step to meeting them.

Frank told us he was very proud of Susie. He thought she did a great job with their children. The children seemed happy. He always felt good and comforted in their home. But lately he too was worried. He saw that Susie was feeling frustrated. She would sometimes cry in the evenings. He would ask her what was wrong and she would say, "I don't know." Frank told us he didn't know what to do. He felt awful that his wife was on edge, which made him distance himself more from her. The problem was snowballing, and it wasn't even clear what the problem was.

Susie needed something from Frank that she hadn't figured out for herself. Somehow, she wanted him to read her mind and give her the right kind of attention exactly when she needed it. Frank loved Susie and would do anything for her. But how was he supposed to give her what she wanted when she herself didn't know what it was?

The whole situation could be remedied if Susie were able to figure out specifically what she needed from Frank and tell him those needs. Heaven is just around the corner for this couple and they don't even realize it. The first step is for both partners to recognize their needs and learn how to communicate them.

Knowing What You Need

In order to get a definitive answer to a question or emotional support from your spouse, you need to think carefully about what you need. Are you feeling blue and want a hug? Do you have a great idea about redecorating the bathroom and want approval? Do you need to find out if your spouse can be home by 6 P.M. next Thursday night for dinner with friends? Sometimes you have a very specific message and need a very specific response. And other times it's not so clear. One of the most important factors in communication is clear thinking ahead of time. It's much easier for your spouse to respond to your needs if you know what they are first. In fact, it's essential. If you don't know what you need, how is your spouse supposed to know?

Soul Mates
If your spouse seems upset about something, ask him or her what's wrong. Then, take the time to help your spouse work it through.

Identifying Your Needs

This quiz will help you figure out what you need from your spouse in general terms. You can also use these questions as a set of guidelines for thinking about what you need at specific times when you know you need something from your spouse but can't think of what it is.

Needs Quiz

1. When do I especially need my spouse?

   _____

2. In what situations do I often need my spouse?

   _____

3. When do I feel alone and unsupported by my spouse?

   _____

4. I feel my spouse should know what I need without my needing to tell him or her.

   True   or   False

5. Why don't I let my spouse know what I need?

   _____

If you think about when and in what situations you need your spouse, you will be on the road to clearer communication.

Resolving Conflicts

We asked Susie these questions. She realized that she had expected Frank to read her mind. She didn't know exactly what she wanted from him when he came home, but she knew it was this time that most frustrated her. She told us she really looked forward to seeing him after being with the children all day. And she wanted him to look forward to seeing her. She was secretly hoping he would give her a big hug when he came home and compliment her on what a wonderful job she was doing with the children. She was tired at the end of the day and felt she needed positive feedback from her husband. In our office, she told this to Frank and he was astonished. He looked at her and said, "The reason I don't take the time to hug you or compliment you is that I rush to be with the kids to give you a break. I know you're exhausted." Frank thought that's what Susie needed most from him, but in fact she needed praise. Once he learned what her needs were, he said he'd be happy to oblige.

Soul Mates
Sometimes what seems to be a big problem can be resolved with a simple hug.

Susie was still crying, but now it was tears of relief. Something that had been bothering her for months was solved in a five-minute conversation. Frank started hugging Susie every single night when he came home from work and told her what a great mother she was. Their evenings together became a time of greater joy, and their marriage became stronger.

Many people feel that if you have to tell someone to bring you a dozen roses, it doesn't show true caring. But which character trait would you rather have in a spouse: someone who does nice things every once in a while or someone who wants to meet your needs when you ask them to? When Susie was specific about what she needed from Frank, he was able to meet her needs and improve their relationship. Even if he had brought her flowers one night, it's far better to have someone who pays attention to what she needs and delivers.

Sending Your Message

You've answered the previous questions, and you're willing to take a chance and let your spouse know what you want. Now that you know what you need, all you have to do is tell him or her. Right? Wrong.

Timing is everything. Telling your spouse that you need him to help with the dishes when he has just walked in the door will probably make him want to walk right back out again. Or telling her that you need more appreciation when she's already going to be late for work would be a disaster.

Approach your spouse when he or she is calm and when there is time for the task at hand. Sit down. Make eye contact. Make sure he or she is done reading and not eyeing the TV. Wait until after a meal if you'll both be thinking better. Your needs are important, and telling them to your spouse requires his or her undivided attention. You worked hard to figure out what you needed. You deserve to be heard and your spouse deserves to be given the chance to hear you. Use the following lists to determine whether you try to talk with your spouse at the right or wrong times.

Think Twice
Don't approach your spouse at an inopportune time if you really want him or her to listen. By waiting for a better time, he or she will be more receptive and will hear what you are saying.

Good Times:

➤ When you are both in a good mood.

➤ When you can both give your full, undivided attention.

➤ When you are both well-rested.

➤ When you both have enough time for the entire discussion.

➤ When the TV is turned off.

Bad Times:

➤ When one of you is in a bad mood.

➤ When you have an unresolved conflict about something else.

➤ When one of you is in a hurry.

➤ When one of you isn't feeling well.

➤ When one of you is hungry.

Make Sure You Were Heard

"Roger" is a code word in radio to indicate that a message has been received and understood. In the old days, you might have sent a radio message that never got there. If you heard the word "roger," you knew the other party got your message. If you sent a message and didn't hear anything back, you would assume that it never got there.

Soul Mates
You can make your spouse feel good by showing that you are really listening. The best way to do this is to get in the habit of rephrasing what he or she says. This simple action will bring the two of you closer.

The same principle applies when communicating with your partner. You need to make sure he or she heard what you have said. The best way to do this is for your spouse to repeat or rephrase what you told him or her. This can accomplish two things. It's comforting to know that your spouse heard you. And if they repeat what you said, you will make sure that you have not only been heard, but understood as well.

The Least You Need to Know

➤ Good communication is key to a good relationship.

➤ Listen when your partner is talking with you. Remember that communication is a two-way street.

➤ You have to know what you need in order to get it.

➤ When choosing a time to raise an issue, good timing is crucial.

➤ Get in the habit of rephrasing what your spouse tells you. It will prevent misunderstandings.

It's Just a Matter of Time

Most people don't think about what they want to accomplish when they are with their spouse. They think just "hanging out" together is enough. Well, it isn't. There are different ways to be with your spouse, and they serve different purposes. This chapter will teach you new ways to think about and organize the time you spend with your spouse. Then you'll make the most out of every moment together!

Rush, Rush, Rush

We all live very busy lives. We can never seem to get caught up with our errands, projects, and future planning. We finish an entire "to do" list just to turn around and start another. In between getting all of our "stuff" done, we realize that we need to talk something over with our spouse. But somehow, there never seems to be any time.

Soul Mates
If you want to spend quality time together, you have to make it happen!

Do you feel like weeks go by before you have a chance to discuss something with your spouse? So you grab him on his way to work to ask him an important question and he mumbles something with his mouth full of toast as he's fumbling for his car keys. You know from reading Chapter 5 on communication that that's not the way to have a discussion. But there never seems to be any time!

Where Does the Time Go?

The following chart will help you think about the time that you spend with your spouse. For each day of the week, list the number of hours you spend with your spouse on a typical day. Then write down what the two of you typically do during the time you spend together.

Day	Hours Spent Together	Activity
Monday	_____	_____
Tuesday	_____	_____
Wednesday	_____	_____
Thursday	_____	_____
Friday	_____	_____
Saturday	_____	_____
Sunday	_____	_____

The Spice Rack
A great way to eliminate arguments over what you want to do is for each of you to write down three places you would like to go on three separate pieces of paper. Pick one out of a hat and go for it!

Look at your answers. What do you notice? How many of your hours together are spent having fun? How many are spent making necessary decisions? Are there hours that go by that you feel you haven't had fun and haven't accomplished anything? You are not alone. Most couples feel they don't have the time they need together.

Don't think that watching TV with your spouse counts as spending time together. People spend an average of three hours a day watching TV. You'll have a better marriage if you watch less TV and spend more quality time with your spouse.

Time Is Like Money

Time, like money, needs to be managed. It's very easy to spend a surprising amount of money on small things, like coffee, soda, or a quick lunch with your colleagues at work. At the end of the month, you feel like you don't have money left over for things that are fun. And yet, you didn't enjoy the extra money that you spent either. If you knew that you were saving for something in the future that you would enjoy, you might get more pleasure from not buying the coffee than buying it. Having goals and looking forward to them can be enjoyable.

The same thing is true with your time together. If the two of you set aside time every week to have fun, you would always have something to look forward to. And if you also set aside time every week to discuss important issues, you would feel confident that you would always have time to work things out.

Soul Mates
Your conflicts won't get in the way of your day-to-day relationship if you put aside time every week to discuss important issues.

It's as Easy as One, Two, Three

When you share your life with somebody, there are countless decisions to make. Some are small, such as what time to make dinner reservations on Saturday night, and other decisions are complicated, like making the annual budget or planning a vacation. By setting aside planning time, you ensure that you will have time to make joint decisions and will free up other time you spend together to just enjoy yourselves.

Every good, healthy marriage needs time set aside for three general activities. These need to be scheduled on a regular basis and treated with respect:

1. Time for planning.
2. Time for resolving differences.
3. Time for fun.

Most couples do not plan for these activities and end up being frustrated. All of these different times serve different purposes, and each is equally important. If you don't make time for each of these important activities, it will interfere with your relationship.

For instance, if your spouse is doing something that is bothering you, it's important to discuss it. It might be a small thing, but if you don't have a chance to talk about it, your feelings of annoyance will build up. You will probably find that you are arguing more and not enjoying your time together as much. Ensuring that you will be there to listen to each other is half of the battle.

Your New Weekly Time Planner

Look at your "Where Does the Time Go?" chart again. How much time do you think you need to discuss issues each week? Most couples need about 30 minutes a week for planning activities and 30 minutes for conflict resolution. Now reorganize the hours that you spend with your spouse every week. Set aside a 30-minute session for planning, a 30-minute session for conflict resolution, and a full evening or afternoon for fun time. If you reorganize the time you spend with your spouse, you will be amazed at how much it adds to your marriage.

When scheduling time together, keep in mind the following:

Think Twice
Don't take your appointments with your spouse lightly. A meeting is a meeting, whether it's with your spouse or with your lawyer.

1. Make sure the times are convenient for both of you.

2. Be sure to reschedule your time together if one of you needs to work late or is going out of town.

3. If you have an especially complicated issue to discuss, set aside extra time to resolve it.

4. It can be useful to mark these appointments on the household calendar or in your personal organizer.

5. Each appointment requires each of you to give your undivided attention.

A Question of Balance

Fred and Paula came to see us because they were arguing constantly. Each of them felt like the other one never listened. Whenever Paula wanted to discuss where they should go on vacation, Fred would tell her that he was busy. When Fred asked Paula if they should get season tickets for the symphony, Paula told him to bring it up later. But "later" came and went and they never made these decisions. They were fighting more than usual and that interfered with their fun time together too.

It quickly became clear to us that Fred and Paula needed to manage their time better. We had them work on their own "Where Does the Time Go?" chart. They soon realized that an entire week would pass and they wouldn't have discussed things that were important to them. Fred and Paula spent a lot of time together, but they never set aside time to make plans.

We had them schedule two 30-minute appointments, one for planning and one for conflict resolution. They chose Wednesday evening and Saturday morning. They also set aside Saturday evenings for going out and a half-day on the weekends to be together without specific plans. Their relationship improved dramatically. They knew they could count on having time together to accomplish everything they needed to every single week.

The Spice Rack
If you spend only 20 minutes a week with your spouse having a heart-to-heart talk, that adds up to over 17 hours a year!

Make the Most of Your Time Together

It's ideal to be able to spend many hours every week with your spouse. However, there are always weeks when that seems impossible. You might be working late, or going to sleep early after being up all night with a sick child. We all have obligations outside our relationship.

When you don't have as much time to spend with one another as you would like, there are ways to maximize your time together:

Soul Mates
Time is more precious than gold. If we treat our time together as such, our relationship will flourish.

1. Keep the TV set off in the evenings. You are much more likely to talk with each other when there are no distractions.

2. Take a walk together in the evenings. Even if you are too tired to talk, it will help you feel closer to each other.

3. Spend 10 minutes every evening talking about each other's day. Even if you don't have a chance to see each other that much, you will at least know what the other person has been doing.

4. Eat breakfast together in the morning. Even if you are rushed and only have 10 minutes, sitting together at the table will make you feel you are starting your day as a team.

5. Talk with each other once each day on the telephone. A five-minute conversation helps couples connect and will be time well spent.

Doing these small things won't take much time, but each one of them will help you feel closer to each other. When you don't have a lot of extra time, you need to make the most of the time that you do have.

Bet You Didn't Know

Q: How can I make more time for my spouse when I am swamped with work and responsibilities around the house?

A: Sometimes it's worthwhile to spend money to buy time. If you are having trouble scheduling time to be with your spouse, you might consider hiring someone to do housecleaning, grocery shopping, or gardening.

Time Is Precious

It's very easy for weeks to go by without having quality time with your spouse. You can keep this from happening to you by making sure you put aside time for planning, for conflict resolution, and for fun activities every single week. You will always know, even if you are very busy, that you and your spouse will have quality time together.

Complete the following chart with different activities that you and your spouse would like to schedule and complete on a regular basis:

Planning Goals	Resolution Goals	Fun Goals
	Daily	
_____	_____	_____
_____	_____	_____
_____	_____	_____
_____	_____	_____
	Weekly	
_____	_____	_____
_____	_____	_____
_____	_____	_____
_____	_____	_____

Planning Goals	Resolution Goals	Fun Goals
Monthly		
_____	_____	_____
_____	_____	_____
_____	_____	_____
_____	_____	_____

By making the most of the time that you do have together, you will keep your relationship strong.

The Least You Need to Know

➤ The time you spend with your spouse needs to be managed. Make a time chart and use it.

➤ Set aside time every week for planning, conflict resolution, and fun activities.

➤ When you don't have much time together, it's worthwhile to make the small moments count. Take the time to eat breakfast together, have a brief conversation on the phone in the middle of the day and in the evening, and ask about each other's day.

What's Bugging You?

All relationships have conflicts. As close as the two of you might be to each other, you're still two separate people with different habits and different needs. That's okay. There are no two people in the world who agree on everything. That would be impossible, and there would be no challenges or room for growth and learning.

This chapter will give you guidelines for identifying your differences. You will learn how to decide how annoyed you really are with something your spouse does. These skills are the critical building blocks to resolving conflicts with your spouse.

Who Am I and Who Are You?

The single best way to learn about yourself is to be in a committed relationship. All of a sudden, every little thing you do, from how grumpy you are in the morning to your 27 magazine subscriptions, becomes an issue in the relationship. Lifelong habits that you never gave a second thought to, like clipping your fingernails while watching TV, annoy

Soul Mates
Being in a relationship often is like looking in the mirror. We see things in ourselves that we didn't see before. Sometimes this can be difficult, but it's our best opportunity for growth.

your partner to no end. Some days it seems every single thing you do bothers your spouse and being married seems impossible.

Don't fret! Figuring out what bothers each of you about the other person is the first step toward resolving your differences. Every couple has conflicts. One of the biggest mistakes couples make is to assume that marriage can be conflict-free. This assumption will guarantee frustration. Learning how to deal with the conflicts is the difference between happiness and misery.

Why Do We Annoy Each Other?

You might think you know what bothers your spouse. But, sometimes things that were unacceptable in your house when you were growing up might be of no consequence to your spouse. And habits that went unnoticed when you were growing up might greatly bother your spouse.

OH!

Bet You Didn't Know

Q: Are successful marriages conflict-free?

A: No. All couples, even happily married ones, have arguments. The difference is that successful couples resolve their conflicts well.

When Mary was growing up, there was a strict rule in her house that the breakfast dishes had to be washed before she left the house in the morning. A pile of dirty dishes at the end of the day was unacceptable to her mother. Anyone who did not clean his or her dishes early in the day would be punished. Mary always hated this rule and vowed that when she was married and had her own home she would leave the dishes until after dinner. Mary assumed that the pile of dirty dishes bothered her husband, Joe, and felt guilty about it every single day. In reality, Joe never gave it a second thought.

However, there was something Mary did that really bothered Joe. When the phone rang during dinner she would always answer it. Most of the time she would not talk long, but Joe considered it a rude interruption of their mealtime together. He never said anything to her about it. However, they often had arguments about insignificant things later in the evening. Mary never even realized that answering the phone during dinner annoyed her husband.

It's very important to communicate with your spouse when something is bothering you. It's also important not to make assumptions about what is important to your spouse. Otherwise you might waste your time doing something you think your spouse cares about, when in reality he or she does not even notice!

Gripes and Grievances

Knowing what bothers each partner is absolutely necessary to the success of your relationship. Otherwise, countless hours will be wasted arguing about things that might easily be resolved. Answer the following questions openly and honestly. The way you and your spouse respond may surprise both of you.

Gripes Quiz

1. What is the single most annoying thing your spouse does?

   _____

2. What does your spouse do daily that bothers you?

   _____

3. Name 10 habits you wish your spouse didn't have.

   _____

   _____

   _____

   _____

   _____

   _____

   _____

   _____

   _____

   _____

4. What bothers you most about yourself?

   _____

   continues

---

continued

5. What do you think bothers your spouse most about you?

_____

6. Name 10 habits you wish you didn't have.

_____

_____

_____

_____

_____

_____

_____

_____

_____

7. Name 10 habits you think your spouse wishes you didn't have.

_____

_____

_____

_____

_____

_____

_____

_____

_____

The Bother Barometer

You might have made a huge list of things your spouse does that bother you. You've been careful to be complete and are ready to discuss your list of the 37 habits that annoy you. The two of you have set aside Thursday evening for this discussion, and you wonder if there will be enough time to lodge all of your complaints.

Slow down! Take a deep breath and read the following section carefully. All annoying habits are not equally bothersome. Before you discuss anything with your spouse, you must figure out how important it is to you. You can't expect your spouse to eliminate all of his or her habits. But you can expect him or her to change or modify some of them, especially ones that really bother you.

The *bother barometer* is a basic tool to help you decide how much something really bothers you. Now use it to rate the annoying habits your spouse has. Once you get the hang of it, you can modify it to rate everything from financial matters to dealing with in-laws.

Use the following bother barometer to rate each of the 10 habits you wish your spouse didn't have:

1. Not an issue. Doesn't bother me at all.

2. I'd prefer it didn't happen, but it's not a big deal.

3. It occasionally annoys me when my spouse does it.

4. It sometimes annoys me when my spouse does it.

5. It annoys me most times my spouse does it.

6. It annoys me every time my spouse does it.

7. It annoys me whenever I'm with my spouse.

8. It annoys me even when I'm away from my spouse.

9. I'm miserable because my spouse does it.

10. I can't stand it. Maybe we can't live together anymore because of it.

Think Twice
Don't assume you know what is bothering your spouse. A simple "What's bother-ing you?" will sometimes work wonders!

Soul Mates
Take the time to find out what would be helpful to your spouse. He or she is the single most important person in your life!

Issues that you rate 5, 6, or 7 can escalate into worse problems if they are not dealt with. You must address them with your spouse while they are still at this manageable stage. Most differences that you rate in the middle of the scale can be resolved between the two of you. In the next chapter, you will learn specific skills to help you resolve these kind of conflicts.

Issues that you rate in the 8, 9, and 10 range will be more difficult to resolve. If something your spouse does annoys you constantly and makes you miserable, there probably are many emotions underlying the issue. You can try to resolve the problem yourselves, but you might find you need outside help.

Think Twice
Don't discuss a problem with your spouse until you've thought through how much it's really bothering you. A problem you thought to be major might rate lower on the bother barometer than you initially thought. You might not even need to bring it up with your partner!

On the other hand, things that bother you very little (2 to 4 on the scale) are probably not worth bringing up at all. It's a good idea to recognize that they bother you somewhat and pay attention if something rises on your importance scale.

Sit down with your spouse and discuss each other's answers to the quiz. Did you correctly anticipate what bothered the other person? Are there some things you had no idea bothered your spouse? Are you clear about what bothers you? This information is a crucial first step to resolving your differences.

Identifying Conflicts

Claire and Robert decided to come see us because conflicts about small things were escalating into fights. We suggested they write down the 10 things the other person did that most annoyed them. Then we had them rate the annoying habits on the bother barometer so they would know which ones they needed to discuss with the other person. Both of them found it easy to come up with a list of 10 things, and they found it interesting that only a few of their grievances rated 5 or higher on the bother barometer.

The following is Claire's list of annoyances and their bother barometer ranking:

1. Leaves his dirty socks on the bedroom floor. (2)

2. Overspends his budget by about $50 a month. (5)

3. Turns on the television while the stereo is still on. (2)

4. Spends too many hours a week watching sports on television. (3)

5. Takes the newspaper to work before I've finished reading it. (5)

6. Doesn't like romantic movies. (2)

7. Puts his feet on the coffee table. (3)

8. Brings friends over without asking first. (6)

9. Often arrives late. (5)

10. Leaves magazines all over the house. (4)

The following is Robert's list of annoyances and their bother barometer ranking:

1. Interrupts me in the middle of a sentence. (6)

2. Talks on the phone for a long time when I'm home. (5)

3. Doesn't like action movies. (4)

4. Spends too much money on books. (2)

5. Takes too long getting ready to go out. (3)

6. Uses the last ice cube without refilling the tray. (6)

7. Leaves wet tea bags on the counter. (4)

8. Doesn't make the bed in the morning. (3)

9. Forgets to return videos on time. (3)

10. Files her fingernails while I'm watching television. (5)

Resolving Conflicts

When Claire and Robert discussed the list, they realized that some of the annoyances were easily solved. Some things were small and the other person wasn't even aware that they were issues. Robert can easily leave the newspaper home, and Claire can easily fill up the ice cube tray and file her nails when Robert isn't home. Some issues are solvable just by making the other person aware of them!

Claire and Robert listed three issues that will be more difficult to tackle: disagreements about money, interrupting when the other is talking, and bringing friends over unannounced. If they haven't already done so, Claire and Robert need to make a household budget. They need to determine a reasonable amount of money for each of them to spend a month at their personal discretion and stick to it. We will discuss financial issues and the household budget further in Chapter 11.

Soul Mates
When you resolve a conflict with your spouse, it gives you the opportunity to become even closer to each other.

For the other two issues, they need to improve their communication skills. Claire needs to become a better listener. They might decide that Robert needs to give Claire at least one day's notice before he brings his friends over to the house. Then Claire would have the chance to make other plans. Deciding what they can tolerate ahead of time will help prevent disagreements later. We discussed the key issue of communication in Chapter 5.

The Virtue of Tolerance

We all wish that our spouse never did anything that annoyed us or made us angry. However, that will never happen. Two people living together will always have their differences. When you identify something that bothers you in your spouse, take the time to consider how *much* it bothers you. But keep in mind that tolerating some of your partner's habits and shortcomings will go a long way to creating a harmonious relationship.

> OH!
>
> **Bet You Didn't Know**
>
> Q: If my spouse has habits that annoy me, does that mean we have a bad marriage?
>
> A: No. When you spend a lot of time with a person, you will always notice things that annoy you. Learning to accept at least some of your spouse's habits is an important part of a good relationship.

The Grass Is Not Always Greener

When you are upset with your spouse, it's easy to feel that he or she is not the right person for you. It might seem that other people's marriages are conflict-free. You might think that a marriage with someone else would be a lot better. The grass looks greener on the other side of the fence.

But, remember that every single marriage has conflicts. Two people who live together need to face their differences. You don't usually see the arguments and frustrations of other couples. Most partners keep their fighting private. The grass is not always greener on the other side of the fence.

When you develp the habit of thinking about how much something your spouse does bothers you, it will be easier to tolerate some bad habits. And for those things your spouse does that *really* upset you, read the next chapter carefully. We will give you guidelines on how to resolve conflicts effectively. You will learn to negotiate your differences from annoying habits to major conflicts.

The Least You Need to Know

➤ All marriages have conflicts. Learning how to resolve conflicts makes the difference between a successful and an unsuccessful relationship.

➤ Good conflict resolution starts with identifying the conflict! Some conflicts are resolvable just by identifying them.

➤ Don't make assumptions about what is bothering your spouse. Take the time to ask him or her!

➤ Use the bother barometer to help you focus on the most important issues with your spouse.

We Can Work It Out

Most couples think that they know how to fight. After all, they do it often enough! Many people, however, don't know there are important ground rules to a fair fight. Arguments with your spouse are inevitable. Learning how to fight fair can help you learn from your mistakes and make conflict resolution more productive.

Set Aside Time

Now that the two of you know how to identify conflicts, you need to learn how to resolve them. The first and very important step is making sure you have each other's undivided attention. In Chapter 5, we mentioned setting aside time to resolve differences. Having a regular time to discuss differences is crucial to a good working relationship for two basic reasons. The first reason is that each person knows that he or she will always have a chance to vent frustrations before they build up.

A scheduled discussion time prevents problems from festering and growing out of control. If both people know that Monday evenings from 8 to 8:30 are always discussion times, they will never worry that their concerns won't be heard. The other advantage to a regular discussion time is that it creates some distance from the problem. By talking about a problem away from the heat of the moment, both people can be more objective.

Soul Mates
If you can't complete an argument, make sure to write down your thoughts so you can pick up where you left off.

Discussing a problem right when it's happening guarantees a more heated argument. When either person is very emotional about an issue, that emotion can interfere with the resolution. Waiting to discuss a problem will ensure both people are as calm and objective as possible.

How much time should you set aside for discussion? Thirty minutes a week works well for many couples. The maximum amount of time we advise is one hour. If you cannot resolve an issue in one hour, you probably need to "sleep on it" to gain perspective. It's important to pick a convenient time for both of you. Times like right before you have to dash off for work or after your usual bedtime are not going to give you the calm, uninterrupted time you need to settle your differences.

Think Twice
Don't waste your time trying to discuss something at the moment of conflict—this can be non-productive. You might be so angry that your perception is distorted. Waiting to discuss conflicts during a regular scheduled time will help both of you be more objective about an issue.

It might seem like a waste of time to do this every week. But actually, it's a *time-saver*, because you don't need to spend time fighting throughout the week. By having a scheduled time for conflict resolution, disagreements will take up a very small part of your week.

Most couples don't plan how they will resolve conflicts because they cling to the notion that in a successful relationship there aren't any conflicts. Nothing could be further from the truth! It's precisely because successful couples take the time to resolve their conflicts that they are successful.

Turning Conflict into Resolution

In Chapter 7, we talked about the importance of identifying conflicts—the first step toward resolving differences with your partner. Once you realize *what* is bothering you, you can use the bother barometer to figure out *how much* something is bothering you.

You and your spouse might not need to discuss things that rank low on your scale. By using this method, you will also know what issues you absolutely must talk about during your weekly meeting.

Harry and Sue spent a lot of their time together bickering and never seemed able to resolve anything. Harry would track mud into the house, and Sue would become angry. She would ask him to take off his shoes and leave them on the porch, and he would say, "Don't bother me now, I'm busy." Sue would attempt to bring up the topic, but Harry never wanted to talk about it. She was becoming more and more frustrated. Lately, she would yell at him for that and other things. She felt like he never listened, but she didn't know any other way to get her point across.

> **Soul Mates**
> Couples often have ongoing sources of irritation that they never take time to discuss. Simple annoying habits can sometimes be resolved in a 10-minute discussion!

On the other hand, Sue would leave magazines all over the house. Harry could not always find the one he wanted to read. He wanted Sue to keep all of the magazines in one place, so he would know where they were. Every time he brought it up with Sue, she was busy and didn't want to talk about it.

Harry and Sue both had a habit that annoyed the other person. It wouldn't take much effort for Harry to take off his shoes when they were muddy and for Sue to keep their magazines in the family room.

They could resolve these issues if they would take the time to discuss them. However, because they waited until the heat of the moment, the intensity of their emotions prevented a productive discussion. What would otherwise have been a minor problem built up and became a constant source of frustration for both of them.

Have a Clear Goal in Mind

Before you talk with your partner, think about how the problem might be resolved. In the above example with Harry and Sue, the goal is straightforward. But, something might be bothering you and it's not clear what would help. If this is the case, stop! Think it through. Take the time to develop some specific ideas on how to make things right. It will be easier for your spouse to change if he or she knows exactly what would help you. A good discussion has a clear end point; if you don't know what that is, why would your partner?

> **Think Twice**
> Don't just say, "This is bugging me." Tell your spouse what you'd like him or her to do about it. Otherwise the issue might not get resolved to your satisfaction.

The following steps will provide clarity and help you focus on what you want your partner to do:

1. Write down what is bothering you.

2. Use the bother barometer to determine how much it bothers you.

3. Try to examine why it bothers you.

4. Come up with three different things your spouse could do to help.

5. During your next discussion time with your spouse, tell your spouse what is bothering you and what he or she could do to help.

Think of Solutions

Melissa and Sam were generally very accommodating toward one another. When something bothered the other person, they bent over backward to do something about it. But recently, they had a problem. Melissa was concerned that Sam was spending far too much time at work and coming home past dinnertime every night. Sam was working on a special project, which would last a few more months, and he needed to put in extra hours at the office to get it done. Melissa felt lonely and neglected all week. When she brought it up with Sam, he became defensive. He did miss the time he spent with Melissa, but when he asked her what he could do, she only said, "You need to come home earlier." He responded, "That's impossible. I have too much work to do." That seemed like the end of the discussion, and Melissa continued to feel frustrated. Sam was usually willing to accommodate her, but this time he could not realistically meet her request.

Finally, instead of brooding over it, she started to think about other solutions. She came up with a good idea. She asked Sam if he could shift his schedule. Instead of coming home at 9 P.M. every night, she asked if he could come home at 11 P.M. one night and 7 P.M. the next night.

OH!

Bet You Didn't Know

Q: What is the difference between a debate and a marital discussion?

A: In a debate, you get points for being right. In a marital discussion, both partners get points for making sure their emotional needs—and the needs of their spouse—are met.

Sam thought about this and agreed. He felt much better, because he felt like the solution accommodated his needs as well. Sam then came up with the idea that on the nights he worked until 11 P.M., Melissa would bring take-out dinner to his office so they would at least have a short chance to talk. If he was going to be working so late, he needed to take a dinner break. By opening the door to a reasonable solution, Melissa shifted Sam out of his defensive mode.

They generally abided by this new schedule for the next six months, until Sam completed his project. Both of them were happier because they had more time together. Sam felt less stressed by his extra workload because he knew he was seeing Melissa for dinner almost every evening. Many problems have reasonable solutions, but they need to be thought of first!

Say "I," Not "You"

Too many arguments break down into yelling, screaming accusation sessions:

> "You did this."

> "You did that."

> "You made me feel awful."

These are fighting words and are very likely to put your partner on the defensive. Sentences starting with "you" are by definition accusatory. They also don't inform your spouse how you are feeling. But sentences starting with the word "I" have the opposite effect:

Think Twice
Don't accuse your spouse during an argument. If you're in the middle of a fight and find yourself saying, "You did this" or "You did that," stop yourself. Take a deep breath and begin your next sentence "I feel..."

> "I feel this way..."

> "I was hurt when..."

> "I get frustrated by..."

These phrases help your partner sympathize with how you feel and are the first step to resolving conflicts. It's easy for your partner to be on your side when you say how you feel. It's much harder for your partner when he or she feels defensive. By following this simple rule, you can make your arguments productive by helping the other person understand how you are feeling.

After seeing us for several months about their difficulties handling conflicts, Harry and Sue, at our guidance, started having weekly discussion sessions. These would sometimes turn into fighting sessions. The most recent discussion involved Sue's habit of leaving the car's gas tank near empty. Even though it was a relatively small issue, they never seemed to be able to resolve it. Harry would say, "You drive me crazy when you let the gas run out in the car. You're so inconsiderate. You can't be thinking of anyone but yourself when you do that." Sue really felt attacked. Harry's words did not make her feel like fixing the problem; they just made her mad. So, both of them were angry, and Sue continued to let the gas run too low in the car.

> OH!
>
> ### Bet You Didn't Know
>
> Q: Sometimes my spouse angers me so much, I just can't stop yelling. What can I do?
>
> A: Take a five-minute break to cool down. When you resume your discussion, start the next sentence with "I." Be careful to avoid the accusatory word "you."

But think how differently Sue would feel if Harry had brought up his complaint using the "I" rule. "I was frustrated yesterday because the gas was very low in the car. I was late to my meeting because I needed to fill up the car with gas. I would really appreciate it if you would put gas in the car when it gets down to a quarter tank. That would help me out a lot." Sue probably wouldn't feel defensive. She would see his point of view and might feel motivated to keep a reasonable amount of gas in the car.

Reality Check

These questions will help you think about your conflicts with your spouse. You might find that conflicts would be more productive if you followed the "I," not "you," rule.

1. How often do you fight with your partner? Every day? Several times a week?

2. Do you feel your fights are resolved fairly? Or are your arguments often unresolved?

3. Do you tend to accuse your partner of something by starting sentences with "you"? Can you remember specific incidents in the last three weeks when you used the word "you" in a fight?

4. How could you have rephrased your sentences to include the word "I"? Do you think the issue would have been resolved differently?

When you think about it, you probably realize that rephrasing discussions using the word "I" instead of "you" would help resolve conflict. During your next discussion, see how it changes the tone of the whole conversation for the better!

Be a Good Echo

In Chapter 5 on communication, we talked about making sure you were heard. This is particularly important when you are trying to resolve your differences. Never assume you have been heard. Everyone is different. While you might need to be told only once to make sure to close the refrigerator door, most people need to be told something several times before it "clicks" in. Be patient and try not to have anger in your voice if your spouse needs reminding. Also, just because you said something once to your spouse doesn't mean that he or she understands what you meant or what you need. Having your spouse repeat what you said is a way of showing you that he or she heard what you said. If your spouse doesn't repeat it accurately, then you have a chance to say it differently.

Melissa and Sam usually understood each other's concerns. But sometimes even they would miscommunicate. They would make an incorrect assumption about what the other person was saying. For instance, Sam didn't like it when Melissa was on the telephone for long periods of time when he was home, especially during mealtime. He wanted her to limit her conversations to about 10 minutes, and if the phone rang during dinner, he wanted her to tell the person she would call them back after dinner. So Sam said, "I don't like it when you're on the phone all night. I like to spend time with you in the evenings." Sam worded his request by following the "I" rule.

Melissa immediately assumed that Sam did not want her to answer the phone in the evenings. The phone rang several times each night, and Melissa usually answered it. She worked out of their home and used the telephone to conduct much of her business. Melissa assumed that Sam's request was unreasonable. So she said, "You mean that you want me never to answer the phone during dinner? What if an important client is calling and doesn't leave a message? And you mean that I shouldn't conduct any business in the evenings? That would be impossible for me!"

"No, no, no. That isn't what I meant." Sam told Melissa that what he meant was that she always answer the phone, but tell the caller she would call him or her back after dinner. And, he asked that she limit her calls to 10 minutes, unless it was something urgent. This seemed reasonable to Melissa. By repeating what she thought Sam meant, Sam was able to clarify what he really wanted from her. If she had just said, "I can't do that," this issue would still be unresolved.

Soul Mates

There is nothing worse than having someone misunderstand what we mean. We all love it when we feel thoroughly understood. That kind of communication takes time and determination, but the rewards make for a thoroughly satisfying relationship.

Stay on Target

It's tempting in an argument to collect every grievance you have ever had against your spouse and throw it in his or her face. This is obviously counterproductive. If you are talking about dirty socks, talk only about dirty socks. That is an issue you can tackle and resolve. If dirty socks turns into wet towels, cold dinners, and too many long days at the office, you will defeat your purpose. You will not have resolved the issue about dirty socks, and you will have succeeded only in making your spouse angry and alienated.

> OH!
>
> ### Bet You Didn't Know
>
> Q: When I bring up all the things that are bothering me, we never seem to be able to resove anything. What can I do?
>
> A: It's very important to discuss and resolve one issue at a time. When you try to resolve many different things at a time, it can be overwhelming and it makes it impossible to find workable solutions. If you make sure to set aside time every week, or possibly twice a week, to discuss conflicts, you will have the time you need to work through one issue at a time.

Sue and Harry were handling their conflicts better. They had set aside time to discuss differences, and they were better at using the word "I" to communicate their needs. But sometimes they would lose focus during an argument. Sue wanted Harry to clean the kitchen table after he was done eating, and asked him to do so. But just as he was about to agree, she began listing several other "dirty kitchen" issues that were bothering her. When she was on her fifth request, Harry lost patience and walked away. She had lost focus and had lost her husband's attention by bombarding him with too much at once.

Sue learned her lesson, and the next week she only brought up the kitchen table. This illustrates another benefit of the weekly discussion sessions. A planned time gives you another chance to work through a problem. Harry agreed, and Sue saved her other grievances for another time.

One-Liners to Avoid

Statements like these stop a fight dead in its tracks. Nothing gets resolved when you say the following:

"You're impossible."

"I'm leaving you."

"We'll never get along."

The person speaking them, in essence, is saying that this process is futile and a waste of time. It's impossible for the other person to respond to such a statement, and he or she will either walk away or come right back with a similar statement. It's very easy to fall into this trap. Sometimes the situation really does seem impossible. But try to stop yourself next time from delivering these "show-stopping" one-liners. Remember that these types of statements will only push your spouse away and you'll be that much further from your goal of having a close, intimate marriage.

Think Twice
Never say the word "divorce." Ever. Don't even imply it. It's one of the most destructive things you can do to your relationship. It weakens trust and creates fear about the future.

Be Honest with Your Limits

Most of us would like to make our spouses happy. If our spouse has a reasonable request of us, we try to be accommodating. But an issue might arise that is not so easily solved. The request our spouse makes might exceed our limits. For instance, in the earlier example with Melissa and Sam, Sam did not agree to come home at 7 P.M. every night. He knew that he could not complete his project without working extra hours. As much as he wanted to accommodate Melissa, he could not agree to her request.

Think Twice
Don't make promises you can't keep. A broken promise can be much worse than no promise at all.

Imagine what would have happened if he had told her that he would try to come home at 7 P.M. At about six o'clock every single night, Sam would become frantic. He would look at the amount of work he had left to do and realize there was no way he would be home on time. He would do as much as he could and then call Melissa at 6:45 and tell her that he would be late. Melissa would be angry because she had prepared dinner and was looking forward to seeing him. Sam would be in a no-win

Think Twice
Don't push your partner away. When a married couple is in the midst of battle with each other, it often feels like they are on opposite sides of the river, as if they are enemies. It's now—in the middle of a conflict—that the two of you most need to work together.

situation. If he came home on time, he would be resentful that he couldn't fulfill his responsibilities at work. If he stayed late, he would upset Melissa.

But Sam had been honest with himself about his needs, and he and Melissa came up with a good solution. It's always better to be honest with your spouse about your own limits from the start. Saying you'll do something and then not following through is usually worse than admitting you can't do it in the first place. When you are both clear about your limits, you can develop a solution using all of the necessary information.

Don't Forget You Are Both on the Same Side

It's important to remember that you and your spouse are on the same side during every argument. You both have the same goal during every fight—to resolve your differences so that both of you are satisfied.

Your goal is not to "win" the argument, but to help develop a workable solution. You care about your spouse and want him or her to be happy. You don't want your spouse to be miserable and upset about an issue you haven't been able to resolve together. Try not to lose sight of that when you are frustrated.

Resolving to Resolve

If you are determined to resolve your differences with your spouse, then you are halfway there! Conflict resolution takes a commitment of time and energy from both you and your spouse. But that time and energy is well spent. When you work together on resolving your differences, you are strengthening your relationship.

There are times you will need to compromise to reach a solution. You might need to do something you don't really want to do in order to accommodate your spouse. And at other times, your spouse will need to do something he or she doesn't really want to do in order to be accommodating of your needs. Remember to look at the larger goals—getting along and resolving your differences. That can make compromising easier.

The Least You Need to Know

➤ Set aside time for conflict resolution, and be clear about your goals.

➤ Avoid using the accusatory "you" in arguments. Try to use the word "I" to describe your feelings.

➤ It's useful to repeat back what your spouse tells you.

➤ Keep your discussions focused.

➤ Don't commit to things you can't do. Figure out a compromise solution that you both can live with.

Chapter 9

I'm Sorry...That's All I Can Say

In This Chapter

➤ The importance of admitting fault

➤ Why it's so hard to say "I'm sorry"

➤ Placing the blame on something or someone else

➤ How to avoid carrying a grudge

When one of you makes a mistake or forgets to do something that you said you would, saying "I'm sorry" can change an angry argument into a constructive discussion. Those two little words can work miracles! There is only one problem. Almost everyone has an aversion to apologizing. Overcoming that aversion is one of the keys to having an extraordinary marriage.

We All Make Mistakes

There is an expression that we use when we make a mistake: "I'm only human." We're saying that everybody makes mistakes, so what we did is okay. And it is okay, as long as we take personal responsibility for our wrongdoing. Saying "sorry" but not meaning it or not intending to improve our actions will cause a lack of trust to develop. Saying "I'm sorry" and admitting that we did something wrong is the first step to self-improvement. Being unable to apologize is a recipe for a brittle marriage. Saying "I'm sorry" gives a marriage the resiliency to weather both partners' mistakes.

Taking Responsibility

Trent had difficulty taking responsibility for his actions. He had agreed to come home at six o'clock every night, which was very important to his wife, Holly. She worked part-time so that she could be with their infant during the day, and she often needed to leave at six o'clock for night meetings. Trent would occasionally come home on time, but many nights he would be 10, 20, or even 30 minutes late. He always had an excuse about something coming up at work or the bad traffic on the freeway. He never once said, "I'm sorry." Trent blamed his lateness on external factors instead of taking personal responsibility.

> **Soul Mates**
> In a partnership, your problem is your partner's problem. (And vice versa!) Often, people don't take the time or make the effort to help their mate with difficulties he or she may be experiencing in the outside world. It's important to a strong marriage that couples solve problems together.

This behavior frustrated Holly to no end. She could never count on him for any of her evening plans. She felt that she had done her fair share by being home with their baby most of the day and that Trent was not living up to his end of the bargain. One day, she let him know how furious she was. Through her tears she said, "You never even say, 'I'm sorry,' like somehow it isn't even your fault. It is your fault. You're the one who's late all the time." Trent took a step back and looked at Holly. At first he wanted to shout back, "Of course, I say I'm sorry," but then he realized it wasn't true. He was always making excuses. It took a while, but he finally apologized. By doing so, he was taking responsibility for his actions rather than blaming external factors.

> **Think Twice**
> Don't spend all your time trying to figure out who is to blame. You have the power to rise above this petty game! Instead, spend that time solving the problem. You will waste less time and accomplish more.

Trent's apology was valuable for many reasons. First, it showed Holly that he cared about her feelings. Second, only after admitting he was wrong could Trent start improving his behavior. And third, Trent and Holly could be a team, rather than acting like they were on opposing sides. The point is that the greater a couple's ability and willingness to say "I'm sorry," the more balanced, stable, and satisfying the relationship.

Rate Your Ability to Take Responsibility

It can be difficult to admit that you made a mistake. But it's a very important part of a good relationship. Take the time to answer the following questions honestly on a scale ranging from 1 (rarely) to 5 (always).

Responsibility Rating

1. If you forget about something you said you would do, how often do you blame somebody else?

    1   2   3   4   5

2. If you are late, do you tend to blame an external circumstance, like bad traffic or bad weather?

    1   2   3   4   5

3. If the car ran out of gas when you were on the way to a movie, would you automatically blame your spouse?

    1   2   3   4   5

4. If you forgot to buy some items on the grocery list, would your first thought be to come up with a good excuse?

    1   2   3   4   5

5. How much do you think it would improve your relationship with your spouse if you took responsibility for your own mistakes (with 1 being not at all and 5 being extremely)?

    1   2   3   4   5

Think about your answers. If you found that you might blame someone or something else for your mistakes, consider why that might be. It will be easier for you to take responsibility for your actions if you understand that it's difficult for you.

But I'm Always Right!

Nobody is always right. Nevertheless, it's hard for most of us to admit when we're wrong. Sometimes we know that we did something we shouldn't have, and we feel badly about it. So the mind plays a trick on us. It pretends that we didn't do anything wrong. Then we don't have to feel badly about it, and we don't have to say, "I'm sorry," because saying "I'm sorry" would mean admitting that we behaved badly.

This logic will make you feel distant from your spouse. There is nothing wrong with making a mistake. But there is something wrong about not admitting it.

Don't Turn the Table Around

One of the most destructive things you can do when you make a mistake is blame the other person. It will make a bad situation worse, and it will cause the other person to become even angrier. Steve and Tricia were finding themselves arguing all the time about relatively unimportant things. For instance, when Tricia pointed out that Steve had used the last of the toilet paper, he would become defensive and say, "You always put it away where I can't find it." When Steve would ask why Tricia opened mail addressed to him, she would say, "You get a ridiculous amount of mail and I didn't want you reading it all night." Steve and Tricia blamed each other for their own mistakes.

Soul Mates
The strongest couples say "I'm sorry" the most! If you make a mistake, let your spouse know. Say, "I'm sorry, I made a mistake. I'll try not to do it again."

Steve and Tricia were so unable to take responsibility for their own actions that they even tried to blame the other person for their own mistakes! If each would just say, "I'm sorry. I'll try not to do it again," and really mean it, it would make a big difference in their relationship; then they could move past a wrongdoing and start enjoying each other's company again.

Apologizing to Clear the Air

Sometimes it's not so clear who is at fault. In many situations, both people contribute to the problem. Sometimes it's a 50/50 split and it's easy to see that you need to apologize to each other. But other times you might have only contributed just a bit to the problem. It's a good idea to apologize anyway. Even if a problem is only 5 percent your fault and mostly your spouse's, apologizing will make it easier for your spouse to apologize. Remember, the objective is to have a happy, harmonious life, not to be right all the time!

OH!

Bet You Didn't Know

Q: I always apologize and my spouse never does. What can I do?

A: Both people in a marriage should be apologizing for mistakes. If you or your spouse never or rarely apologizes, it might be a red flag indicating problems in your relationship. First try discussing your concerns with your spouse. If this doesn't help, you might do best seeing a couples therapist together.

Jose and Penny were invited to a surprise party for a good friend. They needed to be there at 7 P.M. sharp, and they had to park their car several blocks away so they wouldn't ruin the surprise. Their friend was due to arrive at the house at 7:15. Jose knew that Penny had a tendency to run late, so he asked her to be ready by 6:30. The house was 15 minutes away, so they had buffer time. Penny knew that Jose wouldn't stop to ask for directions and sometimes had trouble finding a new place, but he had promised to get directions ahead of time. They both had anticipated problems to ensure getting to the surprise party on time.

But that day Penny was running very late. She had a project due at work and didn't get home until 6. She usually took an hour to get ready, but committed herself to finishing in 45 minutes. She figured that if they left at 6:45, they could still be at the party on time. Penny knew Jose would understand.

Soul Mates
When you apologize, you prevent the other person from focusing on your contribution to the situation. Hopefully, your spouse will be able to take responsibility for his or her actions, apologize, and try to do better next time.

Jose was frustrated, but he couldn't do anything but wait for her. When they were halfway to the party, he realized he had left the directions at work. He had the address and knew the general area, but wasn't sure if he needed to make a right or a left turn at a critical intersection. He was angry with Penny for being 15 minutes late. If they had left at 6:30, there would have been room for error.

Of course, Jose made the wrong turn and they went in the opposite direction for five minutes. When they finally found the house it was 7:10 and they knew they didn't have time to park two blocks away and get there before their friend. Jose and Penny decided they should miss the surprise and arrive at the party at 7:30. They drove the car a few blocks away and argued for 20 minutes.

Jose and Penny were both at fault. They had come up with a buffer system that allowed for one thing to go wrong; unfortunately, two things had gone wrong. Penny should have made more effort to be home earlier, or at least double-checked to make sure Jose had the directions. And Jose, of course, should have had the directions with him.

They went to the party and had a miserable time. They each should have accepted their share of the responsibility and apologized for their mistakes. That apology would have put the incident behind them so the evening could have been fun. But instead, Jose could only see Penny's fault in the matter, and Penny could only blame Jose. Result: No apology and a bad evening.

What if the situation was even more unbalanced? For instance, if Penny were only five minutes late and Jose had forgotten the address and needed to go back home for it, it would still have been important for Penny to apologize to Jose. Even though her behavior contributed minimally to the situation, she was still somewhat at fault and should apologize.

The "I'm Sorry" Quiz

Please take the following quiz to assess how you handle arguments when you know you are in the wrong.

"I'm Sorry" Quiz

1. Try to remember an argument with your spouse when you knew you were in the wrong.

   _____

2. Did you apologize?

   _____

3. If not, why not?

   _____

4. How would things have been different if you had said, "I'm sorry"?

   _____

If you do not usually apologize to your spouse, try thinking about your response to #4 and determining the effect it would have had on your spouse. What kind of an effect would it have on you if your spouse said "I'm sorry" more often?

Don't Hold a Grudge

There are times when it's not so easy to accept an apology. If your spouse hurt you or greatly inconvenienced you by his or her actions, "I'm sorry" might not seem like enough to make things better. If you can, think of something reasonable he or she could do to make it up to you. Or, if you were the one who disappointed your spouse, figure out how to make things right.

Think Twice
Don't hold a grudge against your spouse. Every minute you spend being angry is quality time you could be spending together.

Greg had bought theater tickets for Linda's birthday. They both were very excited. Greg had a tendency to be late, but he really planned to arrive home on time that night. Unfortunately, everything was working against him: his workload, worse traffic than usual, bad weather, and an accident on the highway. He cut everything too close, arrived home 45 minutes late, and missed the theater. Linda was really upset, especially because it was her birthday.

Greg apologized and clearly felt sorry. Linda tried hard not to hold a grudge, but she was very disappointed. Greg also knew that saying "I'm sorry" wasn't enough. So, he bought new tickets using his "personal" part of the budget. He gave up some lunches out and some trips to his favorite coffeehouse. Greg surprised Linda the next week with the tickets—and he came home on time. Linda was thrilled and felt that Greg had made up for his mistake the week before.

Sometimes there is nothing that can be done to remedy a situation. Maybe your spouse said something mean to you in the heat of an argument and your feelings were hurt. Or maybe he or she stood you up for a lunch date that you missed a meeting for. Once your spouse has apologized and taken responsibility for his or her actions, your job is to forgive and forget. Holding a grudge won't accomplish anything and will distance you from each other. A sincere apology is very valuable.

Anger and Forgiveness

There's an old saying that the best part about fighting is making up. We think there is some truth in this. Think about whether you become angry very quickly or whether it takes a lot to make you angry. Now think about whether you forgive slowly or quickly.

Quick to anger and slow to forgive	Quick to anger and quick to forgive
Slow to anger and slow to forgive	Slow to anger and quick to forgive

Which of the above boxes best describes you?

➤ *Quick to anger.* Some people get angry more quickly than others. They are often described as "having a quick temper." Large things as well as small things can make them angry quickly. It's much better to be slow to anger and not let small things bother you. If you're quick to anger, ask yourself when you become angry if

Soul Mates
Apologizing fully to your spouse involves three steps: Step 1: Admit to yourself that you did something wrong. Step 2: Say "I'm sorry" to your spouse. Step 3: Do your best to avoid repeating your mistake.

your anger is justified. Slow yourself down by taking a deep breath or going for a walk. Remember, your goal is to be slow to anger.

➤ *Slow to forgive.* Some people forgive quickly, while others tend to hold grudges. When someone apologizes to you, do you forgive and forget, or do you tend to remain angry for a while? It's very important to be able to forgive someone and move on. If you are slow to forgive, ask yourself what your anger is really buying you. Would you be willing to give some of it up for a better marriage?

➤ *Slow to anger, quick to forgive.* This should be your goal. Always keep in mind that you want to get angry as little as possible and forgive as often as possible. These are character traits that will both improve you as a person and strengthen your marriage. A relationship between two people who are slow to anger and quick to forgive will be an extraordinary one.

Every time you make up with your spouse, you renew your commitment to the relationship. Many important things are implied: You're saying that you accept his or her apology and forgive him or her. You're also accepting that your spouse isn't perfect and showing that you want to move forward.

The Least You Need to Know

➤ We all make mistakes. Accept blame gracefully and admit when you are wrong.

➤ It's important to apologize, even when you and your spouse are both at fault.

➤ Don't hold a grudge. You need to forgive your spouse and move on.

➤ Keep in mind that your ultimate goal is to be slow to anger and quick to forgive.

Part 3
Daily Hurdles

The two of you are getting along better than ever. You're doing nice things for each other and planning fun activities together. You've gotten better at figuring out what is bothering you, which has helped to resolve conflicts. And you're even saying "I'm sorry," when you're only a little bit at fault.

But now you find yourselves facing daily challenges that feel overwhelming at times. Now is your chance to put your new skills to work. This section focuses on the issues that couples deal with on a day-to-day basis. We'll show you how to make healthy financial choices. We'll give you tips for sexual compatibility to help keep your marriage strong. We'll outline planning strategies to take care of the weekly chores. And we'll show you ways to handle your in-laws with kid gloves. By the time you finish reading these chapters, you will have the tools you need to leap your daily hurdles with ease!

...For Richer, For Poorer

In This Chapter

➤ Understanding the emotions behind financial issues

➤ Determining if you have realistic expectations about money

➤ Assessing your spending and saving habits

➤ Making financial decisions together

Money and finances are emotionally charged issues. They can be sore points in an otherwise good relationship. This chapter will help you understand how you and your spouse view money so that financial issues don't become emotional issues in your marriage.

Money Can Be an Emotional Issue

Mary and Joe always fought about money. Mary tried to save every penny that she could. She would spend many hours clipping coupons for the grocery store each week, and she would never order dessert or beverages at a restaurant. Mary grew up in a household where there was never enough money, and now she wanted as much money in the bank as possible. Joe, on the other hand, loved to eat lunch out several times a week, including

Soul Mates
When you and your spouse are having a disagreement about money, take a moment to understand your emotions and explain them to your partner. He or she will probably be more receptive to your point of view.

dessert and coffee. The freedom to eat out meant a lot to him, and not being able to do so would cause him to feel resentful. Joe grew up in a solid middle-class household that had enough money for extra activities. Before Mary and Joe can sit down to do a household budget they can both live with, they need to understand their emotions about money.

The same is true for you and your spouse. When you sit down with your spouse to do your household budget, keep in mind that money issues can become emotional very quickly. Disagreements about money are often not about money, but about something else, such as power and control.

Realistic Expectations

We all grew up with expectations about our adult life. We had ideas about what kind of house we wanted, where we wanted to travel, and how much we wanted to work. Sometimes, we are lucky and most of our financial expectations are met. But many people's expectations far exceed their financial assets, and they become frustrated when they cannot have what they have always wanted.

Think Twice
Don't let managing your finances become a back-burner project. So many couples let petty annoyances fester until they become major problems. Take the time now to make a financial plan with your spouse.

There are so many reasons why your financial situation might be different than the two of you expected. One of you might have been laid off, a business might have failed, or you might have made a bad investment. Perhaps you had visions of marrying a millionaire, and instead fell in love with a pauper. It's so easy to blame our spouse or ourselves and constantly wish that there were more money in the household. But, unless you can realistically change your financial situation, you need to face up to your expectations for what they are—expectations, not reality. The sooner you learn to be content with what you have, the sooner you will find true happiness.

The following questions about money will help you determine whether your monetary expectations are realistic. On a scale ranging from 1 (not at all) to 5 (absolutely), circle the number for each question that best describes your situation. When you finish, add up your score.

Expectations Quiz

1. Are you living the lifestyle, more or less, that you envisioned you would?

        1   2   3   4   5

2. Do you feel you make enough money?

        1   2   3   4   5

3. Do you feel your spouse makes enough money?

        1   2   3   4   5

4. Most of the time, are you able to afford the things you want to buy?

        1   2   3   4   5

5. Do you and your spouse tend to agree about money issues?

        1   2   3   4   5

6. Do you have enough money to feel secure?

        1   2   3   4   5

7. Do you save a reasonable amount of money every year?

        1   2   3   4   5

8. Are you able to spend a reasonable amount of money on yourself?

        1   2   3   4   5

9. Do you try not to blame your spouse for not making enough money?

        1   2   3   4   5

10. Do you and your spouse have a workable household budget?

        1   2   3   4   5

Use the following ranges to determine where you stand.

10–20   Financial disagreements probably play an enormous part in your lives. It's critical for you and your spouse to read this chapter immediately and put it to use right away.

21–30   Conflicts about money most likely interfere with your relationship. When you work them through, your marriage will improve. Make sure you read this chapter carefully.

31–40   You and your spouse probably don't have major conflicts about money, but there are some unresolved financial issues in your marriage. Read on.

41–50   You're a money pro! Reading this chapter will serve to fine-tune your talents.

Are You a Saver or a Spender?

One of the reasons couples disagree about money is that money means different things to each of them. For some people, money provides a sense of security, of being taken care of; this kind of person would tend to be cautious about spending money and would try hard to put money in the bank. For others, money provides a sense of freedom; they might exercise a more carefree attitude. Of course, most of us fall somewhere in between. There is no right or wrong way to think about money, but it's important to create a budget that works for both of you.

The first step is to figure out where each of you stands with respect to money. Go through the following lists and decide what best describes you. If you are a saver, you probably have some of the following traits:

1. You can never have enough money in the bank.

2. It's a waste of money to order drinks in a restaurant. The water is free.

3. I always keep my eye on the time when I'm making a long-distance telephone call.

4. Meeting the household budget is very important to me.

5. It's better to travel at an inconvenient time than spend extra money for an airplane ticket.

6. I rarely buy a hardback version of a book. I wait for the paperback or go to the library.

7. I try to buy everything on sale.

8. I spend a lot of time planning for the future.

If you are a spender, you probably have some of the following traits:

1. I usually buy what I need without much regard for price.

2. A lot of money in the bank is meaningless if you don't let yourself spend it.

3. My convenience is usually more important than the cost of an airline ticket.

4. When I'm eating out in a restaurant, I order whatever I want on the menu.

5. I would rather go over our household budget sometimes than have to constantly be thinking about money.

6. I talk on the phone long-distance without worrying about the time.

7. I don't wait for an item I want to be on sale.

8. Life is to be enjoyed here and now.

Saver and Spender Combinations

Now, go through the spender and saver lists and determine which one best describes your spouse. Determine which combination of traits the two of you have:

➤ One saver and one spender

➤ Two spenders

➤ Two savers

Each pair of traits will result in different sorts of disagreements. Just because both of you are spenders or savers doesn't mean you won't have any money problems. The following sections will show you what to watch out for.

One Saver and One Spender

If one of you is a saver and one of you is a spender, you'll probably have many disagreements about money. But you can also learn a lot from each other about enjoying life (on the one hand) and planning for the future (on the other). The person who is the spender might feel a sense of security being with someone who is more cautious about money. And the person who is more restrained might be able to enjoy life more with someone who is more spontaneous about money.

Read the following list to find out what can be expected in a saver and spender household:

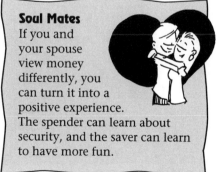

Soul Mates
If you and your spouse view money differently, you can turn it into a positive experience. The spender can learn about security, and the saver can learn to have more fun.

1. You will probably have frequent squabbles about money.

2. When the spender buys what he or she wants, the saver will feel resentful because he or she won't indulge themselves in the same luxury.

3. The spender will feel like his or her spouse is too controlling about money.

4. The saver might secretly feel jealous that the spender can spend money so easily.

5. The spender might secretly feel secure, knowing that his or her spouse is careful about money.

Two Spenders

In a household where both of you are spenders, you will still probably have some financial disagreements. Unless you have unlimited resources, you will also run out of money and run into trouble.

Lisa and Judd both found it very easy to spend money. When they were dating they would go out to fancy restaurants and run up big bills. They didn't think twice about going on vacation and staying in pricey hotels. When they got married, they had no money in the bank and thousands of dollars in credit card bills. For the first few years of their marriage, they continued their same spending pattern and rarely had any arguments about money.

Then they talked about having a family and realized they needed to get rid of their debt and start saving money. Neither of them knew how to change their spending habits. They started fighting about money for the first time in their relationship.

> OH!
>
> ### Bet You Didn't Know
>
> Q: My spouse and I tend to be spenders. What can we do?
>
> A: Recognition is the first step! You have identified yourselves as spenders early on. Get financial advice, make a budget, and stick to it. Then you can prevent bankruptcy and constant arguments about money.

One time Lisa bought a new outfit and Judd chastised her for it. Then when Judd planned a romantic weekend, thinking it would make Lisa happy, she took it as his way of expressing his desire to put off having kids for a while! They were no closer to saving money than before, and now they weren't even enjoying themselves!

Read the following list to find out what can be expected in a two-spender household:

1. Rather than constant squabbles, you will probably have big blowups when the monthly bills come in.

2. When you need to start planning for the future, it will be hard to break your spending habits.

3. You will probably owe money on credit cards.

4. You might not have enough money in savings and investments.

5. You might blame each other for your money problems.

Two Savers

In a household where both of you are careful about money, you might have trouble enjoying yourselves. You might both be spending a lot of energy thinking about the future and not enough focusing on the present.

Melanie and Greg were proud of themselves. They put away money every month into their savings account and into their investment portfolio. Most months, they were even able to save more than they had planned. They never owed money on their credit cards. They both brought bag lunches to work and rarely ate out in restaurants. They were prepared for the future.

But Melanie and Greg had trouble really enjoying themselves. They talked about money constantly. Any time they went out together, they focused on how much it was costing and if it was "worth it." They found it difficult to relax and just have a good time being out. Melanie and Greg were suffering from being too cautious.

OH!

Bet You Didn't Know

Q: Is the answer to money problems to be extremely cautious about spending money?

A: Not necessarily. Every couple needs to strike a healthy balance between spending and saving. Consider setting aside money every week for entertainment, even if it's a small amount.

Read the following list to find out what can be expected in a two-saver household:

1. You won't have substantial credit card debt.

2. You will likely have money in the bank.

3. The two of you might be too focused on money.

4. You might find it hard to spend even a reasonable amount of money on yourselves.

5. You might be focusing too much of your attention on the future and not enough on the present.

Making Financial Decisions Together

Whether you and your spouse are both savers, both spenders, or one of each, both of you should be involved in the financial planning of your lives. If one of you were bringing in more income than the other one, it would be easy to feel that he or she should have more control in the decision-making about the budget or have more discretionary income. The person making less might feel less valuable and give up an equal voice in financial decisions. Money can mean power in your relationship.

Think Twice
Don't fall into the trap of assuming the person who makes more money should have more say in how it's spent. Don't forget that you are part of a team!

Thinking "This is yours, this is mine" can be devastating to a marriage. Although it's valuable for each person to have some of his or her own money, the basic thinking must be "This is ours." Money that either of you makes must contribute to the household, not to the individual. The person making less money might be taking time off to raise the children, starting a new business, or running the household. That partner's contribution, although maybe not financial, is equally critical to the happiness of your family. Making financial decisions together is the healthiest way to approach money.

OH!

Bet You Didn't Know

Q: I want to be more involved with the financial decisions of our household, but I don't know anything about money. What can I do?

A: Learn more about finances! Consider taking a class with your spouse on managing your finances. Or get a book on financial planning and discuss it with your spouse.

The Least You Need to Know

➤ Money can be an emotional issue. Developing realistic expectations about your finances can prevent conflicts about money.

➤ Determining your saving and spending habits can help you anticipate financial problems in the future.

➤ Make financial decisions together. If you feel you don't know enough about money, take a class or read a book on finances.

Chapter 11

Money Management

In This Chapter

➤ The importance of a household budget

➤ Dealing with a reduction in household income

➤ Surprising challenges with an increase in income

In this chapter, we'll give you tips on developing a household budget and guidelines on dealing with a change of income. We'll help you discover a system of managing your money that works for you.

Budget Basics

An ideal budget is a balance between saving and spending. Both of these financial issues are also emotional issues. Saving represents security for most people. Having money in the bank makes them feel they will have enough money for an emergency or for retirement. Not having enough money in the bank makes most people very anxious. On the other hand, the amount of personal spending money you have represents freedom. It's the money you spend without discussing it with anyone else. Not having enough personal spending money makes people feel confined; having enough gives them a sense of freedom that is important.

The following questions will help you think about your own savings and personal money needs, which will help you create your household budget.

---

1. I usually feel that our household has enough money.

    Yes   or   No

2. I tend to worry about money.

    Yes   or   No

3. I am willing to be flexible to create a workable household budget with my spouse.

    Yes   or   No

4. I need _____ in the bank or in investments to feel secure.

5. I need to put _____ in the bank every month to feel secure.

6. I need _____ every week for personal spending money.

Consider your answers. Are they realistic, given your household income? If not, rewrite figures that would be more reasonable. Before you organize your overall budget, have your spouse answer the above questions.

Now take both of your answers and use the following sections to help you determine and agree upon these two key issues:

➤ Savings. (We will save _____ every month.)

➤ Personal spending. (I will have _____ to spend. My spouse will have _____ to spend.)

Once you can settle these two issues, you will have conquered the most emotional part of your budget.

Savings and Investment

This book is not an in-depth finance book, and we cannot suggest to you an exact amount of money you should be saving. Every couple is different, and every situation is different. You might be earning less money now and expect a raise in the future. Or you might be at your peak earning potential and should be saving more now. Your kids might be out on their own, or you might be saving for college.

What we strongly encourage is that you don't skimp on the time and thought you give to this issue. Determining a comfortable, appropriate amount of money you need to save every month is the cornerstone of a good budget.

The amount of money you need to set aside every month is determined by working backward from your long-term goals. The biggest issues facing you might be saving for a house, for a car, for your children's education, or for retirement. The two of you might consider hiring an outside expert to help you develop a solid financial plan. Or you might feel comfortable doing it on your own. There are numerous workbooks and financial planning books out there to help you if you decide to try this on your own.

Soul Mates

When you save money every month, you are strengthening your relationship. Both of you are saying (without words) that you are committed to your future together!

$ _____ is the total amount of money the two of you should save (or invest) every month.

Settling on a figure will give both of you peace of mind. Savers will know that money is being set aside for the future. And spenders will know that by setting aside this money first, their spending habits will not interfere with their long-term goals!

Separate Spending Habits

The other crucial part of the budget is determining how much money each of you gets every month that is entirely at individual discretion. Consider how important this is. The two of you were adults when you got married, so you each made separate financial decisions. At the very least, you were free to splurge on a fancy outfit or order dessert and coffee in a restaurant without discussing it with anyone.

Bet You Didn't Know

Q: What if you and your spouse have similar long-term goals, but still fight about money?

A: No matter what, you are two different people. One of you might like to indulge in a cappuccino every day before work, while the other would much rather save for a big-ticket item. By having some money that is separate, you can each pursue your personal choices by using your own money and not your spouse's.

The amount of money the two of you want to set aside for discretionary income will vary greatly, depending on what you want it to include. Common items to include in personal spending money are lunch and snack money, gas money, gift money, toiletries, and some extra money for unexpected things. This is by no means a hard and fast list. Some people include those items in the regular budget, or they may expand the personal money to include other items. For instance, you could decide that a certain amount of money is reasonable for clothing for each of you and consider that part of the discretionary income. Some couples work better by having as much money as possible separate, while others like to keep closer tabs on everything.

Mary and Joe came to see us because they were tired of constantly fighting about money. Joe tended to be a spender and Mary tended to be a saver. Both of them thought it was a good idea to have separate money they could spend any way that they wanted without interference from the other person. They agreed on $35 a week, which was to include lunch and snack money. This amount was less than what Joe was currently spending and more than what Mary was spending.

The Spice Rack
When you each have a personal amount of money, a gift from you to your spouse means more. It's coming from your money, not the household money.

At first it was difficult, especially for Joe, but eventually they found it easier to save every month. At first Joe was frustrated, but then he learned he could either eat out only three times a week or else go to less expensive places. Initially, Mary didn't spend anything and saved all her money. But, over time, when she really accepted the money was hers and hers alone to spend, she was able to buy things for herself, like a beautiful new wool coat she had always wanted. Both of them grew from the experience, and they have more money in the bank too!

What is the amount of money each of you wants every month that would be totally discretionary? This is money that you can spend without the other spouse interfering in any way.

$_____ His $_____ Hers $_____ Kids

The important thing to remember is that having your own money will give you freedom to make your own financial decisions (and mistakes). Spenders will be able to spend (to a point) without discussing it with their spouse. And savers might find it easier to spend money that is set aside for them.

The Household Budget

This is a topic that many married couples dread: tackling the household budget. But it's important to recognize that sitting down ahead of time to determine the budget not only gives a couple a sense of teamwork, but also allows for more freedom about money, not to mention less anxiety. Having a budget will lessen disagreements about money, because you shift the focus from money to thinking about how to meet your household needs.

In addition to the two *emotional* items we discussed, savings and personal spending, a standard budget will include the following:

Soul Mates
Even if your income and situation does not change, the two of you should reevaluate your budget every year. You might be surprised. There might be some new issues that need to be addressed.

> ➤ Food

> ➤ Shelter (includes utilities)

> ➤ Entertainment

> ➤ Insurance

> ➤ Transportation

> ➤ Health care

> ➤ Clothing

Before you start tackling this part of the budget, do the following calculation:

$ _____   Write down your monthly income.

$ _____   Subtract your planned monthly savings.

$ _____   Subtract your planned monthly personal spending.

$ _____   The money left for your monthly budget.

The amount of money you have left is what you should use to calculate the rest of your budget. The numbers might fall into place. But if you find yourselves arguing over the budget, ask yourselves the following questions regarding how you can save money in each category:

> ➤ *Food.* Do you shop in bulk? Could you eat less meat and substitute grains and beans for some meals? Could you cut down on expensive snacks like potato chips and soda?

> ➤ *Shelter.* Could you reduce your heating or cooling bills? Would it be worthwhile to insulate your home? Could you move to a smaller dwelling or a less expensive neighborhood?

➤ *Entertainment.* Could you see fewer movies in the theater and instead wait for them to come out on video? Could you go to less expensive restaurants or cut out dessert and coffee when you eat dinner out? Could you scale down your vacations by eating fewer meals out and staying in less expensive hotels? If you buy season tickets (cultural or sporting events), could you attend half the events and sell the rest of the tickets?

➤ *Insurance.* Are you fully aware of insurance through your employer? Sometimes insurance plans through work are much less expensive than as individuals. Could you extend your waiting period on disability insurance?

➤ *Transportation.* If you have two cars, could you function with only one? Could you save on gas by carpooling to work together or with other people? Could you sell one of your vehicles and buy a less expensive or older model to lower your car payments (and probably your automobile insurance)?

➤ *Health care.* Do you have the most reasonable plan for your needs? If you have few medical expenses, it might pay to have a less expensive policy with a larger deductible. If you are on long-term medication, are you buying your medicine in bulk? Sometimes plans charge a lot less when you buy several months' worth of medicine through a mail service.

➤ *Clothing.* Could you buy fewer clothes or shop at a more economical store than you do now? Could you put part of the clothing budget under discretionary money?

After you go through these questions, try calculating your budget again. Things might fall into place. If they don't, you'll need to make more drastic cuts than you would like or somehow bring in more income.

OH!

Bet You Didn't Know

Q: I have the chance to make some additional money at work. Should I do it, even though it will mean less time with my family?

A: Deciding to bring additional income into the household is not easy, but the decision must be made with your spouse's input. Working longer hours will bring stress back home with you. Try working extra for one week to see how it feels to both of you. Remember that extra money isn't the only factor to consider.

What to Do When You're Feeling Pinched

What should you do if you cannot come up with a workable budget on your current income and cannot reasonably bring in more money? Or what should you do if your financial situation changes for the worse and you need to pare down your spending even more?

First of all, stay calm. Evaluate whether the situation is long-term (you don't foresee more income in at least a year) or temporary (like an unexpected large medical bill). A temporary change needs both of you to buckle down, cut down on your entertainment or other discretionary items, and pay that bill off. A long-term change demands a new budget.

OH!

Bet You Didn't Know

Q: My wife tells me that I need to be more romantic, but she doesn't want me to spend any extra money on her. What can I do?

A: It's easy to get so focused on money that you forget that some of the best things in life are free! If you're on a tight budget, you can forgo the movie and dinner and still have a great time with each other. Instead, take a long walk, have a picnic lunch, or watch the sunset.

Go through the list of questions again. Are there ways you can tighten your budget without going into your savings? If not, you need to bring in additional income or possibly make some major changes. You will need to scale down. You might need to sell your home or move to a smaller apartment. Do your best to support each other through this difficult time—your relationship will be even stronger when it's over.

Think Twice

Don't be in denial about a reduction in income. Face facts and redo your budget. Not facing the problems now will only prolong the agony.

★*6*@

More Money Might Mean More Problems

It might seem surprising that any problems would result from an increase in income. After all, you have a budget and now you have plenty of money to meet it and then some. It could only be better if the two of you had extra money to spare. Right? Wrong.

Bet You Didn't Know

OH!

Q: If not more money, then what will solve our financial problems?

A: Good communication and a commitment from each of you to have a budget that works.

Think Twice
Don't go on a spending spree if you get a raise at work. Sit down with your spouse and decide together how you want to spend the additional income.

The two of you worked out a careful budget and have worked hard to meet it. More money will make that easier. But what are the two of you going to do with the extra money? One of you might want to save it; the other might want to buy something not on the budget. Or maybe you want to upgrade something that's already in your budget, or go on a great vacation. Sometimes, couples end up spending more money than they make when they have an increase in income. They might fall into the trap of ignoring their budget instead of setting up a new one.

Even though you have more money, you still need to rework your budget. Are you going to increase your savings and keep everything else the same? Should you take that dream vacation you have been thinking about for years? Or maybe it means you just have more money every month that you can spend without thinking about it. The point is that even though you feel richer than before, the extra money is still limited. You can easily go over your budget by upgrading everything.

Three Ways to Organize Your Money

After the two of you have generated a workable budget, you're almost there. The other decision you have to make is how you are going to organize your money. Some couples like to have most or all of the money accessible to both of them. Others like to divide it up more and each take responsibility for different parts of the budget. The following are three ways to organize your finances.

Plan #1: Each of you could have your own credit card and checking account. After putting aside your monthly savings, you could divide up the money appropriately so that each of you takes responsibility for a different part of the budget. For instance, one of you could take care of the groceries, clothing, and entertainment, while the other person took care of the mortgage payment or rent, the utilities, and the car payments.

Plan #2: You could have only one checking account with all of the household expenses, including mortgage, insurance, car payments, and utilities, paid from that account. You could both be involved in paying bills and balancing the checkbook as you write each check. Then each of you could have a credit card and a certain amount of cash each month for more discretionary spending.

Plan #3: One of you could take responsibility for paying the bills each month. That person would take care of the mortgage, insurance, car payments, groceries, utilities, and clothing. The other person would have a monthly allowance for discretionary spending.

The Least You Need to Know

➤ Different households have different conflicts about money.

➤ Monthly savings and personal spending money tend to be the most emotional issues in a budget. Spend extra time deciding amounts that will work for *both* of you.

➤ If your household income decreases, tackle your budget right away, before it gets out of hand.

➤ Even if your income increases, you still need to redo your household budget.

Chapter 12

My Pillow Is Your Pillow

In This Chapter

➤ Why sex changes when you are married

➤ Guidelines for improving communication about sex

➤ Overcoming obstacles to a great sex life

➤ The different ways that men and women view sex

➤ How birth control issues can affect your sex life

➤ Choosing birth control that is right for you

In this chapter, we will give you guidelines to communicate effectively about your sexual needs. We will show you how men and women view sex differently. If you are currently using birth control, we will give you tips to keep it from interfering with your sexuality. This chapter will give you some ideas for improving your sex life.

Marriage and Sex

We all have heard many jokes about sex (or lack of it) in married life. But, sexual satisfaction is much greater in marriage for three reasons. First, the commitment of marriage gives us a comfort that can be found in no other relationship. Second, over time we learn how to better please our mate. And third, communication gets better with time, and good sex is largely a function of good communication.

John and Pamela were attracted to each other the instant they met. They had a very fulfilling sex life many years into their marriage. Now, several years later, things are very different. They have sex much less often and enjoy it less than they used to. Both of them are sad and frustrated by this but don't know what went wrong or how to make things better.

You might be wondering what else is going on in their lives. Well, it's probably no surprise that Pamela and John have a three-year-old and Pamela is pregnant with their second child. They bought a home two years ago and their budget has been tight since then. Pamela is working an extra 10 hours a week to help with the monthly bills, and she is not happy with the child care arrangement for their three-year-old daughter. It's difficult for them to have a fulfilling sexual relationship in the middle of all of this stress.

This scenario, unfortunately, is very common in married life. Slowly, at first imperceptibly, sex with your spouse might get relegated to a lower priority. In the beginning of your marriage, sex might have been one of the main focuses in your life, but it can now take a back seat even to a good night's sleep! This can take a toll on your marriage. Read on to see ways to get your sex life back on track.

Communication and Sex

Communication is the key to a great sex life. You need to let your spouse know that you are interested in having sex. Leaving him or her guessing can lead to disaster. And letting your partner know exactly what feels good to you can lead to a great evening!

Soul Mates
Having a conversation about sexual needs outside the bedroom ensures a better time in it!

Jim and Loretta generally enjoyed their intimate time together, but lack of communication had them sending mixed messages about when they wanted sex. Sometimes, when Loretta gave Jim a hug, he thought she wanted to go to bed, but she just wanted a hug. He tended to think that any physical approach from Loretta meant she wanted to have sex. He also assumed that when he sent her a signal by rubbing her shoulders, she would know he was interested in having sex. But, usually, she just thought he was rubbing her shoulders!

Bet You Didn't Know

Q: Shouldn't my spouse just "know" when I want to have sex?

A: No. It's important to be clear when you are interested in having sex. You will avoid disappointment and improve your sex life in general.

This misunderstanding interfered with their enjoyment of sex because they each felt that the other was playing games. They came to see us to figure out how to improve things. We asked how often each of them wanted to be intimate. Jim answered two to three times a week, and Loretta answered one to two times a week. Then we asked both of them if they felt comfortable agreeing to have sex two times a week, an amount that coincided with both of their answers. They both agreed. We pointed out that they should be direct about their desires, so they would not send mixed messages. We advised them to say, "How's tonight for you?" It took less than one month for their sex life to be better than ever. They began to build trust again because they no longer sent each other mixed messages.

Obstacles to a Great Sex Life

The responsibilities you face as a married couple can be overwhelming and exhausting. You might be working long hours, be concerned about your child who is sick, or be worried about meeting your budget this month. Making the transition to having fun is difficult when you have a lot on your mind. You need to allow yourself to put aside your day-to-day worries and focus on each other.

Early in your married life, having sex was probably a very high priority in your relationship. Now sex might be a lower priority because there are so many other things to get done. It can be difficult to think about having sex when you are thinking about your other responsibilities. There are dirty dishes, piles of laundry, pressures from work, and other members of the family to think about. That list surely doesn't conjure up romantic images!

Exhaustion can also interfere with your sex life. Most people are usually not interested in having sex when they are tired. Married couples (especially those with children) tend to be exhausted at the end of the day.

The Spice Rack
You and your spouse might have difficulty making the transition from being responsible to being relaxed enough to enjoy sex. Try planning to have sex after an evening out together. You'll already have made the transition from work to play.

All they can think about is getting a good night's sleep. Chances are very high that one or the other of you is tired, which does not bode well for a fulfilling sex life. One way to improve the situation is to go to sleep very early one night to rest up for the next special evening together.

Answer the following questions to help you focus on potential sticking points in your sex life with your spouse.

Intimacy Quiz

1. Do you find it hard to make the transition from being a responsible adult to being relaxed enough to enjoy sex?

   Yes   or   No

2. Is sex a relatively low priority in your relationship with your spouse?

   Yes   or   No

3. Do you feel distracted much of the time when you have sex with your spouse?

   Yes   or   No

4. Has your general sex drive diminished since you have been married?

   Yes   or   No

5. Are you often exhausted when you have sex with your spouse?

   Yes   or   No

6. If you have children, do they interfere with your privacy?

   Yes   or   No

If you answered "Yes" to any of the above questions, write down ideas you might have to improve the issue. For instance, if you are exhausted when you have sex, you might try a different time. And if you feel distracted, you could set the mood to help make the transition to intimacy. Discuss your ideas with your spouse and put them into action right away. You will immediately see an improvement in your sex life.

Plan to Have Good Sex

One of the most useful solutions to the obstacles to your sex life is planning ahead to have good sex. We plan many other fun activities, such as going to a baseball game, seeing a movie, or traveling. Why not plan on having sex? Many people feel that sex needs to be spontaneous and carefree to be satisfying. We are often disappointed in our sex lives with our spouse because it doesn't seem to be fun and spontaneous anymore. Look at your answers to the earlier questions. Are you exhausted or stressed out? Do you have less of a sex drive than 10 years ago? Do you have kids? You can't expect a sex life to emerge spontaneously in the middle of all that chaos. It doesn't mean you can't have great sex. And it doesn't mean that you don't love your spouse. It simply means that you are more tired and overcommitted.

As mundane and "unsexy" as it may seem, many married couples would do well to plan their sex life ahead of time. The same principles we discussed in Chapter 4 on dating apply here. You are busy and involved in many other things; time slips by without even realizing it. You need to set aside time for intimacy with your spouse. If you rely exclusively on spontaneity, you might find that you are forever getting and giving mixed messages about when each of you want to have sex.

Here are three things to remember in order to have great sex with your spouse:

1. Make sure you set aside time for a sexual relationship together.

2. Don't bring your day-to-day worries into the bedroom.

3. Communicate your sexual desires and do your best to accommodate each other.

Think Twice
Don't be shy! As in every type of communication, letting your spouse know what your needs are is critical for him or her to be able to provide what you need. The same is true for your sexual relationship. You need to let your spouse know what feels good to you and find out what he or she needs as well.

The Spice Rack
When you plan ahead to be intimate with your spouse you have the added benefit of anticipation!

The Spice Rack
Developing intimacy with your spouse is an ongoing process. Over the years, the trust that develops from good communication and patience will lead to sexual harmony.

Men and Women Are Different

Sex tends to be a more of an emotional issue for women and more of a physical issue for men. While this is obviously not a hard and fast rule, there is a certain truth to it.

For Women Only

The following is a list of things that women need to keep in mind:

1. Men don't always need to be the ones to initiate sex. Your husband will probably enjoy being approached by you first. Your advances will make him feel attractive.

2. Even though men tend to be more physically oriented, they have an emotional side too. From time to time, set a romantic mood for your husband. Prepare a candlelit dinner and play beautiful music. Be creative!

3. Your husband wants you to enjoy intimacy, but he can't read your mind. Communicate with him and let him know what you want.

Answer the following six questions as honestly as possible on a scale ranging from 1 (never) to 5 (always). They will help you identify ways to improve your sex life with your husband.

Intimacy Quiz (For Women Only)

1. How often do you accept your husband's advances?

    1   2   3   4   5

2. Do you feel relaxed with your husband in the bedroom?

    1   2   3   4   5

3. Are you clear with your husband about when you want to have sex?

    1   2   3   4   5

4. Does your husband try to please you?

    1   2   3   4   5

5. Do you communicate to your husband what you like?

    1   2   3   4   5

How did you do? If you answered all of the questions with a 4 or 5, congratulations! If not, write down each issue you answered with a 1, 2, or 3 and list several things you could do to improve the situation. Remember the importance of communication, putting aside other worries, and setting aside time to be intimate with your husband. Be honest and spend time thinking through your answers.

For Men Only

The following is a list of things that men need to keep in mind:

1. Women are generally more emotional than men are. Let her know how much you love her and how close you feel to her.

2. Women like to feel emotionally close to their partner when they are intimate. Unresolved conflicts will interfere with your sex life.

3. Women can enjoy physical closeness without sex. Sometimes she just might want to cuddle and feel close to you.

Answer the following six questions as honestly as possible on a scale ranging from 1 (never) to 5 (always). They will help you identify ways to improve your sex life with your wife.

Intimacy Quiz (For Men Only)

1. How often do you accept your wife's advances?

   1   2   3   4   5

2. Do you think about your wife's sexual needs?

   1   2   3   4   5

3. Do you create a romantic atmosphere if you are interested in sex?

   1   2   3   4   5

4. Does your wife try to please you?

   1   2   3   4   5

5. Do you communicate to your wife what you like?

   1   2   3   4   5

How did you do? If you answered all the questions with a 4 or 5, congratulations! If not, write down each issue you answered with a 1, 2, or 3 and list several things you could do to improve the situation. Keep in mind the importance of communication, putting aside other worries, and setting aside time to be intimate with your wife.

Birth Control and Married Sex

All couples need to consider both whether they want to use birth control and, if so, what type of birth control will work best for them. Issues about having children and whether or not to use birth control can greatly interfere with your married sex life.

You and your spouse need to decide together whether or not you want to use birth control and for how long. If you don't, you will be turning what should be a joint decision into a game of Russian roulette in the bedroom—every sexual encounter will involve thinking about, or fighting about, whether or not to use birth control. For example, if one of you wants to try for a child now and the other wants to wait a year or so, you will feel tension whenever you are intimate. In Chapter 15, we will discuss in greater detail how to work through the issue of whether or when to have children, but remember that disagreements on timing will interfere with your sex life. You and your spouse must discuss these issues outside of the bedroom and come to an agreement that you can both live with.

Think Twice
Don't ignore issues about birth control in your marriage. You can't have a fulfilling sex life with your spouse if the two of you don't agree on whether to use birth control.

If the two of you agree about wanting to wait to have children or about not having them at all, you're ready to think about a birth control method. You might have already chosen one that works well for you. Different methods have certain advantages and certain problems. If you decide to use birth control, take the time together to choose a method that will best suit both of your needs.

Birth Control Pros & Cons

Method	Pro	Con
The Pill	Very effective method. No preparation necessary.	Need to take every day without exception. It might have undesired side effects such as weight gain, headaches, occasional spotting, and mood swings. Most obstetricians recommend waiting three months after you stop taking the Pill to try to become pregnant.

Method	Pro	Con
Condoms	Generally no side effects. Easily available. Can provide lubrication.	Some men describe feeling less pleasure. Interrupts intimacy.
Diaphragms & cervical caps	Generally no side effects. Can be in place before intimacy.	Need a prescription. Need spermicidal jelly or cream to be highly effective. Can be messy.
Depo-provera & Norplant	Long-lasting protection (12 weeks for Depo-provera, 5 years for Norplant). No preparation necessary.	May have undesired side effects such as weight gain, headache, occasional spotting, and mood swings. Most obstetricians recommend waiting three months after stopping method (when the Depo-provera has worn off, or the Norplant is removed or worn off) before trying to have children.
Rhythm method	No side effects. Natural method.	Least effective method. Interferes with spontaneity.
Sterilization: tubal ligation for women, vasectomy for men	Long-term side effects are rare. The method is permanent and 100 percent effective. No preparation necessary.	The method is permanent. You should be absolutely sure you don't want more (or any) children.

OH!

Bet You Didn't Know

Q: Where can I get more information about birth control?

A: Detailed information about birth control methods is available at family planning clinics, student health centers, and many doctor's offices. In addition to information, they usually supply some methods of birth control, such as the Pill or diaphragms.

The Least You Need to Know

➤ Communication is the key to a great sex life. Don't expect your spouse to read your mind.

➤ The day-to-day grind can damper your interest in sex. Planning ahead to have sex can improve your sex life.

➤ For women, sex tends to be a more emotional issue. For men, sex tends to be a more physical issue.

➤ Decide *together* whether to use birth control and what kind to use.

Chapter 13

Domestic Drudgery

In This Chapter

➤ Understanding how you feel about your home

➤ Strategies for allocating chores

➤ Ideas for remembering your responsibilities

➤ How to keep your end of the bargain

➤ When to hire a housecleaner

Domestic chores are impossible to escape. Whether you live in a house or an apartment, a duplex or a mansion, the trash needs to be taken out, the laundry needs to be done, and the dishes need to be washed. If you are one of the lucky ones with a full-time house-keeper who attends to your every need, you might be able to skip this chapter. Otherwise, read on. We will help you understand how your idea of what makes a home can affect your relationship. We will show you how to divide up the chores fairly and give you tips to help you follow through.

Housework Hurdles

Everyone views his or her home in different ways. For some, it's the one place where they can relax and be themselves. They enjoy being able to come home, grab a drink, sit down in a comfortable chair, and put their feet up. They don't want to think about getting a coaster for their drink or taking their shoes off before propping them up on the table. They might throw their jacket on the couch or not rinse the sink out after brushing their teeth.

Think Twice
Don't criticize your spouse for his or her house-keeping style. Remember, it's your spouse's home too. You need to compromise on your different styles to make your living space a home for both of you.

This behavior might drive their spouse crazy. Their spouse might view their home very differently, seeing it as the one place where things are in order, away from the chaos of the outside world. They like to invite people over spontaneously and want the house to always look nice. They are always going around cleaning up for the other person and really resent it. They spend twice as much time on housework as the other person and always feel their spouse is not doing their fair share.

Where Do You Stand?

Before you and your spouse can organize your weekly chores, it's useful to figure out how each of you feels about your home. Decide whether the following statements are true or false as they apply to you. Then have your spouse answer them.

Home Quiz

1. I like to feel totally relaxed in my home.

   True   or   False

2. It's important to me that everything is in its place.

   True   or   False

3. My dirty underwear doesn't always make it to the laundry basket.

   True   or   False

4. I prefer the bed to be made neatly every morning.

   True   or   False

---

5. I like to eat all over the house, not just in the kitchen.

   True   or   False

6. Dishes should be washed as soon as you're finished with them.

   True   or   False

7. I leave magazines and books wherever I read them.

   True   or   False

8. The bills should all be left in one place.

   True   or   False

9. I enjoy putting my feet up on the coffee table.

   True   or   False

10. I always rinse the sink well after brushing my teeth.

   True   or   False

To compute your score, add up your "True" statements in the odd-numbered questions and your "False" statements in the even-numbered questions. Do the same for your spouse's answers.

0–3   You like your home in excellent order and like things in their place.

4–6   A certain amount of order in your home is important to you.

7–10   You tend to be very relaxed in your home and keeping things perfectly neat is not that important to you.

If you and your spouse both fall into the same category, you probably have a similar idea of what needs to be done to make your home livable. If the two of you fall into different categories, you will have more of a challenge creating a home that both of you are happy living in. It's important to realize that both of you cannot have the *exact* kind of home you want. Two people living together always need to compromise. But there are ways to make the house livable for each of you, if you are willing to negotiate.

Think Twice
Don't create unrealistic expectations of how you want your home to look. The amount of time and money it takes to have a spotless house may not be worth it.

I Can Live with That

If you feel that you and your spouse feel differently about your home, it's important to break the problem into manageable pieces. To start, list the 10 most important items that help you make your house into your home. Examples might be making the bed in the morning, keeping laundry off the floor, putting your feet on the coffee table, or having a snack while watching TV.

By listing the most important things to each of you, a problem that seemed huge and difficult to tackle is now more manageable:

1. _____
2. _____
3. _____
4. _____
5. _____
6. _____
7. _____
8. _____
9. _____
10. _____

Go through the list again and do the following three exercises:

1. Mark items on the list that you can easily do by yourself. For instance, if your spouse doesn't care about making the bed neatly, you might decide that it wouldn't be so terrible if you just made it yourself in the morning.

2. Now write down ways you could compromise on some of the items. Maybe the person who likes to eat throughout the house needs to promise to get the dishes back to the kitchen immediately after eating. Or maybe the person who likes to put feet up on the coffee table will first take off his or her shoes.

3. On the items remaining, for those you cannot reasonably do yourself and ones you feel that you cannot compromise on, write down the specific behavior you would like from your spouse. For instance, if your spouse leaves sections of the newspaper all over the house, it would be reasonable to request that he or she pile them in a central place right after reading them.

Now, instead of general frustration, you have a list of your specific needs. Your spouse will be more apt to meet those needs, both because you now have specific requests (which are always easier to follow) and because you have earmarked several items that you are going to do yourself instead of complaining about!

Getting Beyond Stereotypes

There is nothing coded on the XX chromosome that makes women more capable of doing the dinner dishes than men. But people who grew up in traditional households where their mother stayed home and did the majority of the housework and their father worked outside the home will find it hard to shake off these stereotypes. Men might feel deep down that their wives should be doing most of the day-to-day homemaking, and women might feel their husbands are doing them a favor by helping out around the house. Couples may view housework as something that falls into the lap of the woman, rather than as a team issue.

Clarissa tended to do the majority of the housework even though she was also working outside of the home. Her mother did a wonderful job of running the household she grew up in, and she assumed that she would do the same. But Clarissa was run ragged. While she had recently increased her work from part-time to 40 hours a week, she still continued to do all of the grocery shopping, all of the vacuuming, all of the clothes washing, and all of the dinner preparation.

Henry mowed the lawn and occasionally helped with the heavy cleaning. Clarissa never once asked him for help with the other tasks. It never occurred to her that her husband should help out more. She never thought about the fact that her mother, who was a full-time housewife, was not trying to take care of the entire house while working outside the home 40 hours a week! Clarissa and Henry's relationship suffered for it. Clarissa became irritable and felt tired all the time. But she and Henry both grew up in a house where their mothers did all of the housework. Neither of them had a different model.

> **Think Twice**
> Don't forget to divide up the housework in a way that each of you has agreed to. The resentment that will build up if one of you feels you are doing more than your fair share will interfere with your relationship.

Chores Are a Bore

Times have changed. There is absolutely nothing wrong with the traditional division of labor, which includes the man working full-time outside the home and the woman taking care of the house. But now, many women also work outside the home and are still forced to continue taking care of all the household duties. However, it's very important to take into account your outside obligations when dividing up the household chores. Most people are busy and would rather be doing something else than washing the dishes or taking out the garbage. But chores are a fact of life, and they need to get done.

It's useful to create a chore chart that will work for your household. Some items on the chore chart will probably be standard, and others will be specific to your home. You and your spouse need to sit down together to make a list that will work for both of you. If you are currently doing the majority of the housework, your spouse may not be so enthusias-tic about working out a new system with you. But if there is resentment on your part, then you need to explain this to your spouse.

Soul Mates
When you're in the middle of doing a dull chore, remember that you're helping make your house a home.

Holding grudges because of unfair workloads can lead to conflicts in other areas of your marriage. You need to come up with a compromise chore list that you may not be thrilled with, but one that both of you can live with. It should include daily chores, as well as weekly chores. The following list starts with some standard things that most households need to get done, with space left for you to include special chores for your household.

Taking out the kitchen trash	Cleaning the closets
Emptying all the wastebaskets	Vacuuming
Grocery shopping	Dusting
Preparing dinner	Cleaning the living and dining rooms
Doing the dishes	Ironing
Personal laundry	Straightening up the living areas
Household laundry (towels and linens)	Annual spring cleaning
Mowing the lawn	_____
Taking the garbage cans to the street and back	_____
Cleaning the bathrooms	_____
Cleaning the kitchen	_____
Cleaning the bedrooms	_____

Be Fair

When the two of you come up with a complete list of chores, it's time to divide it fairly. You need to take into account how much time each of you works outside the home. If you are working 20 hours a week, and your spouse is working a full-time job, it would be reasonable to expect that you would do more of the housework. But if you are also going to school or taking care of the children, that needs to be taken into account as well.

There are many creative ways to divide up the chores, but it needs to feel fair to both of you. Some couples like to rotate chores on a monthly basis to make the routine less dull. For instance, one month you might clean the bathrooms and vacuum every week, while the next month you might take care of the major kitchen cleaning and grocery shopping.

Hang It Up

After the two of you have come up with a way to divide up the chores in a way that will work, we recommend creating a monthly chart and displaying it on the refrigerator or bulletin board.

OH!

Bet You Didn't Know

Q: What if I forget to do some of the chores that I agree to?

A: Since you have taken the time to agree to them together, do your best to follow through. If you forget, apologize and make it up to your spouse by doing one of his or her chores.

When you have completed your task for the day or week, check it off. By putting a check mark next to a completed chore, it will add to your feeling of accomplishment. You will know that you have done your share that day to help keep the household running smoothly.

No Excuses

It's very important to keep your end of the bargain. If you have agreed to take out the trash every two days, don't forget. It's not your spouse's responsibility to nag you into doing your assigned chores (which would be unpleasant for both of you). It's your responsibility. Doing the dishes is as much a part of your relationship as candlelit dinners. Your spouse needs to know that he or she can count on you and that you will follow through on what you say you are going to do.

Can your spouse count on you? Do you follow through on what you say you are going to do? If you answered "no" to either of the above questions, think of three specific things you could do to improve these traits.

Think Twice
Don't put your spouse into the unfair position of needing to remind you to do your chores. By not keeping your end of the bargain, you are undermining the trust in your relationship.

1. _____

2. _____

3. _____

Hiring a Housecleaner

In many households, finding the time to get all of the housework done is tough. Both of you might be working and be pretty exhausted at the end of the day. A solution that works for some households is to hire someone to help with the weekly housecleaning. People who come to your home every week can help with the weekly chores, such as washing the sheets, vacuuming, and cleaning the bathrooms. While it's unlikely that this person will be able to do all of the chores, he or she will put a large dent in your household chore chart.

Hiring a housecleaner costs money (surprise!). You need to weigh the cost of the service against the benefit you and your spouse will get from it. First, find out what a housekeeper charges where you live. Then, decide if you have room in your budget to add those charges. If you do, and feel it would be helpful, go ahead and try it for six months. Then evaluate with your spouse if it was money well spent.

Soul Mates
Money spent on a housecleaner will free up time for the two of you to be together. It might be more important than a new outfit or theater tickets.

If a housecleaner would not fit your current budget, you need to decide if you can cut down on other expenses. Could you be stricter on your clothing allowance, eat out less often, or cut out a small vacation a year? This is a very personal decision. Having your time freed up on a regular basis might be more important to you than eating out every week at a nice restaurant, or it may not. If the two of you are feeling pinched for time, however, you might at least consider this option.

The Least You Need to Know

➤ Everyone views his or her home differently. Be clear about what you need in your home.

➤ Using a chore checklist is a useful way to remember to do your chores.

➤ It's important to your relationship that you keep your end of the bargain.

➤ Hiring a housecleaner can be money well spent.

I Married You, Not Your Whole Family

In This Chapter

➤ Common family conflicts

➤ Breaking destructive cycles

➤ The importance of creating clear boundaries

➤ Emphasizing good qualities

When you made a lifelong commitment to your spouse, you might not have realized that, to some degree, you also made a lifelong commitment to his or her family. Your spouse also made a commitment to your family. Some of us are blessed with parents-in-laws and siblings-in-laws that we adore. But some of us need to work harder at getting along with our new extended family. In this chapter, we will help you identify conflicts you might have with your family and ways to deal with them. Instead of the extended family being an interference, you'll learn how to bring out the best in them and let them be one of your biggest assets!

Your Mother Is Driving Me Crazy!

According to popular myth, mother-in-laws are meddling, overbearing, and impossible creatures out to wreck an otherwise wonderful marriage. They think they are always right and that it's their job to always tell you the right way to do things (their way!). If this describes how you view your mother or mother-in-law, you probably feel she is interfering with your life rather than being helpful. However, if you would like your relationship with her to be different, read on.

What Is Really Going On?

First of all, it will help tremendously to understand what is happening underneath the stereotyping. It's no accident that mothers are the subjects of in-law jokes. The relationship with your mother, and your spouse's relationship with his or her mother, change more than any other when you get married. Think about it. Mothers nurture us from the moment we are born. Through our childhood they are the ones most involved in our day-to-day life. They know the names of our friends and what our favorite flavors of ice cream are. (We are not excluding fathers from this level of intimacy. However, the fact that there are no father-in-law jokes out there probably reflects a less emotionally complicated relationship.) As we get older, our relationships with our mothers change, but they still are one of the most profound influences on our lives.

Until we are married, our mothers have had the most intense, intimate relationship with us of almost anybody. Friendships and other relationships somehow do not seem to threaten a mother's special role with her child. But when we marry, things are different. We have made a public commitment to a life partner who will share our deepest concerns, our day-to-day life, and our future together.

As it should be, we make our spouse the number one most important person in our lives. Hopefully, our mother is incredibly proud and happy for us. But she also might feel insecure and not know where she stands in her relationship with us anymore. A vicious cycle can start in which the more insecure and left out our mother feels, the more she tries to over-involve herself. And, the more she over-involves herself with our lives, the more we are inclined to back away.

Mother/Mother-in-Law Quiz

1. Describe your relationship with your own mother.

   _____

   _____

   _____

2. Does your mother feel secure?

   Yes or No

3. How does this affect your relationship with her?

   _____

   _____

   _____

4. How does your mother influence your relationship with your spouse?

   _____

   _____

   _____

5. Describe your relationship with your mother-in-law.

   _____

   _____

   _____

6. Does your mother-in-law feel secure?

   Yes or No

7. How does this affect your relationship with her?

   _____

   _____

   _____

8. How does your mother-in-law influence your relationship with your spouse?

   _____

   _____

   _____

Breaking the Cycle

Stephanie's mother stopped by several times a week, often while Robert and Stephanie were eating dinner. It really interfered with their time together and made Robert uptight. Generally Robert was a polite person, but he really considered this rude and tended to show it. He wasn't mean to his mother-in-law, but he wasn't a gracious host either. After she left, he felt frustrated and also guilty that he had not treated her nicely. Stephanie often became angry that Robert had not treated her mother well. She also wished her mother would come by less often, but she didn't know how to improve the situation.

Stephanie and Robert finally sat down and talked about the problem. They realized that what bothered them the most was the lack of privacy caused by an unannounced visit. Stephanie suggested they set up a regular night that her mother would come for dinner. Robert agreed.

Stephanie called her mother and discussed the idea with her. She told her mother that they loved seeing her, but it was difficult for them when it wasn't planned. She needed time alone with Robert. She told her mother that Robert and she would like to invite her for dinner every Thursday evening. Then they would really be able to give her their undivided attention. She emphasized to her mother that she was welcome in their home at other times, but they would appreciate it if she would call first.

> OH!
>
> ## Bet You Didn't Know
>
> Q: Now that I'm married, my mother is telephoning me twice a day. I don't want to upset her, but I don't want her to call so often. What can I do?
>
> A: Perhaps if you telephoned her on a regular basis, she would feel more secure. When you finish a conversation with her, tell her when *you* will next call *her*. Make a point of calling her back when you said you would. If she can count on you to contact her, she might telephone you less often. If that doesn't work, you should talk openly and kindly with her about your needs.

At first Stephanie's mother felt she was being shut out of their lives. Stephanie almost caved in, but somehow found the courage to be firm. She told her mother that she was always a part of their lives, but that they just needed a set schedule to make their lives more manageable. Her mother didn't seem happy at first, but it ended up to be a very workable solution for everybody. Robert was much more gracious and polite to his mother-in-law then he had previously been. He took a genuine interest in her life and became much closer to her than before. Everyone looked forward to their evenings together.

When you are in the middle of a difficult situation, it can be hard to be objective. If you feel your mother or mother-in-law is smothering you, you probably want to push her out of your life. But that will not work, and you will only hurt her feelings and feel guilty for having done so.

You need to make your mother or mother-in-law feel secure. Let her know when you appreciate something she has done for you or some advice she has given you. You don't need to argue with her if you disagree with her suggestions. Just listen and thank her. Ideally, you will come up with ways to include her in your lives. You might ask her advice about certain things if she might be helpful. Make a point of inviting her over for a regularly scheduled time (even if it's infrequent). Having a time that she can count on might calm her down, making her less likely to be over-involved in your lives.

Loving Hearts

All relationships evolve over time, including the ones with our family. If they did not, we would be missing an opportunity for tremendous growth. When we get married, the thing that makes it tough on some members of our families is that on some level they feel the spouse is replacing them. While it's true that our relationship with our family will probably change, it does not mean we will love them less. But sometimes our families feel we cannot possibly love them as much as we used to and also love our spouse. They assume we have a finite amount of love and that their share is smaller than before.

Fortunately, this is not true. Our hearts have the wonderful ability to expand to include everyone in our lives. It's sort of like the way most of us can always eat dessert, even when we are absolutely full. But some people do not see it like this. The result can be an unnecessary competition between family and spouse, which is miserable for everyone involved. Instead, tell your family that you love them on a regular basis. Always make sure they are aware of how important they are to you.

Think Twice
Don't assume you have a limited amount of love to share. Give your love freely to your parents, brothers, sisters, cousins, and everyone else in your families. You will still have plenty of love left to give each other!

It's not necessary to shut your family out of your life when you are married. Having a healthy relationship with both of your families will enhance your relationship with each other.

Common Conflicts

It's much better to decide what you cannot tolerate from family members and take the time and effort to tell them about it ahead of time, than to blow up when it happens. First, try to figure out what is bothering you. This is not always easy. Common conflicts with family members include:

➤ Visiting too often

➤ Staying too long

➤ Calling on the telephone too often or too little

➤ Meddling in your business

➤ Trying to tell you how to live your life

If a family member is really annoying you, take the time and effort to determine what specific behaviors you are bothered by. Many times, resolving a particular conflict can improve your relationship with him or her. It might be that only one behavior is annoying, but many things bother you because of that one thing. If you are having some trouble identifying what exactly is bothering you, it might be helpful to refer to Chapter 7 on identifying conflicts and apply that information to your family.

Jason found his wife's sister really annoying. Sara, his wife, was very close to her sister. They talked several times a week on the telephone, and she came over almost every Sunday afternoon. Sara knew that Jason was annoyed by her sister, but could never figure out why. Jason became irritable whenever she came over and always left the room. Sara and he would often have a fight Sunday evenings after her sister had left.

One Sunday, Sara's sister stayed for dinner, and Jason was clearly upset. He kept his emotions to himself until she went home, but then he yelled at Sara. "Why does your sister always have to come over and wreck our Sundays? It's the one day that we have together and she ruins it for me!" After they talked about it some more, it came out that what really bothered Jason most about Sara's sister was her timing. Sunday was the one day he really counted on to relax, and he felt he had to be a host when Sara's sister was over. He wanted to sit in his lounge chair and listen to his CDs without worrying about a guest.

Think Twice
Don't let conflicts with family members get in the middle of your marriage. Work together to create a clear boundary around your relationship.

Sara let her sister know that Sunday afternoons would not work on a regular basis. Sara's sister changed her weekly visit to Wednesday nights, and she only came over Sunday afternoons when she was explicitly invited. Jason appreciated the privacy he needed on the weekends.

Out-of-Town Visits

Stephanie and Robert had a problem with Robert's parents. They lived out of town and wanted to visit twice a year for a week. While Stephanie and Robert didn't have day-to-day conflicts with them, they always felt like the upcoming visit was looming over their heads. When Robert's parents came for an entire week, it threw their schedules off. They came on relatively short notice, and it was difficult to host them for such long visits.

Stephanie and Robert dealt with their problem by not talking about it. Then every six months or so, Robert's parents would call and announce they were coming the next week. They would tell Stephanie and Robert the flight number and time and expect them to drop everything. Both Stephanie and Robert liked his parents, but they found these visits badly timed and exhausting, even though they looked forward to seeing his parents.

Think Twice
Don't put pressure on yourselves to entertain your parents every minute of their visit. Set up interesting things for them to do. If you turn your schedule upside down, you are more likely to resent them.

Stephanie and Robert needed to take control of the situation. Instead of waiting for Robert's parents to call, they should have called up his parents and given them a choice of two times several months away that would have been good for them to visit. They should have also suggested a five-day visit, rather than a one-week stay. Stephanie and Robert would have enjoyed the visits if they were better timed and shorter.

Here is a list of things that will help you establish better out-of-town family visits:

1. Determine the date of arrival early enough in advance, to everyone's agreement.

2. Establish plans of what you and your relatives would like to do when they visit.

3. Decide ahead of time how long you want your relatives to stay and let them know.

4. If you will have other obligations during their visit, let them know ahead of time to prevent disappointment.

Keep Your Problems to Yourselves

You might think that talking about problems you are having with your spouse might help you become closer to your mother-in-law. Don't do it! Asking advice about a recent argument with your spouse is a severe breach of trust. Never, ever, talk about negative things in your relationship with anyone except your spouse (or a therapist). It's extremely destructive. Even if you do not mean any harm, you are undermining the trust that the two of you have. You will not only alter other people's perception of your spouse, but whatever you discuss will be remembered by the other person long after you and your spouse have resolved the issue.

Bet You Didn't Know

Q: Is it wrong to talk with my friends about my marital problems?

A: When you discuss problems you are having with your spouse with another family member or friend, you are undermining the trust in your marriage. If you compliment your spouse to others instead, you will be strengthening your marital bond!

Accentuate the Positive

Sometimes a conflict with a family member does not have a workable solution. The only thing left to do is to focus on the person's good qualities. It's easier to tolerate some things that bother you about your father-in-law if you try to think about the things you do like about him. Every member of your family is going to be part of your lives in one way or another. You will only benefit if you think about them in positive ways.

Family Profile

Make a list of any member of your family with whom you have a less than perfect relationship. Do the same for your spouse's family. Write down something that bothers you about each of them. Then, next to your annoyance, write down a positive quality that the person has. Use the following tables.

Her Family

	Annoyance	Positive Quality
Mother	_____	_____
Father	_____	_____
Sister	_____	_____
Brother	_____	_____
Aunt	_____	_____
Uncle	_____	_____
Grandmother	_____	_____
Grandfather	_____	_____
Cousin	_____	_____

His Family

	Annoyance	Positive Quality
Mother	_____	_____
Father	_____	_____
Sister	_____	_____
Brother	_____	_____
Aunt	_____	_____
Uncle	_____	_____
Grandmother	_____	_____
Grandfather	_____	_____
Cousin	_____	_____

Once you have your list, figure out ways to help bring out each person's good qualities. For instance, if your mother-in-law (who is controlling and overbearing) is a great cook, have her cook for you. She might bring unwanted cooking advice along with the casserole, but you will get a delicious, homemade meal out of it. Or maybe your uncle is difficult to be around because he is always saying negative things about everything. But deep down he is a very caring, generous person. Ask him to help you fix something around the house or go on an errand for you. He might grumble while he does it, but he will feel helpful and you will feel better about the relationship.

The bottom line: Remember to *accentuate the positive.*

Sometimes You Need to Grin and Bear It

Soul Mates
Supporting each other when someone in your family is being difficult can bring the two of you closer together. Use a frustrating situation to strengthen your relationship!

Unfortunately, there may be some members of your family who are completely aggravating even after you have discussed your concerns with them, made suggestions, and tried to focus on their good qualities. Unfortunately, you are stuck to some degree. There is no solution that will make everyone happy. Keep your marriage strong by making sure you deal with the difficulties together. If one of you is having trouble with a family member, do your best to make the family member feel welcome, while at the same time respecting your privacy and your limits. Always keep in mind that your goal is to have as good a relationship with every family member as possible.

Your Family Can Be Your Biggest Asset

Soul Mates
If you grew up in a less-than-perfect family, your spouse's family might provide you with the warm, loving family you always wanted as a child. It can be a wonderful opportunity to be part of a happy family.

It's easy to forget how important and wonderful your family can be. There are some things that only a relative can provide, like a memory of you when you were young. And whether they show it or not, everyone in your family loves you and wants the best for you.

When it comes down to it, most families will be there for you during the difficult times. Ideally, they will be there for you during the good times as well. By recognizing how special your relatives are to you, you will have taken the important first step to being closer to them.

Bring Everyone Together

Some families have drifted apart over the years and all they need is for someone to bring them together. Why don't you and your spouse step in to make it happen? You could start a monthly Sunday brunch, or have an annual party during the holiday season. It's a great way to reconnect with everyone, and your effort will be appreciated. You can even start a family newsletter to keep everyone informed of family happenings.

Think Twice
Don't leave anybody out if you have a family party! Keep a list of family addresses and phone numbers in a separate place in your phone book. Then when it's time to invite people, you can just pull out that list.

The Least You Need to Know

➤ Sometimes a family member who interferes is insecure about his or her role in your lives. Don't push this person away. That will only make matters worse.

➤ You have enough love for your spouse and everyone in your family. You don't need to skimp.

➤ It's important to know your limits and create clear boundaries with your families. Otherwise, you will be frustrated, which will interfere with your relationship.

➤ Don't share your marital difficulties with your family. It will be destructive in the long run.

➤ Bring out the best in members of your family. Remember that your family can be a big asset.

Part 4
We're a Family Now

One of the most powerful ways a married couple expresses love for each other is deciding to raise a child together. Deciding when or whether to start a family can be difficult. Most of the time, a child in your household is a completely joyous experience. But it can be trying at times too. The relationship with your spouse will change, and you need to readjust accordingly. In this section, we'll give you many parenting tips to keep your family happy and your relationship strong. Learning how to manage all of these issues effectively will make raising your children more fun and fulfilling than either of you ever imagined!

Chapter 15

Planning the Unplannable

In This Chapter

➤ Deciding whether to start a family

➤ Deciding when to start a family

➤ Dealing with infertility

Some couples are sure they want children, while others are sure they don't. If you don't fall into either of these two categories, you may feel caught in the gray area in between—unsure about having children, how many children, or when to start trying to have children. In this chapter, we will help you think about these issues and develop a plan.

Decisions, Decisions

It's very important to clarify how each of you feels about having children. Any unspoken disagreements about the issue can cause damage to your relationship because the issue is so central to your lives. You don't have ultimate control over whether you can have a child, but that does not mean the decision of whether to try should be left to chance. There are many steps that you can take to think through this important decision. The first step is to sit down with your spouse and decide whether you want children, and if so, when. We designed the following questions to help guide you through these issues:

1. Do you think about being a parent?

2. Is raising a family a major goal in your life?

3. If you think about yourself in 20 years, can you imagine not having children?

4. Do you want children, but you want to wait?

5. Will the reason you want to wait to have children still be there in the future, or will it be resolved (or modified) over time?

Think Twice
Don't make decisions about when or whether to have children when you are in a rush. Set aside time to give this very important issue the attention it deserves.

If you and your spouse agree about whether you want children and when you want to try, congratulations. You have just passed a major hurdle in your relationship. However, it's not uncommon for there to be a lot of tension surrounding the issue of when or whether to have children.

Common Concerns About Having a Child

Deciding to have a child is a big decision that brings up fears for many people. The following are some of the concerns people have shared with us:

"It's a huge responsibility."

"It will interfere with my marriage."

"I will lose control of my life."

"My career is very important to me."

"Raising a child costs a lot of money."

"I'm afraid I won't be a good parent."

Soul Mates
Getting married and starting a family are enormous commitments. But remember that the biggest responsibilities in life are usually the most rewarding.

If you are feeling some or all of these things, you are not alone. Having these concerns does not necessarily mean you don't want to have children, though it may mean you want to wait. But it means that you are aware your life will change when you have a child.

Discuss your specific concerns with your spouse. He or she may be able to give you the reassurance you need. It's easier to respond to a specific concern, rather than trying to respond to someone saying, "I don't want children."

Also consider talking with friends who are parents. They will probably be happy to share the concerns they had and how they overcame them. And they will be able to share with you the joys of parenthood as well.

Deadlock

Ken and Beth had been married for three years. Beth was ready to start a family. She always knew she wanted to have children and thought about having two or three. On the other hand, Ken really liked their life. He had no interest in having children now and said he would consider it in "five years."

Beth was convinced that she could change Ken's mind. She was especially nice to him and brought up the subject of children when he was in a good mood. But nothing worked. Ken didn't want to think about children. He liked their relationship and his freedom and felt that children would completely interfere with his life.

Beth became discouraged. She was definitely getting the message that Ken did not want a family now. But it was so important to her! She talked herself into waiting several years so that she would be on the same schedule as Ken. Beth felt that would be a workable solution. The only problem was that Beth was miserable. A very important goal of hers was being postponed a long time, and perhaps indefinitely. Ken and Beth began to fight more than ever before. Beth became more critical of every little thing Ken did. Their marriage turned from a good one to a disaster. Both Ken and Beth were miserable.

Bet You Didn't Know

Q: I don't ever want to have children, but I don't want to hurt my spouse's feelings. What should I do?

A: You must be honest and tell your spouse how you feel. It's not fair to keep your partner waiting for years, hoping you will change your mind. Your spouse might—or might not—be able to accept your decision. But better now than later.

Several years later when Beth talked about children again to Ken, he said "No way." Now he was really sure he didn't want a family. Ken had all of the same reasons as before and now the added reason that their marriage was not very good. Beth was devastated. She had counted on the fact that waiting would be the solution. Ken and Beth are still together, but they have an unhappy marriage. And Beth is still hoping that Ken will change his mind about having a family.

You cannot have a fulfilling marriage and disagree on this fundamental issue. Don't fool yourselves into thinking that it will work itself out, or that time will resolve it. You need to make a decision together that you both can live with. If you cannot resolve the issue by yourselves, it would be wise to see a skilled therapist together. A neutral third party might be the best way to get beyond the deadlock you are facing on this important and emotionally charged issue.

Timing Is Everything

In our society, we are given the illusion of control about many things. We can preprogram our coffee makers to have fresh coffee in the morning, watch close to one hundred cable channels on TV 24 hours a day, and zap frozen food in the microwave for a three-minute dinner. We tend to assume that we can apply this control to everything in our lives.

Unfortunately, many things do not work this way. Planning to have a family is one of them. You might have decided to wait two or three years before having a child, but became pregnant even when using birth control. Or you might be trying to become pregnant and are disappointed month after month.

But, within reason, it's important to think through when to start a family. While we hope you find the following ideas helpful, we caution you against thinking you can plan exactly when you will have a child. It's beyond your control!

Personal Goals

While your own life does not stop in its tracks when you have children, it does slow down quite a bit. Infants are wonderful and beautiful creatures, but they are incredibly time-consuming. You will be exhausted from lack of sleep for many months. Your life will dramatically shift from going after your own goals to meeting the needs of your baby. By waiting to have children for a year or two, you might be able to complete something important to you and be in a better position to focus on your child.

Think Twice
Don't think there will be a perfect time to have children. Remember that there is no way you can reach all of your personal or financial goals before you start a family!

If you are completing a segment of your education or starting your own business, you might consider giving yourself some time to reach a reasonable goal. For instance, you might decide to get your bachelor's degree before having children. If you have a vocational goal, such as getting a business off the ground, you might decide you need to be able to hire an employee to help before you have a child.

We are not suggesting that you wait until everything is perfectly settled before you start a family. You'll be waiting forever. But if there is some major, obtainable goal you can reach that won't take longer than a year or two, you might feel much better prepared to make the transition to being a parent.

Financial Responsibilities

Raising a child is expensive, from diapers and food, to child care and education. If waiting a year would change your financial situation, the two of you might consider waiting. Maybe completing a degree in school would allow you to get a higher-paying job. Or maybe paying off your credit cards would let you start your family with money in the bank instead of with loans to pay off. It might allow one of you to stay home with the baby instead of working full-time just to pay your debt and child care costs.

Again, the answer is not to wait until you have a huge amount of money in an investment portfolio. Rather, it's to consider whether the two of you might enjoy a more favorable financial situation in a year or two. It might make the difference between always struggling to meet the monthly bills because you are still paying off your debt, and having a tight but reasonable budget that allows you to save for your future together.

There is, however, one major caveat to waiting for your finances to be settled before you have kids. *Very few people ever feel that their finances are settled!* Even people who have more money than they used to will find new ways to spend it or worry about how to manage it.

Think Twice
Don't let finances alone stop you from having children. Concern about finances may be a way for you to avoid the issue, rather than face the real reasons why you may be postponing becoming a parent.

Your Relationship

It's very important for the two of you to have a good working relationship before you start a family. It can be helpful to be married for a year before starting a family. Even though you will get a lot of joy from a child, you will also get a lot of new stress. The stronger your relationship with your spouse, the better parents you will be.

OH!

Bet You Didn't Know

Q: My spouse and I are having difficulties in our marriage. If we have a child, will that bring us closer?

A: Many people think that having a child will fix a troubled marriage. But, in fact, once you have children, you will need to work harder to keep your relationship strong. Ideally, you should work on and improve your marriage *before* you have children.

Now or Later?

Joe and Fran were unhappy. Joe wanted to start a family and was genuinely surprised that Fran was reluctant. Fran said she wanted kids "someday," but would never talk about when. She would withdraw and become sad when they discussed children. She rarely wanted to have sex because she was worried she would become pregnant.

Joe was feeling desperate and insisted that he and Fran go to therapy. When they came to see us, we asked them to picture themselves as parents. Fran looked up and started sobbing. In between tears, she choked out, "I'd be horrible. I'd mess up my kids. They'd be miserable." Joe was speechless. He knew Fran well, but he had no idea that she had been thinking these sorts of things.

Soul Mates
When you are making the decision to start a family, you will feel many emotions. Try to understand what your spouse is feeling and why he or she might be having difficulty with the decision. Be especially supportive of each other.

Over the next six months, Fran and Joe came to see us weekly. Joe began to understand Fran's concerns better. She was terrified of repeating her past. She had had an unhappy childhood and felt that she didn't want to raise a child who would suffer like she did. Her parents divorced shortly after she was born, and she felt it was her fault. She was worried that Joe would leave her after they had a child. Over time, she was able to see how Joe was different than her own father. Joe was supportive, stable, and wanted to raise children with her.

If both of you want to try for a child, but one of you wants to wait for a while, the person who wants to put it off needs to consider why. If the reason you or your spouse wants to wait is a long-term issue, such as being worried about being a good parent or concerned about the time raising children will take, it should be worked through right away. Postponing the discussion will only postpone dealing with the issue. On the other hand, if the reason for waiting is short-term, such as having the chance to complete college first, then the other person might feel different about compromising and waiting.

Don't Put It Off Too Long

While it's often a good idea to wait a while before trying to start a family, don't wait too long. The biggest risk in waiting too long to have children is that you increase the chances of infertility. Some couples are infertile for reasons that have nothing to do with age. But nowadays, it's not unusual for people to delay having children until their thirties or even forties. A couple who might easily have conceived in their mid-twenties might have fertility problems in their mid-thirties and need medical intervention to have a child.

Infertility

It's absolutely heartbreaking to want a child with your spouse and not be able to get pregnant. You go through countless months or years of disappointment and tears. At some point, many couples make the decision to see a fertility specialist. This option frequently helps couples become fertile. But be prepared. It can be a stressful and expensive undertaking. If you and your spouse are planning on pursuing fertility treatment, always keep in mind it's a difficult process and you need to support each other through it.

If you and your spouse decide to try fertility treatments, you will want to research the various fertility clinics and specialists in your area. The following issues are important to consider when choosing a facility and physician:

➤ *Find out the success rate for different interventions.* There is some variation from location to location. By doing your homework in the beginning, you will keep from using a center with a much lower success rate than other centers. Protect your time, money, and energy by starting with the best!

➤ *Get referrals.* Ask friends if they liked their physician and the atmosphere of the center. Was the staff supportive? Were they able to answer all your questions to your satisfaction? Feeling comfortable is an important factor in reducing your stress level.

Think Twice
Don't blame each other for your fertility problems. Blaming will not help the situation and will only cause both of you to feel worse. Instead, support each other through this stressful time.

➤ *Consider the location.* While the other issues are obviously more important, the location of a facility might be a tiebreaker. If you undergo fertility intervention, you will need to visit the clinic often and on specific days in your cycle. Having a clinic convenient to your home or work will make things easier.

➤ *Consider the cost of the treatment and how much (if any) your insurance will cover.* Some plans will cover certain treatments and not others. And sometimes certain clinics are covered and not others. It's important to know this information ahead of time to help you make your decision.

Adoption

If you cannot have children with your spouse and fertility treatment either does not work or seems too stressful to pursue, another option to consider is adoption. Choosing to adopt a child is a big decision. One of the best ways to get started is to talk with people who have adopted a child. Most people are happy to share their experience about how they adopted their child. You probably will hear some interesting stories. Find out what route they took to adopt their child to help you decide what might work best for you.

There are many types of adoptions, including local adoptions, statewide adoptions, national adoptions, and international adoptions. Each state and country has different adoption laws, including waiting periods, rights of the birth mother, and age requirements of the adoptive parents. An adoption agency or an adoption broker can help you through this process.

Soul Mates
Work as partners when you go through the adoption process. Make sure you fill out applications, go to appointments, and make decisions *together*. Being part of a team will give the two of you strength, rather than both of you feeling alone.

Some of the issues you should think about when you are considering adopting a child include:

➤ Will you accept either a boy or a girl?

➤ Will you accept a child of any ethnic background?

➤ Will you accept a child who is not an infant?

➤ Do you have an age limit for a child you will accept?

➤ Will you accept a child with disabilities?

These are very difficult questions to answer. It's important to think about them ahead of time. The more flexible you are, the more easily you will find a child to adopt. Most adoption agencies will ask you these questions as well.

The Least You Need to Know

➤ Deciding if and when to have children can be difficult. There might be many reasons why your spouse does not want children; openly talk about those reasons together.

➤ Sometimes waiting a year or two to have a child can give you time to mature and reach some personal and financial goals.

➤ Having a child will not fix a troubled marriage and is likely to make it even worse.

➤ Putting off having children too long might result in fertility problems. Undergoing fertility treatments can be stressful. It's very important to support each other during this difficult time.

Chapter 16

And Baby Makes Three

> **In This Chapter**
>
> ➤ Adjusting to family life
>
> ➤ Rethinking past decisions
>
> ➤ Changing outside relationships
>
> ➤ Making special time for each other without the kids

From the moment you make the decision to start a family, your relationship with your spouse changes. It's no longer just the two of you. There is a new element in your lives. You will probably need to rethink your work hours and your household budget. You should be aware that relationships with friends and family will change. And you also need to remember to spend time alone together. In this chapter, we will show you how to make the adjustment as smooth as possible, while keeping your relationship strong.

Bringing the Baby Home

Bringing a baby into your home will be one of the most memorable times of your lives. You are the proud parents of a beautiful bundle of joy. You are beaming with delight. Your entire world has changed. You now have the breathtaking responsibility of raising a human being to adulthood.

The transition from couple to family is one of the biggest adjustments you will ever make. Every little thing is new, from having someone dependent on you for everything to not being able to make many concrete plans for a while. You have the awesome responsibility of the full-time care of someone who is totally dependent on you!

Caring for Each Other

It's very common for one of the new parents (often the dad) to feel left out. The new baby makes his or her needs very obvious. Somehow it seems that the two adults in the house don't need to be taken care of, and the focus is always on the baby. But this is not true. You are both probably feeling insecure and sleep-deprived. Pay attention to each other's needs and support each other as much as you can. Do your best to communicate how much you love each other.

Marilyn loved being a mother. She felt particularly lucky because she fell into the role easily. Nursing was easy for her, the baby was thriving, and he had a good temperament. Marilyn spent more time with her mother, who also loved being with the baby. The moment her husband, Jim, came home from work, she would tell him in great detail about all the things the baby did that day. She would describe how many hours he slept, how much he ate, and how many times he spit up. They would eat dinner quickly, and then Marilyn would nurse the baby, sing the baby songs, give the baby a bath, and put the baby to sleep. After that, she would tell Jim she was going to bed so she could get in a few hours before the baby's nighttime feeding.

Think Twice
Don't get so caught up in your beautiful new baby that you forget about your spouse. Make special time for each other.

Jim loved being a father, but after several months of having every evening revolve completely around the baby, he started to feel left out. Marilyn used to ask about his day, and they would discuss some issues from his work. He knew that they would be able to go out less often with a baby, but he didn't think he would have to give up his entire relationship with Marilyn!

Over the next few months, things escalated to the point where Jim would come home late every night because he didn't even feel that it was worth it to come home. He pitched in with the baby on weekends, but he was feeling distant and somewhat hostile toward Marilyn. They were beginning to have many fights, and the fights were worse than before the baby was born. Jim was feeling very guilty about how he felt, but he didn't know what he could do about it.

They came to see us and talked about what was going on. Jim described feeling his relationship with his wife was almost nonexistent. Marilyn said she didn't know what to do because all of her time and energy were taken up with the baby and she didn't have anything left for her husband. We assured them that the things they were experiencing were very common with a new baby in the house.

We suggested Marilyn always, without fail, ask Jim about his day when he came home. We also said Marilyn didn't need to share every single detail of the baby's day with her husband. Jim assured her that he was very interested in the baby, but not necessarily in exactly how long he slept or how many diapers were changed that day.

Now that Marilyn was not nursing exclusively, we thought it would be beneficial for Jim to feed the baby a bottle in the evening so that he would have some time alone with the baby. Marilyn could use that time to relax or talk with someone on the telephone. At this point, Marilyn suggested that maybe her mother could come over one evening a week to give her and Jim a chance to go out for coffee together. Marilyn didn't feel ready to leave the baby for a long stretch of time, but she knew that she and Jim needed time together. When Marilyn and Jim made these minor changes in their evenings, they noticed a big difference. Jim felt more involved as a father, and more important, he felt valued again as a husband. Things became even better as the baby grew older and began interacting with Jim.

> **Soul Mates**
> If your spouse has been home with the baby all day, surprise him or her by bringing dinner home. This will give you more time together and your spouse will appreciate it.

> **The Spice Rack**
> When you are parents, it's still important to show that you care about each other. Ask each other about how the day went, and try to do one nice thing a day for each other. By doing these things, you can make sure that you are reserving some much needed attention for your spouse!

It's Not Just the Two of You

The sooner you adjust to the demands of a new child, the better. One of the hardest things about the transition from being a couple to having a child is coming to terms with the fact that your life is going to change in every way. If you try to do all the things you used to do and add a baby in there too, you are setting yourself up to be really over-whelmed. The baby needs a certain amount of attention and will make that clear to you. You will need to make choices, especially about time and money, that take into account the fact that you are now a family.

Bet You Didn't Know

Q: Now that I'm a parent, my plans keep getting changed. What can I do?

A: As a parent, many plans you make will not work out. Being flexible is one of the most valuable traits you can have. Just remember it's all for a good cause! Your sacrifices now will grow a loving (and hopefully appreciative!) human being.

Time Management

Managing your time when you have a child can be quite a challenge. In the past, you would estimate how many hours a task would take and set the time aside so that you could get it done. While the basic principle still applies, there is one major difference: Taking care of a child is a 24-hour-a-day, seven-day-a-week job. You can make a schedule based on the expectation that your child will sleep through the night and not be too sick

Think Twice
Don't forget that one of you will need to take time off from work when your child is sick. Consider setting up your schedules so that you alternate times you are available.

to go to child care. But your schedule can easily be thrown out of whack. Imagine that your baby cried for most of the night. You're pretty tired, but you're set on going to work anyway. When you pick up your baby to get him ready, you realize he has a fever. Someone needs to stay home with him today, and maybe take him to the pediatrician. A big wrench has been thrown into your schedule. This can be very frustrating, but if you expect unexpected problems, they will be much easier to deal with. Understanding and accepting the fact that you need to be flexible will prevent many conflicts between you and your spouse.

Alice planned to go back to work part-time when her baby was three months old. After her baby was six months old, she planned to switch to full-time work. Her husband, Robert, worked full-time. Since the baby was so young, they decided to hire a nanny to watch her at home. Ideally, they wanted to find a nanny who would work part-time for three to six months and then would work full-time when Alice went back to working full-time. But they found when they interviewed people that no one was interested in that arrangement. Most of the potential nannies wanted a full-time job. And the ones who wanted to work part-time had other obligations like school and would not be able to switch to full-time.

This couple's carefully conceived plan was ruined! They realized they needed to hire someone full-time now, even though Alice was not going to be working full-time. It was going to be more expensive than they had planned; in fact, it would cost Alice's entire part-time salary to pay for a full-time nanny. Initially, Alice and Robert were upset, but then they began to see some of the advantages. Alice would have a chance to get to know the nanny because she would be home half of the time. It would also give Alice the opportunity to rest and get caught up on much needed sleep.

They hired a nanny and things went smoothly while Alice was working part-time. She had time to do errands, catch up on her sleep, and even had a little time for herself. Everything changed when she went back to work full-time. Even though the baby was sleeping through the night, she was exhausted. Before the baby, she would do all of the errands and have personal time after work. Now, she needed to be home by 6, which gave her only enough time to drive home from work. Alice didn't have time for the grocery shopping, let alone time to get her hair cut or talk with a friend on the phone.

Alice became irritable, and she and Robert began to fight more. They came to see us because they wanted to work things out before the situation became even more unmanageable. When they described their situation, it was clear that they had a time management problem. They just didn't have enough hours in the day to get everything done that they needed to, let alone have time to relax. We asked them if it would be possible for either of them to work less than full-time, so they would have some time during the week to do errands. They said that right now it wouldn't be possible, but that it might be a reasonable solution in the future.

We asked if Robert could pitch in with more of the errands. In the past, Alice did the majority of the errands because her job was less demanding than Robert's. But that was no longer true because now she was taking care of the baby when she came home. Robert agreed to do the grocery shopping every week. Robert also planned on coming home twice a week at 6 to relieve the nanny. On those nights, Alice would have a chance to do an errand, catch up at work, or go to the gym. This new schedule made a big difference. It took into account the fact that either Robert or Alice needed to be home at 6 every day, and it divided their new obligations more fairly.

> **Think Twice**
> Don't forget that taking care of a child is a 24-hour-a-day, seven-day-a-week responsibility! You need to take that fact into account when planning your errands and work schedule. Otherwise, you might find yourself short on hours at the end of the week.

Your Time Costs Money

It can be quite a shock when you realize you cannot go out to a movie with your spouse without thinking about it ahead of time. And unless you happen to live next door to your baby's doting grandmother, it's probably going to cost money! All of a sudden, you need to spend money just for the privilege of being alone with each other.

Soul Mates
Make sure to cherish and appreciate your time alone together even more now since it's harder to come by!

It can also be a big surprise to realize that if both of you work you are not bringing in two paychecks, but actually two paychecks minus child care costs. You must rethink the value of your work when you have a child. Sometimes paying for child care takes an entire paycheck (after taxes are considered). If you are working and receiving personal satisfaction from your job, it still might be worth working. But if you are working solely to bring in additional income, you will definitely need to reconsider the financial benefit. Either way, you will probably need to compute a new budget to meet the additional expenses of a child.

Don't forget to consider the hidden expenses of a two-job family. Items such as gas, dry cleaning of work clothes, and costly convenience foods really add up! When you add in the cost of child care, you might find there is little financial benefit to both of you working.

Outside Relationships

When you have a child, you will need to readjust your relationships with other people. This doesn't mean you need to give up close friendships or never see your family. It might even mean the opposite. But the rhythm of your lives has changed, which means the other parts of life will change as well.

Family Involvement

The reaction that your family has after you have children will vary. It might depend on how close you were to begin with, or whether your child is their first or their seventh grandchild. But, you can bet that most of the time they will want more involvement with you, rather than less. Bringing a child into your lives is a family event. Your lives are more public than they were before. You are carrying on the family for your parents, and they have a stake in how your child is raised.

Hopefully, your family's involvement will be mostly a positive thing. For the most part, your children will benefit from involvement with them. Don't deny your children access to a family member because you are carrying a personal grudge. Children can bring out the best in others and might help you put aside past grievances.

Thinking back to Chapter 14 on dealing with your family, there are often family members who are interfering and might become more so when a grandchild or niece or nephew is involved. If you have a particularly difficult relationship, or if a relative has been abusive, you will need to be more cautious.

Bet You Didn't Know

Q: My relationship with my parents is not great. Does that mean my children won't get along with them as grandparents?

A: If you have a grudge against one of your parents, remember that he or she is your child's grandparent, not parent. The relationship between a grandparent and grandchild is different than a parent-child relationship.

When you have children, you have many new responsibilities. If your family lives nearby, they can share these with you. Encourage your family to help out. If either of your parents is able to baby-sit, say yes. It's a great way to have time alone together without having to pay for it, not to mention the value for your child. Welcome your parents and siblings into your family; they will enrich the lives of your children. And, if they are willing to baby-sit, they can give you much needed time alone with each other!

Friendships Change

All of a sudden, you will start seeing your friends as those with children and those without children. The ones with children will understand your new rhythm of life. They will realize that it's not always so easy to get a baby-sitter and get together with them. They will probably enjoy getting together with you and your whole family.

Your friends without children might need some education. Your relationship with them might change. They might be offended that you don't want to pay for a baby-sitter to go out and get a bite to eat; you would rather have them over for dinner. They might get annoyed that you cannot finish a thought completely before your child needs something. If this happens with some of your friends, don't write them off. Explain your new constraints (involving both money and time) to them. Hopefully, they will understand and you will be able to enjoy each other's company in different ways than you did before you had children.

Think Twice
Don't forget yourself. Many people spend so much time and effort trying to make everyone else in the family happy that they forget about themselves. Always remember that the most important factor to ensure the happiness of your family is for you and your spouse to be happy!

Making Special Time for Yourselves Without the Kids

The single most important factor in having happy children is to be happy in your relationship with your spouse. If the two of you feel close to each other and are supportive of each other, your children will feel secure. That's why it's very important to have time alone with your spouse. Your kids might throw a tantrum when you walk out the door together, but don't feel guilty! You will be better parents if you spend time alone together, and they will be happier kids!

Ideas for Dating When You Have Kids

Some parents are very good about going out every week or so without the children. Unfortunately, these days it's more common for parents to forgo time together for family time. Don't let that happen to you! The following suggestions take into account the huge time commitment and general exhaustion most parents have:

➤ See an afternoon movie on the weekend and have an early dinner afterward. That way you can have family time with your kids in the morning before you go and still be home around their bedtime. The baby-sitter could have them ready in their pajamas with their teeth brushed, and you could tuck them in bed. Then, you can get to sleep at a reasonable hour too!

➤ Go out in the evening after the kids have gone to bed. You can be together as a family during the dinner hour and not lose that time together.

➤ Spend an evening together without spending money if you are on a tight budget. Browse through a bookstore together and take a walk. It might seem silly to hire a baby-sitter if you are not going to a movie or out to dinner, but everyone needs that carefree feeling once in a while, even if it must be paid for!

Maybe you won't be able to date as regularly or elaborately as couples without children, but there are still things you can do that will be fun. All things that you enjoy doing together or any suggestion from Chapter 4 would be great ways to spend time with each other.

Ideas for Getting Away Without Your Kids

It's extremely difficult to get away overnight without your children. Many couples simply don't do it until their children are older. If it's at all possible, try to go away, even for one night. It takes planning to find someone to watch your kids. You might be extremely lucky and have grandparents or other relatives around who will watch your kids overnight for you. That's great. Most people need to use a combination of a hired sitter and friends or relatives.

Keep in mind that it might be more refreshing to go away for a short time in a more expensive, luxurious setting than a longer vacation that would be less special. Every night you spend away from your kids will entail some expenses or worry. If you go away for only one or two nights and spend as much money as you would on a five-day vacation, you might have a better time. Plus, you will have to spend less on a baby-sitter, or impose less on other people. Start small. Even one night away can be refreshing.

The Spice Rack

If you can only get away for one or two nights with each other, make the most of it. Be sure to relax, have romantic dinners, and just be together in a beautiful setting.

Think Twice

Don't forget that a TV in a hotel room can interfere with good conversation. Try to find a bed-and-breakfast without TVs in the rooms. Or just unplug the TV set when you check into your room. You'll have a more meaningful vacation.

The Least You Need to Know

➤ Be sure to remember to give each other attention and not give it all to the baby.

➤ When you plan out your time, be realistic and take into account your full-time responsibility to your child. You also need to be flexible and ready to change your schedule if it's not working out.

➤ It's worthwhile to reconsider your reasons for working when it will cost a substantial part of your paycheck to pay for child care.

➤ Your family will become more involved in your lives after you have children. Use this to your advantage.

➤ Make a commitment to regularly spend time with your spouse alone. Try to go away overnight with your spouse at least once a year.

Parenting as Partners

In This Chapter

➤ How your relationship affects your children

➤ Tips on disciplining your children effectively

➤ How to make the most of family routines

➤ Ideas for family traditions

All of us want our children to grow up in a loving, happy home. Some days it seems easy enough. Everything is going well, your kids are hugging each other and playing together, and they tell you that they love you at bedtime. Other days, you're not so sure. Your kids are fighting, you feel stressed, and nothing seems to be working. While all families have their good and bad days, there are many things you can do as parents to create more of the good days.

Building Blocks

The foundation of a happy family is a strong, loving relationship between the two of you. The single, most important thing that you can do for your children is to do everything in your power to have the best possible relationship with your spouse. If they see the two of you getting along and supporting each other, they will mirror you and will likely get along with each other and their friends. Every single ounce of energy that you put into your relationship will come back to you tenfold through your children.

On the other hand, children are also great imitators of less than perfect behavior. If they see the two of you arguing constantly, calling each other names, putting each other down, or hitting each other, you will probably see them repeating these negative behaviors. They will probably feel insecure, and this insecurity might be reflected in poor grades, bad behavior at school or home, or even depression. If the two of you are going through a rough period, work on your relationship! The entire family will benefit, not just the two of you.

The Great Imitators

George and Tina's 11-year-old son, Eric, had been acting up for a few months. Before, he was a solid "B" student and was well liked in school. Recently, however, he had been failing some of his exams, not doing his school reports, and neglecting his friends. Eric had also started to talk back to his parents, walk away from the dinner table, and slam the door to his room. George and Tina just didn't know what to do. The worse Eric's behavior got, the more they worried and the more they fought. They blamed each other for his behavior, and rather than come up with solutions, they kept focusing on the problems.

Bet You Didn't Know

Q: Is it bad for my children to see my spouse and I disagree?

A: No. It can be instructive for your children to see the two of you disagree *and* resolve the issue. They will learn valuable skills. On the other hand, yelling, screaming, threatening, or calling each other names is counterproductive. If you do have an unproductive argument in front of the children, be sure to *make up* in front of them as well.

When George and Tina reached the end of their rope, they came to see us about Eric. We listened to their description of his problems and then asked them how things were going for the two of them. They admitted they had been fighting a lot lately, even before their son was having problems. They were struggling financially, and both were working overtime to bring in extra income. They weren't going out together anymore in an effort to save money, and in general they weren't even enjoying each other's company. They never discussed their problems in front of their son because they didn't want to worry him.

As they talked more and more about their problems, Tina and George started getting the message that their behavior had really affected Eric.

Over time, George and Tina worked through a lot of their financial worries. They changed their budget so they could reduce their work hours, and they started to go out together again. They made a point to have a nice meal every night and talk about everyone's day. Their son gradually returned to his old self. He started inviting friends over to the house and completing his assignments. Eric's behavior problems had been a reflection of his parents' problems. When his parents worked through their difficulties, Eric's behavior began to improve.

Think Twice
Don't underestimate how much your relationship affects your children. If your relationship is suffering, work on it right away. If it goes on for too long, your children will suffer as well.

Disciplining Your Kids

One of the most important things you will do for your children is discipline them. It's an important part of helping them feel secure. Children need and want structure, even though they often will fight you every step of the way. It would be nice if children always listened to us the first time we asked them to do something. But even the best of children don't behave every minute. Disciplining kids is part of being good parents even when it's more troublesome to discipline our children than it would be to just let them have their way. Disciplining kids can also be a source of conflict between parents, but there are ways to keep arguments about discipline to a minimum.

The Three Times Rule

Often what happens when we try to discipline our children is we tell them to do something over and over again until we are incredibly angry and frustrated. For instance, if you say, "Johnny, stop hitting your brother," and he doesn't stop, you will probably say it again. If he still doesn't stop, you might say it several more times until you become furious. Then, you might grab him and put him kicking and screaming into his room, turn off the TV set, or take away a toy he's playing with.

A method that works much better for both you and your child is the three times rule. First, you simply say, "Johnny, stop hitting your brother." The second time, you say it with a consequence: "Johnny, stop hitting your brother or you will have a time-out in your room, you can't watch TV anymore today, or I will put away the toy that you are fighting over." And the *third* time, *no matter what,* you apply the consequence. The third request is usually accompanied by counting slowly one…two…and, at three, *boom,* they're in time-out, or have met whatever consequence you warned them about.

You have to use this rule every single time for it to be effective. Don't give in! If you follow through with your punishment, your child will really learn that you mean what you say. And he or she will know that not listening to you will bring a consequence, not just a threat. It also will give your child a sense of control because he or she will always have a warning before the punishment is actually carried out.

It's also important to choose the punishments carefully. You should keep two things in mind. First, the punishment should be something that you can and will carry out. If you tell Bobby that he can't come to the party with you and you know you will take him anyway, that is not an appropriate choice. Second, you should also get in the habit of making the punishment fit the crime. If Susie is coloring on her sister's book, you should give her a time-out in her room, or put the crayons off-limits for the rest of the day. Taking away dessert after dinner would not be as fitting a punishment. The closer the consequence is (in time and relationship) to the inappropriate behavior, the more likely the child will understand the relationship of his or her actions to the punishment.

Keeping a United Front

It's also vitally important to keep a united front with your spouse when disciplining your children. If one of you starts to carry through a punishment, and the other one tells them that it's not necessary, you will have undermined your authority. Your children will be the ultimate losers because it will not be clear what is expected of them. Even though they might feel good that they were not punished at the time, they will be generally confused about how they should behave. Further, you will have eroded trust in your marriage. Therefore, you must *always* stand by your spouse at the time, even if you disagree strongly. Afterward, in private, you can discuss how you might have handled the situation differently.

OH!

Bet You Didn't Know

Q: What if my spouse and I disagree on how to discipline the children?

A: Keep in mind that your goal *as a team* is to give your children limits. Your children must have consistent discipline from both of you. It's very confusing if each of you disciplines differently. You must put your differences aside and make a plan. If you cannot come to an agreement, you might find a book on discipline helpful.

The absolute best thing for a child is to see that his or her parents are a strong unit and are in agreement, even about a punishment. Of course, all kids will try to break parents down. They are experts at sniffing out differences and trying to push two parents apart.

Your child might play one of you against the other. This is very normal behavior for a child. The quickest way for a child to outgrow this phase is for his or her parents to stand strong. When a child learns it's possible to get what he or she wants by playing one parent against the other, the child is more likely to continue doing it.

The following is a list of discipline Dos and Don'ts:

DO	DON'T
Discipline firmly and consistently.	Let your child play you against your spouse.
Discipline with love.	Punish inconsistently.
Use time-outs instead of hitting or yelling.	Yell and scream at your child irrationally.
Use the three times rule.	Call your child names.
Choose appropriate punishments.	Notice only negative behaviors and not positive ones.
Keep a united front with your spouse.	Shame or insult your child.
Compliment your children frequently.	Threaten punishments that are impractical to follow through on.

Bet You Didn't Know

Q: Sometimes I'm just so angry that I can't keep from yelling at my child. What can I do?

A: If you find yourself starting to yell, take a deep breath and count to five. (The child will likely stare at you wondering what you're up to!) Then you'll be able to handle the situation like a pro—calm, cool, and collected. You'll also show your children by your *actions* how to handle their anger.

Merging Different Parenting Styles

Ted came from a very strict household. Children were to be seen and not heard. He was very strict with his children, and he did not tolerate any misbehavior. His wife, Millie, also came from a very strict home. She had bad memories about it, though, and tended to be more lenient with their children. When the kids were alone with their father, they were usually unspontaneous and relatively quiet. When they were with their mother, they knew they would get away with more and tended to be wild, loud, and rowdy.

Ted and Millie came to see us because they found themselves arguing more and more about the children. Ted was frustrated with Millie's leniency and felt the children were out of control. They would argue about discipline all the time in front of the children. And Millie often became upset with Ted when he disciplined the children because it reminded her of how strict her own father was with her. She wished the kids behaved a little better, but she wanted to do it without being as strict as her parents were.

When we asked Ted and Millie to describe their goals for their children's behavior, they listed similar things. They wanted their children to listen to them when they asked them to do something. They wanted them to behave at school and around other people. They didn't want them to talk back to an adult. They wanted them to say "please" and "thank-you." Ted and Millie were surprised that their lists were so similar, because it generally seemed to them that they had very different goals for their children.

Soul Mates
Rewarding your children for good behavior is the fun part of disciplining. Make it a point to "catch" your children being good and praise them. At the end of the day, talk with your spouse about all the wonderful things your children did that day and do so in front of them. Appreciating their positive behaviors will bring you all closer to each other.

We taught them to use the three times rule. Ted used it more than Millie, but she would not interfere when he did. It worked well because their children had an opportunity to correct their behavior when Ted was upset with them. Sometimes they were still punished, but many times they managed to stop what they were doing and calm down before a threat was carried through. Millie also found the three times rule useful. It made it easier for her to discipline their children when she needed to.

Differences in parenting styles can often be reduced by sitting down with your spouse and coming up with a list of behavior goals for your children. Then you can figure out which behaviors are intolerable and use the three times rule for discipline. Remember to always work these issues out with each other.

Family Routines

One of the most valuable things you can do is to provide your children with a stable, nurturing environment. Children like security, and one of the ways they feel secure is to have things they can count on. It's not surprising that they like to read the same book over and over again and have the same bedtime routine. You can, as parents, give them many things they can count on.

Morning Routine

Having a morning routine can make the difference between total chaos and a smooth start to the day. Everyone in the family will benefit when the first hour of their day is calm. The day should start with an established wake-up time that gives everyone enough time to get everything done without rushing. An example of a morning routine is as follows:

➤ Rise and shine

➤ Eat breakfast

➤ Get dressed

➤ Brush teeth

➤ Collect things needed for the day, such as lunch, homework, or jacket

➤ Off to school

Think Twice
Don't leave everything for the morning if you are on an extremely tight schedule. Make lunches and lay out coats the night before. That will make the morning less hectic.

Dinner Routine

Dinner is usually the one meal of the day when there is a chance for everyone to be together. Nowadays, people often rush through dinner or eat separately. That is a shame. Sitting down to a family meal can be a wonderful time in the day. It can give you the chance to hear about everyone's day and reinforce the family unit. Even if you realistically can't all have a sit-down dinner together every night, try to establish several nights a week that are meant for family dinners. Even if you are eating take-out food, set the table properly with plates, utensils, glasses, and napkins.

Think Twice
Don't just gobble the food down in front of the TV set. Turn it off! Dinnertime can be valuable family time that your kids will remember long after they've established families of their own.

Bedtime Routine

One of the most important routines for a child is the one at bedtime. Children who have a set of things to do every night before they go to bed will be calmer and able to fall asleep more easily. Bedtime should be the same every night, and the routine should start 30 to 45 minutes before "lights out." A suggestion for a bedtime routine for younger children is as follows:

Soul Mates
If you teach your children to go to bed easily by establishing a routine, then you will have more quiet time for the two of you.

➤ Take a shower or bath

➤ Put on pajamas

➤ Brush teeth

➤ Read a bedtime story

➤ Talk about the day

➤ Bedtime with hugs and kisses

As your children get older, they will establish their own routine. But it's still important to give them a regular bedtime and make sure they stick to it.

Sunday Pancakes

One fun routine is to have a special weekly meal. As a family, you might make pancakes every Sunday for breakfast. Each child could be given a task: help measure the flour, crack the eggs, or stir the batter. You could try different recipes and even create your own family pancake recipe. Or you could make Wednesday night "macaroni and cheese night." By having an enjoyable routine on Sunday mornings or another time in the week, you will be creating wonderful memories for your children, as well as providing them with something to count on.

Birthdays

Birthdays are fun for everyone in the family. Here are some ideas to make birthdays special in your house:

The Spice Rack
On mommy's or daddy's birthday, celebrate first with your family and then with just the two of you. Create your own tradition and do something special each year.

➤ Have a traditional family birthday cake.

➤ Create and sing a family birthday song.

➤ Tell family stories on birthdays.

➤ Look at birthday photos from the year before.

➤ Make breakfast in bed for the birthday person.

Family Vacations

Family vacations play an important part in our memory of childhood. They are times when everyone is together, on the same schedule, eating meals together, and having a good time. Hopefully, everyone is less stressed than usual and the emphasis is on being together and having fun. But remember, what is fun for an adult is not necessarily fun for kids.

What's fun for children? Well, we can start by naming what is not fun for kids. Fancy meals, grand hotel lobbies, art museums, and good shopping. Kids like simple foods, outdoor activities, parks, swimming pools, and games. And they often need physical activity each day to release energy!

There are many ways to ensure that your children will have their needs met and that you will also have some time with each other on your next vacation. Here are three ideas:

> **Think Twice**
> Don't assume that what is fun for the two of you will be fun for your children. If you consider your children's needs when you make your vacation plans, then the whole family will have a good time.

1. Many hotels now have children's programming on weekends and during the summer. It ranges in price, so be sure to ask ahead about the rates. Your children will be able to get some exercise, eat hamburgers, and spend the day or evening doing things that children like to do. Meanwhile, you and your spouse can do things that the two of you enjoy. Try to use the children's programming about half of the time so that you will still have family time too.

2. Go to a family camp. There are more and more family camps cropping up. They usually have dormitory-style food served three meals a day with activities for different age groups at various hours throughout the day. You have a set price for the vacation, so you don't need to worry about being surprised with the restaurant bill. The activities for your children are also included in the price, and if you are taking a full week of vacation, it will usually be less expensive than a hotel's children's programming. Plus, at a family camp, family activities tend to be built in as well, such as arts and crafts and a talent show.

3. You might consider bringing along a baby-sitter or your parents. In exchange for the plane fare and food, you can trade for a certain amount of baby-sitting every day. This can be especially useful in the evenings when your children are asleep anyway. You can spend most of the day with your family and have many of the evenings for the two of you. If you are driving to your vacation destination, this can be a very cost-effective way to get some time to yourselves.

Creating a Happy Family

You and your spouse will create a happy family if the two of you are happy. Keeping your relationship strong is the single most important thing that you can do for your children. Don't fight in front of your children, and spend time and energy working on your marriage. Be consistent when you discipline your children, and help create great memories for your children with family traditions and fun family routines. If you truly parent as partners, you will raise wonderful children. They will have fond memories of their childhood and will have a good relationship with you for the rest of their lives.

The Least You Need to Know

➤ A strong relationship between the two of you is the foundation for creating a happy family.

➤ Keeping a united front with your spouse will help your child feel secure. If you disagree with the way your spouse is handling something, discuss it later, not in front of your child.

➤ Discipline firmly, consistently, and with love.

➤ Children find comfort in routine. Having family routines and traditions will give your children things they can count on.

➤ Family vacations can create great memories for your children.

Part 5
Transitions

Your lives seem to be going along smoothly, when suddenly there's a change. Perhaps one of your work schedules has shifted or you have moved to a new place. Perhaps one of your parents needs more attention. Or, if this is your second marriage, perhaps your past is catching up with you. Your relationship has shifted, and you don't know how to handle it. Just when you thought things were going well, a wrench is thrown in the machinery. You feel frustrated and maybe even hopeless about your situation and your relationship.

Don't panic! All of these feelings are common when there is a change in your life. But take heart: There are also many ways to handle them. The following chapters will help you tackle different transitions that couples often face in their marriages. We'll give you useful tools to help you adapt to these changes and that build on the skills you have learned in the previous chapters.

Chapter 18

Employed, Unemployed, Reemployed

In This Chapter

➤ How your job can affect your relationship

➤ Analyzing your current employment situation

➤ Avoiding pitfalls of long working hours

➤ Adjusting your schedules to make time for the chores and each other

➤ Staying close when one of you travels for work

In this era of downsizing, you should be prepared for changes in your job. Perhaps your department had a cutback so you are working less hours than before, making less money. Or perhaps you've kept your full-time job but are expected to work extra hours every week to make up for a colleague who was let go. Perhaps you've been lucky and were promoted, making more money, but now you are traveling a lot or have been asked to relocate to a different city. All of these changes will affect your marriage. In this chapter, you will learn how to adjust to changes in the workplace so you can take care of the most important relationship in your life, and we don't mean the one with your boss!

Love and Work

Although you usually develop your relationship and your career separately, we all know through experience that they are connected. The quality of your love life will affect your work. If you're feeling stressed about your relationship, you will be on edge at work and less productive. If you're feeling great about your partner, you will sail through your day at work.

Soul Mates

If your spouse is miserable at work, this will have a definite impact on your relationship. Be supportive if he or she wants to change jobs. Even if it's a rough time temporarily, you will both be happier in the long run.

The opposite is also true. How your work is going will affect your relationship. This shouldn't be surprising, because most people spend more time at work than they spend awake with their spouse! If you are happy with your work, that will enhance your relationship. You will probably be in a good mood when you get home. You will be relatively relaxed and will have an enjoyable evening with your spouse. On the other hand, if your job is sheer drudgery, you will probably be stressed when you get home from work. You might spend your evening in a bad mood and complain about work.

How's Work?

Some people are lucky enough to really enjoy their work and would do it even if they made no money or a lot less money. But the main reason most people work is to earn a salary. That doesn't mean you need to be miserable at work. You can like your job and still be doing it because it pays a salary.

The first step toward maximizing what you get from your job is asking yourself the following questions:

1. Do you generally like your job?

2. Do you dread going to work in the morning?

3. Are you treated well at work by coworkers and by your boss?

4. Are you paid a reasonable amount of money for the sort of work that you do?

5. Do you feel completely drained at the end of the day?

6. Are you working more hours than you can handle?

7. Does your job keep you on the path to where you want to be five years from now?

8. If you are unhappy at your workplace, do you think that doing similar work at another place would potentially make you happier?

9. If you are unhappy at work, have you ever considered making a complete career change?

10. Do you feel that your spouse would be supportive if you changed jobs or careers?

Consider your answers to these questions. If you are reasonably satisfied with your work, great! If not, make sure you consider whether there are ways you can improve your current job. For instance, can you change or shorten your hours, shift your job description, or work for a different boss? If your current job is so miserable that you don't think it could ever be reasonable, then is it possible for you to find a better job?

Soul Mates

If your spouse is miserable at work, that will affect you. Be supportive if he or she wants to change jobs. Even if it's a rough time temporarily, you will both be happier in the long run!

Stressed Out

Diane and Brad have a good relationship. They have been married for three years and are thinking about starting a family soon. One day Brad was very excited when he came home from work. He told Diane that he had received a promotion to assistant manager at his company. The company could not promise him an increase in salary, but said he would probably get a bonus at the end of the year. Diane and Brad celebrated by going out to a special dinner on Saturday night.

Eventually, the reality of the situation hit them. Brad's entire personality seemed to change. He came home after 8 o'clock every night. He was irritable and often snapped at Diane. He would eat his cold dinner without talking much about his workday. Diane had been prepared for him to work longer hours, but she was not prepared for his grouchiness. When they went out on Saturday nights, they often got into arguments about unimportant things.

Diane didn't know what to do. She felt sorry for herself. Every time she asked Brad how he was doing, he would simply say, "Fine." But things weren't fine. What was happening to their marriage? Diane finally told Brad that she was very unhappy and that they needed to talk. Brad said, "Sure," but became very defensive when Diane expressed her concerns about his new behaviors. "What do you want from me? I'm tired all the time and I'm working hard for our future."

Diane asked him if he liked his new job. "Of course I like it, I'm an assistant manager now, aren't I?" Diane then asked him a simple question, "What are some of the things that you like about your job?" He thought about it and couldn't answer. After a while she asked, "What *don't* you like about your job?" "Oh, I hate the stress and responsibility that goes with it. I had to fire a perfectly nice guy because my boss didn't like him. If someone gets sick at work, I have to make sure that his or her job gets done anyway. I used to go in, do my job, and come home. Now I have to make sure that several other people do their jobs too. I come home feeling miserable."

Diane was amazed that Brad felt like this. "Brad, I never want you to be miserable at your work. Even if it's a promotion, if you're unhappy, who needs it? Maybe you're just one of those people who doesn't enjoy being a manager. It's much better to find that out now than later. Maybe you should talk to your boss about this."

Brad talked to his boss the next day. He told him that he did not feel suited to his new job and explained why. His boss was disappointed because he liked Brad. So Brad asked if he could have his old job back. His boss felt that he was overqualified for his original job, but told him that he needed a day to think about it. When Brad went back, his boss had created a new job for him. He restructured it so that Brad was no longer in charge of the entire division, but rather had responsibility for specific projects. Brad was very excited about this idea. He still worked slightly longer hours than he had before the first promotion, but now he was energized when he came home.

Think Twice
Don't assume that a promotion will automatically mean a better job for you. It's always important to evaluate your job from time to time and determine whether you find it satisfying.

Brad had been miserable in his new job, but when Diane confronted him with her concerns, he was able to take action. By finally being honest with himself and his boss, he changed his work environment and, subsequently, his relationship with Diane. In your own relationship, see if there is a mismatch between either your or your spouse's work and how that work fits into your lives. If there is a mismatch, consider whether there are any possible ways you can change or improve the situation.

Are You Married to Your Work or Your Spouse?

Some people are fortunate enough to really love their work. They put tons of energy into their job and receive a lot of personal satisfaction from the results. They tend to work long hours and talk enthusiastically about their jobs to whomever will listen. Most of their friends tend to be from the office. They often have little energy left over for anything or anyone else—including their spouse.

There is an expression to describe such people: They are married to their work. What does this imply about their marriage to their spouse? Usually it means that their spouse comes second, which is a recipe for disaster. Even though someone might receive a great deal of satisfaction from his or her job, he or she still needs to put the marriage first. Work shouldn't be at the expense of your relationship.

Overworked and Loving It

Doug and Laura both had jobs that were important to them. Up until now, they had managed to put enough time and energy into their relationship to have a great marriage. But recently, Laura was becoming more and more engrossed in her work. She was very excited about the new project she was working on. She worked 12-hour days, brought work home with her, and worked most weekends. All she could talk about was her ideas on the project and where her career was heading. Laura was totally consumed by her work.

Doug was beginning to feel left out and resentful. In general, he was very supportive of Laura and proud of her accomplishments. But lately she had no energy left for him. Every time they went out she talked about her work. She never asked him how he was doing and never seemed to think about their relationship anymore. She even stopped doing small, nice things for her husband. Her commitment was exclusively to her job. Laura was married to her work and was putting her marriage to Doug in serious jeopardy.

When Doug brought up the issue about her work, Laura would always say, "Don't you care about my career? It's so important to me, and I thought it was important to you too." Doug really felt like he was being taken for granted. After a particularly bad argument about their situation, Doug blurted out, "Don't assume I'll always be there for you. You haven't exactly been there for me lately!"

Laura was shocked. She had been working so hard and had made the false assumption that her marriage would survive the stress with no extra effort from her. Doug and Laura had a very serious talk about how Laura could invest a lot of time in her work and still have time for Doug. What was most important to Doug was that Laura really put work out of her mind when she was with him and focus solely on him and their relationship. Laura needed to manage her time at work more efficiently. She realized she could save an hour a day, five hours a week, by using her cellular phone to make business calls while driving to work. And she changed half of her dinner meetings to breakfast meetings.

Soul Mates
If both of you are working full-time, try to talk with each other in the middle of the day to catch up.

By making all of these changes, she had more time to invest in her relationship. Laura was much happier and so was Doug. They really improved their marriage once Laura learned she needed to put time and effort into the relationship, even when she was busy at work.

Where's Your Priority?

Priorities can make a big impact on your life. If you have them in the wrong place, you can be miserable. Below is a list of statements that will help you find out what priorities you have in your life. Decide whether the following are "True" or "False."

Priority Quiz

1. I try to be in a good mood at work.

   True   or   False

2. I try to look my best at work.

   True   or   False

3. I generally give my undivided attention to my work.

   True   or   False

4. I put my best foot forward at work.

   True   or   False

5. I would never be late for work.

   True   or   False

6. I give 100 percent effort to my work.

   True   or   False

7. I try to be flexible at work.

   True   or   False

8. I am reliable at work.

   True   or   False

9. I am committed to my work.

   True   or   False

---

10. I am loyal to my work.

   True   or   False

11. I try to be in a good mood for my spouse.

   True   or   False

12. I try to look my best for my spouse.

   True   or   False

13. I generally give my undivided attention to my spouse.

   True   or   False

14. I put my best foot forward for my spouse.

   True   or   False

15. I would never be late for my spouse.

   True   or   False

16. I give 100 percent effort in my relationship with my spouse.

   True   or   False

17. I try to be flexible with my spouse.

   True   or   False

18. I am reliable for my spouse.

   True   or   False

19. I am committed to my spouse.

   True   or   False

20. I am loyal to my spouse.

   True   or   False

How many of the first 10 questions did you answer "True" to (those about your work)? How many of the last 10 questions did you answer "True" to (those about your spouse)? Did you answer "True" more often to the work questions? What do you think this might mean about how you view your relationship? What could you do to change this? List the qualities that you answered "False" to about your spouse and "True" to about your work. Start bringing these qualities into your marriage.

> ### Bet You Didn't Know
>
> OH!
>
> Q: I work at a demanding job and like to be relaxed at home. Is this okay?
>
> A: Yes, of course you can relax at home! But you still need to put effort into your marriage as well as your work. You will be a lot happier and more personally satisfied. People forget that their jobs are often temporary and their marriages will hopefully last their entire lives.

All I've Got Is Time

While it's obvious that a relationship can suffer when one person is working long hours, the opposite can also be true. Surprisingly, if one of you spends *less* time at work than the other, it can also put stress on your marriage.

Joe and Cynthia both used to work full-time. Joe worked for an accounting agency that decided to reduce the number of employees after the tax season, when they had less work. Joe was one of the unlucky ones and would be off work for several months. He looked for a temporary job, but didn't have much success. He decided to make the best of his time off and planned to do some projects around the house and improve his golf game. Joe rationalized this decision by seeing the benefits of having time off and telling himself that he could use the rest. Cynthia, too, liked the fact that Joe had more time because he was able to do some errands.

However, after a few weeks of the new schedule, Joe became restless. He was lonely in the afternoons and felt jealous that Cynthia had a full-time job. When Cynthia came home in the evenings after a full day of work, she needed to unwind from her day. Joe, on the other hand, had plenty of time to relax during the day and had energy to go out in the evenings. Another problem was that Cynthia started expecting Joe to prepare dinner every night and assumed that he would do all of the grocery shopping. But she never discussed this with him.

Eventually, all of these unspoken issues became intolerable. One night Cynthia came home after a particularly difficult day at work. All day she had been looking forward to a delicious home-cooked meal. When she walked in the door, she found Joe comfortably sleeping in a recliner in the family room with a book laying across his stomach. Not only was there nothing cooking for dinner, but the refrigerator was empty. Cynthia was fuming. She woke up Joe and demanded to know why he hadn't cooked dinner.

Joe looked at her dumbfounded. "I was reading and I fell asleep," he said. He didn't mind cooking dinner sometimes, but they had never discussed the issue. Cynthia went on a rampage. "Well, what do you do all day when you're home? You should be making dinner every night, cleaning the house, and doing the grocery shopping. I'm tired. I work all day. You're not even making any money now. It's the least you could do." This made Joe furious, and they both went to bed that night angry at each other.

When Cynthia and Joe finally sat down a few days later to talk, they were in a better mood. Cynthia apologized and Joe was able to accept her apology. Cynthia realized she had specific expectations of Joe that she had never even verbalized. Joe agreed that he should take on more of the chores during these few months, but he also wanted to use the time for other things. Cynthia hadn't realized that there were projects around the house he wanted to complete in these three months. Joe agreed to prepare dinner three nights a week and take on some extra errands. Otherwise, he wanted to take advantage of the time he had in other ways.

If you or your spouse has a major change in your work hours, then you need to renegotiate your chore list. Don't make assumptions about what your spouse will or will not be able to do. Redoing your chore list as soon as possible will prevent conflicts before they happen. You might also need to reschedule your planning time, discussion time, fun time together, or all three! But always remember that your goal is to have the best relationship you can possibly have—and that takes effort and planning!

Money Isn't Everything

If one of you is absolutely miserable at work and there doesn't seem to be a way to improve the situation, it's important to consider quitting your job. Depending on the situation, it might be relatively easy to find another job or it might be difficult. You might be unemployed for a while or need to take a salary cut. You also might need to go back to school for a period of time in order to get a different type of job. As difficult as this transition might be, the two of you will probably be much happier in the long run.

Randy was absolutely miserable in his job at the bank. He especially hated his boss, who was unsupportive and gave him unrealistic tasks. Randy came home every evening feeling exhausted and stressed out. His wife, Pam, was supportive of him and helped Randy unwind and relax at the end of the day. But after months of focusing on Randy, she was feeling stressed as well. Pam liked her job, but she also had some difficult days when she needed support from Randy. She knew that Randy was very unhappy at work, but focusing on his problems every evening was taking a toll on her.

Both Pam and Randy were feeling stressed, and now their marriage was suffering. They were arguing more and were both irritable. They were having trouble enjoying time together, even on weekends. One day, after an especially bad time at work, Randy talked the entire evening about how much he hated his job. Pam was sick of hearing about it and said, "Why don't you just quit? I don't want to hear about it anymore."

OH! Bet You Didn't Know

Q: I hate my job, but I feel stuck. What can I do?

A: If you hate your job, consider it an opportunity to change your employment to something that you like better. Sometimes it takes being in a miserable situation to let yourself make a change or take a chance.

Randy looked at her and wondered if she was kidding. "There's no way that I can quit. We need the money." Pam answered, "Of course we need you to earn money, but that doesn't mean that you have to do this exact job to earn it." They had a long discussion about it and decided that Randy would quit and look for another job.

Think Twice
Don't think that money can buy happiness. It's very important to consider all options if you are stuck in a job that you hate. Quitting is not easy, but it might be the best choice for you and for your relationship in the long run.

At first Randy felt depressed (especially because they had to borrow some money from his brother), but when he started seeing job opportunities that sounded much better than his previous job, he began to feel excited. In the month that Randy looked for a job, their marriage completely changed. He felt much better and was renewed by the chance to look for another job. After six weeks he found a job at a bank that not only had a more reasonable boss, but was closer to their house as well.

Traveling with Work

There are many things to consider if you travel for work and still want to maintain a great relationship. It's easy to lose some degree of connection with your spouse when you are away from home. There are many things that you can do to ensure that your marriage is strong when one of you travels a lot. Here are some things you can try:

1. Talk to each other at least once every single day. There is absolutely no excuse not to have a daily phone conversation with your spouse. It's so important to maintain the contact with each other. Even a brief conversation that lasts only a few minutes will help keep the two of you connected and will prevent each of you from feeling lonely and like separate people rather than the closely bonded couple that you are!

2. Spend as few nights as possible apart from each other. If you are away from your spouse for only one or two nights, it's much easier to maintain the day-to-day closeness in your relationship than when you are apart for a week at a time. Take the time to evaluate how important each activity is on your trip. You might be able to trim a day or two from your time away by rearranging your schedule or eliminating some less important activities.

3. Go together. If it's feasible for both of you to go together when one of you needs to travel for work, do it. It will give you a chance to have some time together in a hotel room that is already paid for! Especially consider doing this when one of you needs to travel to an interesting city or pretty resort.

4. Greet each other warmly when you are reunited. It's especially important to treat each other well when one of you returns home so you don't forget how much you enjoy each other's company.

5. Spend time catching up on your time apart when the traveler returns home. Arrange a special date or a quiet dinner at home to catch up on each other's activities. Don't just ignore the days that went by. Make them part of your marriage by talking about them with each other.

> **The Spice Rack**
> When you are traveling, send your spouse flowers or a basket of fruit with a note that says, "I miss you."

The Least You Need to Know

➤ Your job affects your relationship. If you are miserable at work, you will be bringing that to your marriage.

➤ Even if you love your work, you need to think carefully about your hours and still focus on your spouse. Make sure that your relationship is number one!

➤ Shorter work hours doesn't automatically mean more quality time in the relationship. You need to renegotiate your household chores and your time together.

➤ Sometimes, the solution to being unhappy at work is quitting and finding a new job.

➤ If you travel with your work, make sure you keep your trips as short as possible and talk to each other every day. Reunite with gusto!

183

Chapter 19

Home Away from Home

In This Chapter

➤ Evaluating whether you should move

➤ Common concerns when moving

➤ Ideas to help reduce the stress of moving

➤ Hints for settling into a new place

➤ Exploring your new community together

For better or worse, we live in an extremely mobile society. The average American moves many times in his or her lifetime. People move for many reasons: a better job, a calmer pace of life, warmer weather, or to be near relatives. We will give you guidelines to help you evaluate whether or not you should move. If you decide to move, moving to a new locale may put stress on your relationship. In this chapter, we'll outline ways to minimize that stress. And we will also give you ideas on settling into a new place.

The Big Decision

If you're like most couples, the decision of whether or not to move is a tough one. There are so many factors to consider. If both of you work, you would each need to find a new job. Maybe you would be moving closer to family and friends or maybe you would be leaving them. Your economic situation might be better or worse in a new locale. If you have children, you have their education to consider as well.

Think Twice
Don't decide to move without thinking it through carefully. Being in a new place will affect many aspects of both of your lives.

Usually, if you're thinking about moving, something is prompting you. In most cases, work is the motivating factor. You might have been offered a promotion in a new city, or your current job is being moved to a new place. Or you might be looking for a different lifestyle: a change in climate, cost of living, or city size. The important thing is to think the decision through very carefully. It's a major life change.

Moving Questionnaire

The following questions will help you to consider your reasons for moving. If you have already decided to move, you can skip over them and head to the later section, "We're Moving!"

1. What is your main reason for moving? Is it a preference or a necessity?

2. Will both of you be able to find satisfactory jobs in the new city?

3. Will there be a change in your economic status in the new place? You need to consider cost of housing and living as well as your salary.

4. Will you be leaving friends and family who are important to you? Do you think you will be able to reorganize support in the new place?

5. Will your leaving have an impact on other people (i.e., family members who rely on your practical and/or emotional support)?

6. Can you anticipate hidden costs to living in the new place (i.e., higher telephone bills or transportation costs)?

7. Will the climate be better or worse in the new place? Is this important to you?

8. Will the new locale be a city that is similar in size or much different (i.e., a much bigger city or a rural area)?

9. Do you have special needs as a couple that can be met in the new place (i.e., place of worship, medical needs, etc.)?

10. If you have children, are you satisfied with the schools where you would be moving?

We hope your answers to these questions will encourage you to consider issues you might have overlooked.

Should We or Shouldn't We?

Jack was offered the opportunity to move to a new city 500 miles away. He would be given a promotion and his salary would increase by almost 50 percent. At first he was very excited and couldn't imagine turning down the offer. He went home to tell his wife, Sally, so they could celebrate.

However, while driving home he started to realize that there were really a lot of factors to consider. When he got home he told Sally about the opportunity and suggested that they go out to dinner and talk about it. They went through the "Moving Questionnaire" that you just took. Here are their answers:

> **Soul Mates**
> Make the decision to move together. Be honest about your needs and communicate them clearly to your spouse.

1. They would be moving so that Jack would have an opportunity to have a promotion and make more money. They did not *have* to move, because his company was willing to keep him in his current position.

2. It was not clear whether Sally would be able to get as good a job in the new city. She had been with her company for seven years and had a lot of security in the company. Sally didn't particularly love her job, so she wouldn't mind working somewhere else, but she did have a good salary and reasonable working conditions.

3. Jack would be making substantially more money, although Sally would likely make somewhat less money. Housing would cost approximately 10 percent to 15 percent more than where they currently lived. The general cost of living was approximately the same in both places. Overall, they would probably have more money than they currently did, but not as much as they initially thought.

4. Jack and Sally would be leaving Jack's sister and her family, as well as his mother. They saw them every few weeks. But when they thought about it, they had really enjoyed having the family around. Another factor to consider was that Jack and Sally were planning to have kids in the next few years. It would be especially nice to have family around then.

5. Jack's family would miss them, but no one was currently relying on them for support.

6. Jack and Sally realized that they would spend close to $1,000 every year on telephone bills and plane travel to visit Jack's family.

7. The climate would be somewhat better in the new place. It would not be as cold in the winter and there would be less snow. Sally did not like winters and would prefer them to be milder. Jack didn't have a preference.

8. The new city was bigger than the one they currently lived in. It had more cultural resources, but also more congestion and a higher crime rate.

9. Jack and Sally felt that the new city would have a church they would like. They couldn't anticipate any other special needs that they would have.

10. Jack and Sally didn't have children yet. The schools were good in some of the neighborhoods where they would be living.

When they looked at their answers, they realized that the only real advantage to the new city was Jack's job, both the opportunity for promotion and the salary increase. When they considered the increase in housing costs, Sally's possible decrease in salary, and the money that they would have to spend to keep in touch with friends and family, the salary increase seemed much less than 50 percent. They realized that it was not a good enough reason to move. Jack was excited about the chance to have a promotion and do more challenging work. But Sally and Jack realized that they wanted to be near family when they had children.

> OH!
>
> ### Bet You Didn't Know
>
> Q: Doesn't moving because you were given a raise usually mean more money?
>
> A: A salary increase doesn't automatically mean that you will have extra spending money in your pocket each month. You need to consider both of your incomes, as well as your expenses. Conversely, a salary decrease might not mean that you will have less money. Your expenses might be lower in a different place, resulting in the same amount of money left over every month.

Jack talked to his boss at work and let him know what he was thinking. He was wondering if there was a chance that he would eventually be promoted if he stayed at his current job. His boss said that he was a very valued employee and that he would probably be promoted eventually. But he cautioned him that the salary increase could not match the one they were offering in the new city. After much deliberation, Jack and Sally decided not to move.

When you and your spouse are thinking about moving, remember to consider all of the factors so that you can isolate your real reasons for moving. Always keep in mind that you are a team and that you need to jointly decide whether to move.

We're Moving!

If the two of you have decided to move, you are probably feeling somewhat overwhelmed with all of the things that you need to do. You need to pack all of your belongings and find a new place to live. There are so many unknowns: Will you make new friends? Will you like your new jobs? Who will be your neighbors? You might even be wondering if you're making a mistake.

All these feelings are normal. There are, however, some things that you can do to relieve your stress. Here are 10 stress-reducing tips that can make moving easier for the two of you:

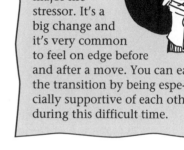

Soul Mates
Moving is a major life stressor. It's a big change and it's very common to feel on edge before and after a move. You can ease the transition by being especially supportive of each other during this difficult time.

1. Rent for at least six months in the new place. You don't need the extra stress of buying a house. And if the move doesn't work out, it's much easier to leave an apartment or rented house than a home you own. The exception to this would be if you are moving back to a place the two of you lived before and you are sure you'll be staying for at least three years.

2. In a separate box that you mark "Urgent—Open First," pack a bottle of champagne, two glasses, photo albums, and a cozy blanket. It will help you feel at home in your new place. Drinking champagne while looking at a photo album of your honeymoon can make the piles of boxes look less imposing.

3. Separate your photo albums from your negatives. You might even have friends or family keep your negatives and forward them when you are sure that your photo albums have arrived safely in your new home. Losing those memories would be a big loss.

4. Make sure you notify the post office of your new address. Your mail will be forwarded for one year. You can notify businesses of your new address as you pay your monthly bills.

The Spice Rack
Pack a small wrapped gift in your suitcase for your spouse. It will be a nice surprise when you get to your new home.

5. Magazines are generally forwarded for one month. If you have magazine subscriptions, inform them of your new address in writing or by telephone.

6. You can save yourself the trouble of mailing out a huge pile of moving cards to everyone by including your new address in your annual holiday cards.

Soul Mates
Try to arrange to have several days to unpack and settle in before you begin work. This will help give the two of you a good start.

7. Keep copies of addresses and phone numbers in several different places. You especially don't want to lose contact with old friends and family now.

8. Arrange to have your utilities (water, power, gas) and telephone turned on one or two days before you arrive. That way you can be assured that they will be working the moment you arrive. The small amount of extra money you will spend will eliminate the possibility of having your first day without a telephone or hot water.

9. If you have children, register them for school as soon as you know that you are moving and what neighborhood you are going to live in. You can't always assume that they can go to the school down the street or that it's any good. By registering your children ahead of time, you will be able to tackle any problems that arise in a timely manner.

10. Pace yourself. Unpacking and settling in is a big job and takes days if not weeks. Give yourselves permission to take time out to be together. Explore your new surroundings. Take a long walk around the neighborhood or see a movie.

Making Your House into a Home

You've unpacked all of the cardboard boxes and put them out to recycle. Your favorite wedding photo is sitting on the mantle above the fireplace. You've stocked the kitchen with your favorite spices. Your dishes are neatly stacked in cabinets above the sink. But somehow, the two of you still feel unsettled. Even though everything is where it should be, you feel like nothing is in place.

You've found out the hard way that settling into a new place is much more than unpacking. It's feeling at home, knowing your neighbors, having friends to invite over for dinner, knowing who you can trust at work. If you have children, then it's knowing other families who have children the same age as yours. Of course, all of these things take time. But there are ways to speed things along so that you can feel settled as soon as possible.

The Spice Rack
When you first move in, take the time to completely unpack and set up your bedroom. Then you will have a room where you can retreat from the mess and really feel at home!

Welcome Home

If you don't know many people in town, you can't sit around waiting for people to welcome you. Be direct. Give yourselves a welcoming party! Invite everyone on your block or in your apartment building. Keep it simple. Put Xeroxed, handwritten invitations in people's mailboxes. Have it in the afternoon with drinks and chips. No one will expect you to serve a feast. In fact, they will be impressed that you did it at all. You'll at least briefly meet your neighbors (at least the ones interested in meeting you). And people who can't make it to the party may stop by and say hello.

You will have accomplished so much with relatively little effort. Rather than wait for a chance meeting with all of these people, you will have told them a lot of things all at once—that the two of you are new in town, that you are friendly, that you are interested in your neighbors, and that you welcome a future relationship.

Think Twice
Don't wait for your neighbors to introduce themselves to you. People are busy. Just because they haven't invited you over doesn't mean that they don't want to meet the two of you. It's okay to make the first move.

It's Party Time

Linda and Paul moved into their new house and felt frustrated that they had only met one of their neighbors. They wanted to feel like part of the neighborhood. They had two children, aged six and nine. It was summer and school hadn't started, so their kids hadn't made new friends yet either.

They decided they would invite everyone on their block over for a Sunday open house. They put invitations on everyone's doorstep. Linda and Paul kept things simple. They went to the grocery store and bought chips, dips, and cut-up vegetables. They bought several cheeses, cut them in small blocks, and put them out with crackers. They used paper plates and cups, and plastic utensils. That Sunday they were very nervous and were wondering if they had done the right thing. When the first person rang the doorbell, they were immediately relieved. The family introduced themselves and apologized for not meeting them sooner. They commented that they had been very busy this summer and had been out of town a lot. They were very glad to have a family on the block, and even had a child who was nine years old who would be going to the same school as Linda and Paul's nine-year-old.

By the time the day was over, they had met people from over half of the homes on their block. Several of them had children close to the ages of their own. Their kids were immediately happier and had friends to play with for the rest of the summer. Their neighbors now invited them to dinner and were interested in getting to know them better.

By taking the initiative, Linda and Paul made a huge step to feeling more at home. By making a small investment in time and money, they integrated themselves into their new neighborhood.

Exploring Your New Neighborhood

When people move to a new location, they often don't spend time exploring stores they use frequently for their errands. They often just use the stores that are closest to their house. For instance, they will go to the supermarket nearby and assume that is where they will shop. They will develop their photos at the local drug store without comparing quality.

Think Twice
Don't underestimate how important the little things are to making you feel at home. The sooner your day-to-day life is in order, the sooner you will feel settled.

You need to feel secure in your day-to-day life before you can feel settled in a new place. It's so important to trust your hair stylist, as well as your grocery store, and know the best place to have your photos developed. It might seem unimportant or a waste of time to check out several supermarkets or have your photos developed at different places. But it's very important and a good use of time. In fact, it's a critical step to helping you feel at home. Think about how much time you devote to your errands. Use the following to decide what is important to you:

➤ *Grocery shopping:* What is important to you in a grocery store? The produce? The selection of non-food items? The availability of money-saving large sizes? Check out several grocery stores to see which one best suits your needs. Don't just go to the one closest to your house and assume you'll feel at home there.

➤ *Photo developing:* There are many different places to have your photos processed, from the corner drug store to the mall to an expert photo lab. Consider issues like convenience as well as your particular needs when it comes to having your photographs developed. How choosy are you about your prints? Do you usually get two for one prints? Is one-hour developing the most important consideration, or is the lowest price key for you?

➤ *Haircut:* This is a tricky one. The person who cuts your hair is a very important person in your life. It's important to like him or her *and* like the way he or she cuts your hair. Ask your neighbors, coworkers, or even a stranger in the line at the video store (whose hair style you admire) where they get their hair cut and what they like about their stylist. If you don't have anyone to ask yet, visit several shops and chat with some stylists. You can find out if they listen to what you want and are open to new clients.

➤ *Clothes shopping:* If you moved to a city with the same department stores as where you used to live, then you have a good place to start. Otherwise, spend some time browsing the local mall. Go when you don't need to buy anything in particular so you won't get frustrated. Evaluate the store's styles, brands, and prices. Figure out where you feel the most comfortable. Then, when you need something, go right to that store.

➤ *Dry cleaners:* Do you do a lot of dry cleaning or just the occasional sport coat? Is a very fast turnaround time important to you? What about extended hours? Do you often need mending or altering done? Again, you can start by asking your neighbors their preferences. It gives you something to talk about, and they are usually happy to help out. The first time you use a place, only give them one or two items. If you are not happy with their work, you can go elsewhere.

➤ *Parks:* If you have kids, it's critical to have a few parks that you really enjoy going to. It's a great way to meet people, and it will help your children feel at home. Make it a family adventure. Pack a picnic lunch, bring your favorite old blanket, and make an afternoon out of it. Try out several different parks until you find one that you and your children really enjoy.

➤ *Specialty items:* Did you have a favorite bakery where you used to live? Or a boutique where you could buy cosmetics? Or a sporting-goods store? Again, this is a time to explore. Look through the phone book; then take an afternoon and check out several different places. It's fun to browse when you don't need to buy anything in particular.

> **The Spice Rack**
> Exploring new restaurants together can be fun. Get dressed up when you go out and really make it feel like a date!

Settling In

Sit back and take a minute to think about what activities you most enjoyed where you used to live. Did you enjoy trying different restaurants, playing golf, or listening to live music in coffeehouses? Dive right in and do those same things immediately!

Now think about where the two of you received most of your social support. Did you mostly spend time with friends from work or people in your church, temple, or synagogue? Did you have a group of friends to go bowling with or have a weekly poker game? After you identify two or three activities that were important to you, try to replicate them as quickly as possible.

Make an effort to acquaint yourself with a new person from work each day. If you can't find a bowling team to join, start one! If you like to read books, join a book club. If you were a member of a church or religious organization before, get involved! It's very simple.

193

You will meet people you have things in common with if you put yourself in the right situation. Don't be shy. Your effort will really pay off to help you settle in as quickly as possible.

> **OH!**
>
> ### Bet You Didn't Know
>
> Q: How can I help my children feel at home?
>
> A: If you have kids, it's critical to have a few parks that you really enjoy going to. It's a great way to meet people, and it will help your children feel comfortable. Make it a family adventure. Pack a picnic lunch, bring your favorite old blanket, and make an afternoon of it. Try out several different parks until you find one that you and your children really enjoy.

Joining In

Linda and Paul were very busy settling into their new house. In the fall, once school had started for their children, they realized that they needed to do more than just talk to their neighbors and go to work. They decided to join a church, and looked at several within five miles of their house. They joined the one that was the farthest, because it felt the most like the one that they had liked where they previously lived. It was smaller than the other churches, but people seemed really involved and there were wonderful programs for their children. Within a month of joining the church and getting involved in church activities, they felt more at home than ever. Paul also started playing basketball once a week after work, which gave him an outlet that he had not had before. Now they were meeting interesting people all the time. They were busier than ever and were really feeling like part of their community. They knew that they had done something right when one of their children told them, "I really like it here. I have so many friends and there are tons of fun things to do." When they thought about it, they felt that way too!

Soul Mates
If you have children, get them involved in activities that they like to do. They will be happy, and as a bonus the two of you will meet other parents who might become your friends.

Giving It Your Best

When you and your spouse move to a new place, give it your best. Really try to meet your neighbors and get involved with community activities. Get to know your neighborhood and have fun exploring together. You will be on the way to making this new place your home.

If after doing everything you can to make the new place work for you, you still feel that it's not meeting your needs, then it's time to rethink your decision. Go through the first section of this chapter, and reevaluate why you would move and what would be better in a new place. You might decide to stay put or move to a new place. You might even decide to move back to where you came from! The important thing to remember is to not get so caught up in the details and logistics of the move that you forget the goals you are trying to accomplish by the move in the first place!

The Least You Need to Know

➤ Carefully think through whether or not moving is a good idea. There are many factors to consider, such as salary, size of city, housing costs, and climate.

➤ Take special care when packing personal mementos and belongings. They are the things that you cannot replace.

➤ Meet your neighbors by throwing yourselves a party. People will appreciate the invitation and will enjoy meeting you.

➤ Spend time choosing your grocery store, dry cleaners, and hair stylist. Feeling comfortable with the day-to-day things in your life will help you feel at home.

➤ Get involved in your new community as soon as possible. You will have a chance to meet people with similar interests if you involve yourself in activities you find interesting.

Chapter 20

When Those You Looked Up to Look Up to You

In This Chapter

➤ Being aware of your emotions when dealing with aging parents

➤ Supporting your spouse

➤ Redefining your relationship with your parents

➤ Preventing resentments and grudges from playing out

It's very difficult to think about people that you love growing older, developing medical problems, and eventually having difficulty taking care of themselves. You wish that everyone that you cared about would live forever, or at least be perfectly healthy. But, aging is a fact of life. Most couples deal with one or more of their parents becoming unable to take care of themselves. When this happens, most people end up being involved with the care of their parents to some degree. Taking care of your parents is an emotional undertaking. In this chapter, we will help you understand your emotions and give you tips on supporting each other through this challenging part of life.

Emotions You May Be Feeling

As your parents or your spouse's parents get older, they will probably need your help. They will also possibly need professional help with their daily care. The very people whom you depended on in the past will be turning to you for assistance. The fundamental nature of your relationship with your parents will change in a more dramatic way than you have ever experienced. Now you and your spouse will be the caregivers.

Caring for your parents as they get older is often a stressful experience. There are many emotions you might experience along with your new responsibility. When you become the caretaker of your parents, it's very important for you to be aware of your emotions. It can make the difference between having a meaningful, rewarding experience and having one of the worst experiences of your life. The following sections describe the most common emotions people feel when they are faced with their parents becoming older and less independent.

Denial

One of the first things you might feel when facing a parent's decline in function is—nothing. It's very common to initially be in denial about a difficult situation. When you are in denial about something, you are trying to convince yourself that it's not really happening. For instance, imagine that your father, who lives alone, is slowing down and becoming weaker. You want to keep thinking of him as strong and healthy, so you tell yourself that he's generally fine. In the short run, that makes you feel better. But, your father probably shouldn't be living alone. And you won't be able to help him find a safer place until you are able to acknowledge his limitations. Denial can prevent you from facing facts and making necessary plans.

Anger

Think Twice
Don't take your anger at the situation out on your spouse. Instead, discuss your feelings of anger or resentment with him or her. Remember that your spouse can be your strongest source of support during this difficult time.

Another emotion you might feel is anger at your parents for being unable to take care of themselves. For example, you might feel that it's their fault for not staying healthy, even though you know that they are not getting sick on purpose. You might resent the fact that they are taking so much of your time and energy. You are especially vulnerable to feeling anger if your relationship with your parents was less than perfect. It's more difficult to take care of someone that you feel some resentment toward. But, even if you have a great relationship with your parents, caring for them might feel like a huge burden. It makes sense that you might feel angry because you have been shouldered with a big responsibility.

Helplessness

Even though you are grown up, you might feel like your parents should always be there to take care of you and still help you through difficult times. Seeing your mother or father helpless can make you feel helpless. You might think, "If my parents can't take care of me, who will?" You are your parents' child, even as an adult. And when one of your parents is weak, part of you is going to feel like a scared, helpless child. Even though you know that you can take care of yourself, you still might feel that you need your parents to take care of you.

Guilt

Guilt is one of the strongest emotions people feel as a parent becomes older and less able to care for him- or herself. There are many reasons that you might be feeling guilty. You might feel that you are not doing enough to help your parents. This might be true, or you might be doing more than a reasonable amount and feel guilty anyway. You might feel that if you had done something different years ago, then your parent would not be so ill now. For instance, you might think that if you had taken your mother's complaint about feeling weak and tired more seriously, her cancer would have been diagnosed earlier and she would be cured.

Bet You Didn't Know

Q: What can I do to help alleviate the financial responsibility that goes along with taking care of an aging parent?

A: One possibility is to talk to the human resources department where you work. Many companies are adding benefits that will help you with the monetary responsibilities of taking care of aging parents.

If one of your parents is very sick and needs a lot of expensive care and a lot of your energy, you might be secretly wishing that he or she would die so that it would be over. This thought would probably cause you to feel incredibly guilty. It's very common to feel this, and it's a completely normal reaction. It doesn't mean that you don't love your sick parent and it doesn't mean you are a terrible child. It means that it's very difficult and possibly very expensive to care for an ill person—realities that can prompt all kinds of unexpected thoughts and feelings. The best way to deal with these feelings is to acknowledge them but still do as much as you can to care for your parents.

A Sense of Loss

When your parent is no longer functioning at 100 percent, that is a big loss. It's normal to feel sad, and it's actually a mature feeling. Feeling sad when your parents are ill and unable to take care of themselves means that you have accepted the situation and the loss that occurs when your parent's health declines. You shouldn't hold back tears. Crying is part of feeling sad and it's okay to express your emotions. That doesn't mean that you should spend years moping around and crying as your parents become more and more ill. But sadness comes with loss, and you should give yourself permission to feel it.

Mortality

Parents are the buffer between you and your mortality. Most people are able to ignore the inevitability of their own death as long as their parents are alive and healthy. But as your parent's health declines, you will probably become highly aware of your own mortality. You might start thinking about the end of your own life or have frequent nightmares about dying. You might start examining where you are in life and reevaluating your long-term goals. When you face the death of someone close to you, it will often spark thoughts about your own life. This is good, and the way to make use of this constructively is to realize how precious life is and what is really important to you.

Some Things Never Change

Your relationship with your parents has a long and powerful history. As much as you might want some aspects of it to change, that is very unlikely. What *can* change is your ability to accept your parents the way they are. It will make their final years much better for both of you.

Theresa's mother always felt that whatever Theresa did wasn't good enough. As a child, when Theresa would bring home a report card from school with A's and B's, her mother would ask why she hadn't received all A's. When Theresa excitedly told her mother about her first job, all she said was, "You should have asked for a higher salary." When Theresa's children were young, her mother always made critical comments to her, such as, "Why can't you keep your children from crying?"

Theresa has tried to please her mother all her life. Now, her mother is in her early eighties and really needs Theresa's help. Theresa felt that this was her final chance to make her mother happy. She turned her life upside down to accommodate her mother. Theresa took a job with flexible hours so she could drive her mother to the doctor. She spent time with her three afternoons a week and did all of her errands for her. But, much to her dismay, her mother still made comments, such as, "Why didn't you see me yesterday afternoon?" or, "You should have known that I would run out of milk."

As Theresa's mother became sicker and weaker, Theresa continued to do more and more for her. She kept hoping that eventually her mother would appreciate her efforts. Of course, this never happened. After a particularly upsetting evening with her mother, Theresa returned home in tears. She told her husband, Carlos, that she felt like she was giving her whole life to care for her mother who was still always critical.

Carlos wisely pointed out that Theresa's mother would never appreciate her *no matter what she did.* Carlos helped her see that it would be much easier to be with her mother if she realized her mother would never give her the approval she was looking for. She must accept the limitations of their relationship and stop expecting more. Over time, Theresa started accepting her mother the way she was. Theresa was able to help out her mother several times a week, but no longer felt that she needed to sacrifice her own needs to such an extent that she was miserable.

Think Twice
Don't wait for your parents' approval. You might never get it and feel disappointed. You need to learn to know for yourself when you have done the right thing and completed a task well.

Digging Up the Past

Before you can accept your parents the way they are, you need to identify their shortcomings. These questions will help you understand the weaker parts of your relationship with your parents. Circle the appropriate number on a scale ranging from 1 (never) to 5 (always):

Parents Quiz

1. Do you feel your parents treat you like an adult?

      1   2   3   4   5

2. Do you feel your parents really listen to what you have to say?

      1   2   3   4   5

3. Do you feel your parents treat you with respect?

      1   2   3   4   5

4. Do you feel your parents favored one of your brothers or sisters over you?

      1   2   3   4   5

continues

---

continued

5. Do you feel your parents have been helpful to you (with either time or money) as an adult?

    1   2   3   4   5

6. Do you feel your parents appreciate what you do for them?

    1   2   3   4   5

7. As a child, did you feel taken care of by your parents?

    1   2   3   4   5

8. Do you feel your parents have unrealistic expectations of you?

    1   2   3   4   5

9. Do you accept your parents the way they are?

    1   2   3   4   5

10. Overall, on a scale from 1 (not very good) to 10 (excellent), rate your relationship with each of your parents:

    Mother: 1 2 3 4 5 6 7 8 9 10

    Father: 1 2 3 4 5 6 7 8 9 10

Look through your answers. If you have resentments toward your parents or are carrying grudges, try accepting your parents the way they are.

Taking Care of Each Other

Watching a parent decline in health is one of the hardest things in life. You will probably experience many of the emotions that were discussed. There are many ways that you and your spouse can be uniquely helpful to each other. Each of your contributions can make all the difference in the world in both practical and emotional ways.

Bet You Didn't Know

OH!

Q: My mother-in-law's health is starting to decline. How can I help?

A: Pay attention to the health and overall functioning of your parents-in-law. It might be easier for you to see and accept a decline in health in your parent-in-law than it is for your spouse. In turn, your spouse might notice things that you aren't able to see in your own parents.

Be Supportive

When your spouse is dealing with an aging parent, he or she might be less available to you both physically and emotionally. Your partner might need to visit a nursing home, do errands, and spend more time in general with his or her parent. It's difficult to give up some time with your spouse, but it's part of being in a supportive marriage.

Your spouse might be more moody than usual as well. He or she is probably dealing with a lot of the emotions we talked about earlier: anger, helplessness, a sense of loss, a feeling of mortality. These can create very powerful feelings. At times he or she might need to be alone, and at other times he or she might want a shoulder to cry on.

Your partner will also appreciate your help. Offer to take your parent-in-law to the doctor or go grocery shopping. If your parent-in-law is in a nursing home, go along on some of the visits. Your spouse will remember your involvement for many years to come.

Soul Mates
Praise your spouse often when he or she is dealing with an aging parent. Let him or her know how difficult it is and how well he or she is managing things. Your praise will go a long way when your spouse is handling such an emotional issue.

Don't Forget Your Relationship

It's especially important to keep your relationship with each other strong. You might be feeling overwhelmed by time and energy commitments to a parent, but don't forget each other. Keep doing nice things for each other, treating each other nicely, and spending time together. Even if you cannot spend as much time together as you used to, make every effort to spend at least a reasonable amount of regular time together. You will best be able to support each other if you continue investing in the relationship.

Outside Support

Many couples feel overwhelmed by their emotions when dealing with an aging parent. Maybe they were handling things well at first, but over time their marital relationship can really suffer. This is especially true if the situation is long term. This can be a difficult transition, and going outside the relationship for support can be a wise move.

There are several options when looking for outside support. There are many support groups that deal with aging parents. You can contact retirement communities, nursing homes, or religious organizations for information. It can be extremely helpful to be in a room full of people who are all going through the same thing that you are. Being in a support group can help you to feel like you are not alone. The other members will understand your emotions and will often have practical advice that you might find helpful.

When his father needed to be moved to an assisted-living facility, Ralph felt terrible. He was racked with guilt for not having his father live with them. He was having trouble sleeping and not enjoying the time he was spending with his wife, Linda. One day when he was visiting his father, he saw a notice for a support group on the bulletin board. It took place once a week in the assisted-living facility. He thought he would give it a try.

Ralph found the group incredibly helpful. The first few times that he went, he just listened to everybody else. He was amazed at how many people had similar feelings. Finally, he felt brave enough to talk and felt relieved when he was supported by others. After several months, he noticed that his sleep was improved, he was able to be more objective about his father, and he was better able to enjoy his time with Linda.

Soul Mates
Accompany your spouse once or twice to a support group. You will better understand what your partner is experiencing.

Ralph continued going to the group for the three years that his father was in the facility. He felt that the connection with the other people in the group was important. Ralph knew that they would be there for him and he could also be there for them when they needed support. He also ran into some of the group members when he was visiting his father, which he enjoyed. Linda realized how much the group was helping him too, and she was grateful to the facility for having the support group available.

For some people, individual therapy is particularly helpful during this time. Childhood issues often come to the surface when you are caring for a parent. Issues that you identified in the earlier quiz, such as not feeling appreciated by a parent or feeling a sibling was favored over you, are going to effect how you deal with your parent. Therapy can help you sort out your emotions so that you will be better able to care for your parent.

Couples therapy can also be useful, especially if the situation is going to be long term. A therapist will be objective and can help you to make decisions that will affect both of you. If the situation is particularly stressful and is interfering with your marriage, this therapy is particularly useful.

The Least You Need to Know

➤ Caring for your parents as they become older is a very emotional time. It's common to feel angry, helpless, guilty, or sad.

➤ Your past relationship with your parents will impact your current relationship with your aging parents.

➤ As the spouse, your role is very important. You can help tremendously by being objective, praising your spouse, and lending a sympathetic ear.

➤ A support group can be very helpful when you are dealing with an aging parent.

Chapter 21

Second Chances

In This Chapter

➤ Making a second marriage successful

➤ Learning from your experience

➤ Building memories together

➤ Accepting the reality of alimony

➤ Dealing with each other's children

If this is not the first marriage for you or your spouse (or for both of you), the two of you will probably face some special challenges in your relationship. Second marriages carry unique problems, but they also offer opportunities for growth and contentment. In this chapter, we will show you how to learn from your past mistakes so you can make this marriage work. We will give you guidelines for building your relationship with each other and not letting your past get in the way. And we will help you deal with alimony and involve children from a previous marriage in your current relationship.

Learning from Your Mistakes

Many people who have been divorced spend a lot of time telling other people just how horrible their first spouse was. For example, they might talk about how tight he or she was with money, or how he or she never showed appreciation. They might even tell other people about issues that are very private.

While it might feel good to put down your ex-spouse all the time, it's extremely destructive to you and to your relationship with others. You should do everything you can to stop yourself. Are you trying to prove that everything that went wrong in the marriage was your former spouse's fault or that he or she was an impossible person that nobody could ever stay married to?

Think Twice

Don't insult your ex-spouse in front of your partner. When you do this you are undermining your marriage. If you say negative things about a past relationship, how will your partner know that you aren't saying negative things about him or her to others?

When you frame everything as the fault of the other person, you are also missing the opportunity for self-examination and growth. Two people are involved in a marriage, and two people are involved in a divorce. It's very important to examine your own behavior. Even if your spouse was really, truly awful to you, it's still useful to figure out what role you played in the situation. You need to consider these difficult issues if you are going to prevent the same things from happening again.

Searching for Destructive Patterns

Jane left her husband of six years because he was too controlling. Jane had married at a young age, and initially she had appreciated feeling taken care of. But over time, she started resenting the total control her husband demanded. He insisted on making all of the major financial decisions and gave Jane a weekly allowance. As Jane became older, she realized that he was not treating her like an adult.

Jane wanted to start fresh in a new marriage and planned on finding a husband who would treat her as an equal. Six months after her divorce was finalized, she met Max, whom she quickly fell in love with. He treated her well; they went out to dinner, to the theater, and dancing—always paid for by Max. Max seemed to be everything that her first husband wasn't. He seemed funnier, calmer, and more sure of himself. Jane was thrilled when he proposed to her after they had dated for several months.

Max was very different than Jane's first husband in many ways. He was kinder and more generous. But ultimately, he was every bit as controlling as her first husband. For example, when Jane became pregnant, Max assumed that she would quit her job to take care of the baby. Jane loved being a mother, but six months after the baby was born, she and Max were fighting constantly because she missed her job. Most of the arguments revolved around issues of control, from small things like what restaurant to eat at to larger issues like whether Jane should go back to work.

Jane was attracted to controlling men, but she ultimately resented them. This does not mean that her relationship is doomed. It does mean that she needs to recognize this pattern and understand the role that she plays in keeping it going. This was a negative pattern for Jane. If she could recognize this in herself, she would soon be able to be clearer about her needs and tell them to her husband.

OH!

Bet You Didn't Know

Q: Besides a therapist, who can I talk with to work through issues about my ex-spouse?

A: Discuss them with a close friend who knew both you and your spouse. Remember that your goal is not to put down your ex-spouse, but to determine *your* contribution to the problems. Then, you can prevent these same problems in your current marriage.

It's very common for someone to get divorced and go on to marry someone a lot like his or her first spouse. People get involved in a relationship that feels familiar to them. At an extreme, a person who was abused as a child often marries someone who is abusive to him or her. Then that person might get divorced and marry another person who is abusive to him or her. Even though it's a horrible, destructive cycle, the role of being abused is familiar and may initially seem normal.

Don't Fall into the Same Trap

It can be very useful to think about negative patterns in your past marriage to prevent them from recurring in your current relationship. For instance, if you felt unappreciated, you could use that information to help you figure out how you might have contributed. Did you tend to undervalue yourself? Did you let your ex-spouse know specifically how to show his or her appreciation? In this case, when you figure out your role in being unappreciated by your ex-spouse, you can take steps to prevent it from happening in your current marriage.

The following questions are designed to help you identify possible destructive patterns in your past marriage. These are difficult questions that will require a lot of thought. Be sure to answer them when you have time and can give them your full attention:

1. What was your main reason for getting a divorce?

2. How did you contribute to this main conflict?

3. List five major conflicts that you had with your ex-spouse.

4. Could any of the conflicts have been worked out with better communication?

5. Would you describe your role in the relationship with your ex-spouse as passive, controlling, or an equal in a partnership?

6. Is your role different in your current marriage?

7. List five major conflicts that you have with your current spouse.

8. Are any of them the same ones you listed in question #3?

9. Do you see any patterns in your relationships?

10. Do you feel that with time and effort you would be able to overcome falling into the same pattern?

Think Twice
Don't blame your ex-spouse for everything that went wrong in your marriage. If you allow yourself to recognize how you contributed to the problems, you will learn from your mistakes. Putting that knowledge to use in your current marriage will maximize its potential.

If you didn't notice any similarities in your relationships, you either have already learned from your mistakes (great!) or you are having trouble being objective. It's very important to think about the role you play in the relationship with your spouse. Repeating the same mistake over and over will only cause disappointment. When you are able to see patterns in your conflicts, you will have taken an important step toward resolving them.

Healing Old Wounds

It's painful when any meaningful relationship ends, and it's especially painful when a marriage ends. The anger that many people feel is usually covering up a lot of pain. Covering up your emotional wounds with anger will prevent them from healing properly. You must get past your anger to fully participate in your new marriage.

Eva came to see us in therapy because she had been very unhappy since her divorce, even though she had expected to feel much better after she remarried. We asked her how often she thought about her ex-husband. Eva said she thought about him constantly because she was still very angry at him, his attitude, his insensitivity, and even his habits. We pointed out that her ex-husband was consuming a lot of her time and energy.

We asked Eva if she felt anything besides anger towards her ex-husband. At first she wanted to answer, "absolutely not," but when she thought about it, she knew that she felt hurt by him. She felt he had lost interest in her and their marriage over the years. She felt he had neglected her and had lived a separate life. Eva had not talked about or even thought much about these feelings. Her relationship with her first husband made her feel alone, unloved, and even unlikeable at times. Deep down, she felt like her current husband would never be able to love her either.

Eva came to see us regularly for the next six months. She talked about her feelings of insecurity and her fears that her current husband would abandon her too. As she became able to admit her concerns, her anger at her ex-husband lessened. Over time, Eva moved her focus from her ex-husband to her own emotions and finally to her relationship with her current husband. When Eva covered up her fears with anger, she remained stuck. But when she confronted her insecurity and fear of abandonment, she was able to overcome them and move on.

OH!

Bet You Didn't Know

Q: Can't I just put my first marriage out of my life completely?

A: No. The first step toward getting beyond your hurt is admitting it. Then you can face your insecurities and prevent them from interfering with your current marriage.

Building New Memories Together

Many people come into a second marriage feeling scared. They may feel they are a failure at marriage, and they don't necessarily believe they can have a successful one. In order to make your new marriage successful, you need to give it a chance. Give yourself permission to start over completely and make this marriage work.

Here are 10 ideas you can use to start fresh with your spouse:

1. Start a new photo album and keep it out on your bookshelves.

2. Store your old photo albums and other reminders of your previous marriage in your closet or garage.

3. Find a new favorite restaurant. Make a point to eat there once a month.

4. Discover a charming bed-and-breakfast within several hours of your home. Spend a romantic weekend there several times a year and make it your place.

5. Create special traditions all your own. For example, take Sunday walks around your neighborhood or read the newspaper in bed on the weekends.

6. Get matching T-shirts and wear them!

7. Choose art for your walls together. Whether you buy posters or original paintings, you will be creating the mood for your home together.

8. Try new recipes together and choose a few favorites. These can be part of your signature meals when you entertain.

9. Over time, replace your daily use kitchen items that you used during your previous marriage. Have a garage sale, or give away pots, pans, silverware, and dishes.

10. Carefully wrap and store all valuable wedding gifts from your previous marriage. You can decide what you want to do with them later, but for now, they shouldn't be part of your day-to-day life.

Bet You Didn't Know

Q: I'm newly remarried and keep comparing my spouse to my ex-spouse. What can I do?

A: You need to fully accept that your past marriage is over so you can completely move on. This will be more difficult if your spouse left you. If even a little part of you is hoping your ex-spouse will come back, you will not be able to fully commit to your current partner.

It's Just a Check

You have done everything possible to start over with your new marriage. But, if you have an alimony agreement with your previous spouse, you will have an annoying monthly reminder of your past marriage. The key to dealing with alimony is to keep your emotions out of it. Remind yourself that it's part of your budget, just like any other item.

If you are paying alimony, it's an expense. It's an amount that you need to pay every month, just like the rent, the car payment, or the telephone bill. It's not optional. It's not going to get lower just because you took a vacation last month. It's a fixed amount of money that you will need to pay every month to your ex-spouse. Be fair. Your ex-spouse depends on it for his or her expenses every month.

The one way to avoid writing a monthly alimony check is to arrange for the amount to be deposited automatically every month to your ex-spouse's bank account. You can do your duty without the painful monthly reminder of writing a check.

If you are receiving alimony, it's part of your income. Your alimony plus income from work or investments is your total income. You must work out your budget within this income. Don't spend every month being angry that your ex-spouse doesn't give you more money. You will probably need to change your expenses to work within your new budget. Reorganize your budget ASAP so you can get on with your life. Do it now!

If your new spouse needs to pay alimony, be reasonable about it. When you got married you knew that your partner had been married before. You need to accept the fact that alimony payments often go along with that. Your spouse is probably not thrilled about writing the check every month. Don't make him or her feel even worse.

Yours, Mine, and Ours

One of the biggest challenges facing second marriages is blending your families. Many people who remarry have children from a previous marriage. Whether the children live with the two of you, with their other parent, or on their own, they will affect your new marriage.

Give It Time

Developing a relationship with stepchildren takes time. Even if you have the best intentions, they might feel animosity toward you in the beginning. Sometimes, no matter what you do, your stepchildren are unfriendly. They don't accept your invitations, they don't want to talk to you, and they basically want nothing to do with you. In short, they don't want to acknowledge your marriage to their parent.

Think Twice
Don't expect your stepchildren to instantly feel close to you. They have wounds to heal too.

Keep in mind the following when developing a relationship with your stepchildren:

➤ Listen to your stepchildren.

➤ Invite your stepchildren over to your house on a regular basis if they don't live with you.

➤ Include your stepchildren in family activities.

➤ Make your stepchildren feel welcome.

➤ Don't forget to celebrate your stepchildren's birthdays.

➤ Respect your stepchildren's privacy.

➤ Be sensitive to your stepchildren's feelings.

Keep at it. Continue inviting your stepchildren to be part of the new family. Continue being nice to them. Continue showing an interest in them. The more you follow these steps for including and respecting them, the sooner they will include you and show you respect. If you keep making it clear that you want to have a relationship with them, they will accept it when they are ready.

Don't Take Sides

Whether they realize it or not, your new spouse and your children will be fighting for your love and attention. They will try to prove to themselves that you love them the most. When they get into an argument, they might turn to you and ask who is right. They are setting you up. Don't take sides! You will only end up making one person happy and disappointing the other one. The relationship between the stepparent and the stepchild needs to develop without interference. If you are asked to take sides, step out of the room saying, "I'm sure you can work it out by yourselves!"

Sue, her new husband, Keith, and her daughter from her first marriage, Maggie, came to see us because of all the arguing in their house. Maggie and her stepfather constantly got into arguments. Whenever her mother was around, Maggie would call her in to help settle the argument. Most of the time, Sue would step in and decide who was right. They would stop fighting, but either Keith or Maggie would end up being angry at Sue.

We focused on Keith and Maggie's relationship in therapy. Maggie was angry that her mother had remarried. She felt that it took time away from their relationship and that her mother "just wasn't the same anymore." Keith liked Maggie but felt that she was too dependent on her mother. Plus, he admitted that he would like to have more time alone with Sue.

Soul Mates

One of the most important ways to show your love, both to your spouse and to your children, is to stay out of their arguments. They need to develop their relationship with each other by themselves. Over time, they will learn to resolve their differences.

Each of the relationships needed time to be nurtured. We suggested that each of the "couples"—Keith and Maggie, Sue and Maggie, and Keith and Sue—needed separate time alone for their relationships to flourish. Keith and Maggie were not enthusiastic about spending time together, but each liked the idea of having time alone with Sue. Over time, as Keith and Maggie felt more secure with their relationship with Sue, they began to develop their own relationship with each other. It took many fights and a year of hard work, but they were finally able to function like a family.

If you find yourself feeling distant from your stepchildren, or your spouse feels distant from your children, give those individual relationships a chance to flourish. Plan time alone with your stepchildren on a regular basis, or encourage your children to spend time alone with your spouse. It will take time, but if you are sincere about wanting the relationship to work, it will.

The Other Parent

If you have children from a previous marriage, it's likely that you will have regular interactions with your former spouse, the parent of your children. It's definitely a challenge both for you and for your new marriage to continue the relationship with your ex-spouse. And it's important to your children to keep your differences with your ex-spouse between the two of you.

The children from your previous marriage have two parents—you and your ex-spouse. Their relationship with each of you is very important to them. Do your best to facilitate your children's relationship with their other parent. If you have a lot of anger and resentment toward him or her, this will certainly be difficult. But everything you can do to help your children through this confusing time is worthwhile and will add to their mental and emotional well-being.

Think Twice
Don't say negative things about your ex-spouse in front of your children. Remember that you are talking about one of their parents.

Older and Wiser

When you get married for the second time, you bring along the past from your previous marriage. To make your marriage work, you need to give it the best chance possible. Take the time to learn from your past marriage. Don't just start where your last marriage left off! Instead, create a strong foundation with your partner that you can build on for years to come. You are older than you were when you married last time. Don't miss the opportunity to be wiser too!

The Least You Need to Know

➤ It's important to take your share of responsibility for the problems in your past marriage. Only then will you be able to learn from your mistakes and grow.

➤ Every relationship needs a strong foundation to be successful. This is true of a second marriage too.

➤ Alimony is a fact of divorced life. You will be showing strength of character if you give or receive it gracefully.

➤ Absorbing each other's children into your marriage can be difficult. Keep an open mind and give the new relationships time to work.

Part 6
Bridge Over Troubled Waters

Some couples face situations that can change everything in their relationship. It's common for couples to ignore what is happening, which can be destructive to their relationship. It's very important to learn how to handle the situation in a productive and emotionally stabilizing manner.

In this section, we'll help you confront many situations that can be difficult to handle. We'll show you how to deal with illness and give you tips for keeping your relationship strong. We'll show you how to identify alcoholism and other addictions and point you in the right direction to get help. In addition, we'll discuss infidelity, show you ways to handle it, and give you ideas for keeping it out of your marriage. In the last chapter, we'll give you guidelines for finding a therapist and getting the most out of therapy.

By the end of this section, rather than feeling like a victim of circumstance, you'll have concrete guidelines on how to handle these problems. Most important, you'll have the confidence to act rather than waiting for the problem to simply go away by itself.

Chapter 22

...In Sickness and In Health

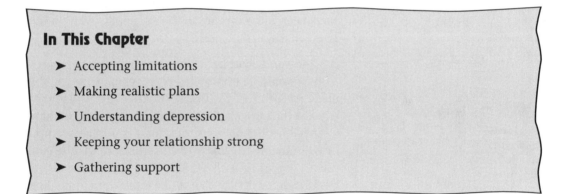

In This Chapter

➤ Accepting limitations

➤ Making realistic plans

➤ Understanding depression

➤ Keeping your relationship strong

➤ Gathering support

Illness puts stress on a marriage, whether you have something short-lived, such as the flu, or something long-term and serious, such as cancer. All couples will confront sickness during their marriage, and some will face a serious illness. In this chapter, we will give you the tools to keep your marriage strong and healthy when one of you is sick.

Accepting Limitations

When you or your spouse is ill or functioning at less than normal capacity, your life is going to change. If the person is ill for a short time, your life will change for a short time. But if the person has a long-term illness, then your life will change indefinitely. In a successful marriage, the couple will accept the fact that their life has changed and will work out a new plan together.

Mindy and Scott always went on an annual ski vacation together. They were great skiers and always tackled challenging slopes successfully. But this year they weren't so lucky. Mindy took a hard fall, broke her leg, and needed surgery. She was in the hospital for 10 days and needed to recuperate at home for six weeks.

When she came home, Mindy was in a full-leg cast. Everything went smoothly at first. Scott took some time off from work and was able to take care of Mindy and do all of the errands. But once he went back to work, Scott's time was limited. Mindy was isolated at home and quickly became bored with daytime TV and magazines. She started feeling very lonely.

Think Twice
Don't assume you can't do anything if you are sick. Consider catching up on letters or phone calls or doing work from home. You might even learn a project-oriented hobby, such as painting or needlework.

Mindy felt badly that she was so helpless, and Scott felt badly that he couldn't help more. They both became increasingly irritable and bickered constantly. Mindy felt deserted and became angry at Scott, even though she knew it was irrational. And Scott felt that Mindy should have been more careful on the ski slopes, even though he knew that was ridiculous.

The Spice Rack
If your spouse is home sick, call from work in the after-noon. Ask what you can get for him or her on your way home.

If Mindy and Scott had completely accepted the fact that Mindy would be immobile for six weeks, they could have made a plan to deal with the situation. They would have realized that she would become lonely and could have arranged for frequent visitors. Scott could have temporarily hired someone to help with the chores so that he could spend more time with Mindy. The problem was that six weeks didn't initially sound like a very long time. By the time they realized how long it really was, they were not getting along, which made it even more difficult to make a plan.

Keep in mind the following when one of you is sick:

➤ The person who is sick usually cannot meet all of his or her responsibilities. You may need to let less important chores slide.

➤ The person who is well cannot do everything and might become exhausted too.

➤ The person who is sick will probably get lonely if he or she is alone many days in a row.

➤ The person who is sick might be able to catch up on letters or phone calls or even get work done from home.

➤ It's a good idea to get a friend or a relative to help out.

If you both accept your limitations, you will be able to adjust to the situation. There are practical matters to consider, such as chores, as well as emotional matters, such as the sick person becoming lonely. Being aware of the issues is the first step to making a constructive plan.

Soul Mates

You can avoid unpleasant arguments if you acknowledge the limitations an illness causes. The sooner you make a plan that accommodates your new situation, the sooner you will be able to fully adjust to it. It's important to be flexible.

Long-Term Limitations

Some illnesses are short-lived and then you're back to normal. Others are chronic and leave you with long-term limitations. It's very hard to admit that you cannot do everything you used to do. For example, if you were in a car accident that resulted in broken ribs and back pain, your ability to lift or even sit in a chair for many hours might be limited. Your back pain might leave you unable to do your household chores or your current job. If you tried to do everything you used to do, you would probably end up having more pain, being grouchier, and eventually injuring your back even more. That certainly would not be good for you or your marriage!

Brian had chronic back pain and was constantly in pain, but he continued to do all of his activities. He took a mild pain reliever, but it did not help much. By the end of the day, Brian was usually in a bad mood and was not very pleasant company. His wife, Ann, was becoming more and more concerned. It was clear that Brian's pain was getting worse.

When she suggested he see a doctor, or rest more, he would say, "Stop nagging me." Brian did not want to admit to himself or anybody else that he had a physical problem.

One morning Brian was in such pain he could not get out of bed by himself. Fortunately, Ann was home and ran into the bedroom when she heard him moaning. Brian finally agreed to see a doctor. Ann called one of their friends to help get him into the car. After talking with Brian and examining him, the doctor explained that there were many things he could do to keep the pain under reasonable control.

Soul Mates

If your spouse will have ongoing limitations, it's very important that you both accept them. When you have realistic expectations, you will be able to be truly supportive.

The doctor suggested physical therapy and regular exercises to strengthen his back and stomach muscles. He also suggested getting an ergonomic chair at work and not lifting heavy objects.

Over time, Brian's pain subsided. He did his exercises faithfully, went to physical therapy, and got a new chair at work. Brian and Ann went on walks together as he built up his strength. Brian slowly changed his lifestyle to accommodate his back pain and matured in the process. Even though Ann still worried about Brian's back pain, she was relieved to see him feeling better and accepting his limits.

Making a Financial Plan

In addition to accepting your physical limitations, some long-term illnesses will require you to accept your financial limitations as well. Your household income might be less because the person who is ill now works fewer hours, or not at all. In addition, depending on the severity of the illness, you might need to hire someone to help around the house or to help care for you or your spouse. You need to consider the following items:

➤ *Medical expenses (including insurance deductibles and co-payments).* Discuss these issues with your insurance company ahead of time to find out what is covered by what percentage to help you prepare for future expenses.

➤ *The cost of extra help.* Having someone come to the house to help with laundry, grocery shopping, cleaning, or cooking can help tremendously.

OH!

Bet You Didn't Know

Q: We don't have a lot of extra money, but we need help with the chores. What can we do?

A: One good resource is high school or college students who want to earn extra money.

➤ *The cost of a caretaker.* This can range from someone to help out a few hours each day to a full-time professional nurse. Evaluate your needs and look into all your options.

➤ *New income from disability or social security.* Private disability insurance and SSDI start paying after a specified period of time away from work. When you are redoing your budget, make sure to consider this additional source of income.

➤ *Reduction of income.* This can result from the sick person not working. Initially the person who is ill might be able to use up his or her sick or vacation time, but eventually that will run out. The sooner you accept the fact that you will no longer be receiving your paycheck, the sooner you can make thoughtful financial plans.

Caring for Each Other

When one of you is sick, whether it's for several days or for many years, you need to take care of each other. Your relationship will change with an illness, but that doesn't have to mean it will change for the worse. There are ways to keep your relationship strong when one of you is ill. You need to keep communicating with each other and keep having fun together.

Keep Communicating

The two of you need to keep the channels of communication open more than ever. You will be each other's safest place during this difficult time. Remember to do the following:

1. When you need to be alone, tell your spouse as kindly as you can.

2. Try your best to always give each other your full attention.

3. If you are feeling scared and fearful, tell your spouse. As much as you might want to push him or her away, try as hard as you can to pull him or her closer to you. Give your spouse the chance to support you.

4. Physical contact is healing and creates closeness. Hug each other often.

5. Your love for each other will keep your relationship strong. Saying "I love you" to each other reinforces your commitment.

Bet You Didn't Know

Q: Does a positive attitude about an illness help?

A: Imagine if someone tells you there is a more than 90 percent chance that things will turn out well. That sounds pretty good. On the other hand, if someone tells you there is a 10 percent chance that things will turn out badly, that doesn't sound too great. But they describe the exact same probability! It's always worthwhile to think positively. In fact, some people believe that a positive attitude enhances your immune system and will actually increase your chances of a full recovery.

Keep Having Fun

Even though you might not be able to go to a movie or out to dinner every week, the two of you need to keep having fun together. Set aside time just for the two of you to be alone together without any interruptions. There are many things that you can do to have fun, even if you don't have much energy. Here are some things to try:

➤ Play a board or card game.

➤ Buy a box of markers and draw some colorful pictures together.

➤ Rent a classic movie and watch it together.

➤ Read a book aloud to each other, one chapter at a time.

Understanding Depression

Depression is one of the most common and most misunderstood illnesses. Many people think that if they are feeling depressed, they should just be able to get over it by themselves. When depression becomes severe, this isn't true. Many times depression has biological causes and can be treated with medication. Depression can be overwhelming and out of the person's control. Depression can last for many months, or even years, if it's not treated.

Sometimes, depression is triggered by a stressful event in your life, such as an illness or a job change. At other times, it can seem to come out of nowhere. Often, people who are depressed feel worthless. They have trouble concentrating and are usually unable to enjoy things. It's common to have difficulty sleeping when you are depressed. You can get into a vicious circle where you have low energy from your depression, are unable to sleep well, and then feel even more tired and exhausted.

Down in the Dumps

Lisa was miserable. She was laid off from her job when her company downsized. At first, she handled it well. She and her husband, Doug, took a one-week vacation, and then she started looking for another job. But after three weeks of looking, she hadn't found anything. Lisa had sent out 50 resumes and had only been called back for one interview. After the interview, the company told her that they liked her but she was overqualified for the job.

Lisa was quite discouraged. She lost all interest in hunting for a job. She started sleeping late every day. When Doug came home from work, he would ask how her day was, and she would say, "What do you think? It was terrible." Lisa started losing her energy and couldn't enjoy anything.

Doug didn't know what to do. When he suggested that they should go to a movie, Lisa would say, "I'm too tired," even though she had slept late that morning. When he suggested going out to brunch on a Sunday, she would say, "I'm not hungry." When he gave her ideas on looking for another job, she would say, "No one would want to hire me."

Doug was worried, but he also became angry at Lisa. He felt like she needed to snap out of it. Doug thought Lisa just wasn't trying very hard to get better. Over time, his concern turned into frustration. He started arguments with her, but most of the time she didn't argue back. Lisa had stopped caring about much of anything, including herself and her marriage.

It never occurred to Doug or Lisa that she was suffering from a curable illness. Lisa developed a major depression, which was probably triggered by the loss of her job. Over time, she lost interest in anything, wasn't eating very much, was sleeping poorly at night and awakening late in the morning, and she felt worthless. There were even some days when she woke up wishing she were dead. After several months of Lisa's exhaustion, Doug thought that maybe cancer or another illness was making her so tired. He dragged her to their primary care doctor who immediately recognized that Lisa was depressed. The doctor started her on antidepressants, and within a few weeks she began to feel much better.

Think Twice
Don't make the mistake of assuming that you should be able to cure depression by yourself. It takes someone very strong to admit he or she needs help.

Are You Depressed?

Recognizing depression early can prevent needless suffering. Depression is curable most of the time. If you think you might be depressed, answer the following questions "yes" or "no":

1. Do you frequently feel unhappy or down in the dumps?

2. Are you uninterested in most of your usual activities?

3. Has your appetite either increased or decreased significantly?

4. Has your sleep been disturbed and/or have you been unable to get out of bed in the morning?

5. Do you feel fatigued or low on energy most days?

6. Do you feel worthless or guilty most days?

7. Do you have trouble concentrating?

8. Do you have thoughts about wishing you were dead or killing yourself?

If you answered yes to three or more of the questions, you might be depressed. Make an appointment right away to be evaluated by your primary care doctor or a psychiatrist.

Gathering Support

Many couples make the mistake of trying to do everything by themselves. They hate the idea of admitting that they are not self-sufficient. This puts a lot of pressure on the two of you. If you or your spouse is sick, you not only have extra things to do, you also have one less of you to do them! It's so important to ask friends and family for help. You need their emotional support as well as their practical support.

Your friends and family would love to be useful to you. You can help them help you by being specific about what they can do. Here are some ideas to get you (and them) started:

Think Twice
Don't assume that you and your spouse should only rely on each other. You can have a strong marriage *and* have others helping out. Be sure to ask friends or family for help when you need it, especially during the difficult time when one of you is sick.

➤ Cook a meal.

➤ Visit the person who is sick while his or her spouse is at work.

➤ Take the person who is sick to his or her doctor's appointment.

➤ Go grocery shopping.

➤ Wash, dry, and fold a load or two of laundry.

These may not seem like big things, but they can be time consuming. If you do them all yourself, you will take valuable time away from the two of you being together.

The Least You Need to Know

➤ The sooner you accept any limitations you might have when you are sick, the sooner you can make a sound plan that will accommodate your needs.

➤ Long-term illnesses will usually require you to reexamine your budget.

➤ Communication is more important than ever when one of you is sick. When you communicate well with your spouse, you are showing how much you care for him or her.

➤ Even if you have physical limitations, don't forget your fun time together. Enjoying each other's company is especially important now.

➤ Depression can become overwhelming if it's not treated. Don't assume that the depressed person can get better on his or her own. If you are unsure, it's always wise to get an evaluation.

➤ You need all the help you can get when one of you is sick for any length of time. Tell friends and relatives specific things they can do to make your life easier.

Just One More

Addictions interfere with a healthy life and a healthy marriage. When you are addicted to something, it becomes all-consuming. It's impossible to have a good relationship with someone if he or she is always thinking about something else. In this chapter, we will describe alcoholism, show you how to identify someone who is addicted, and tell you what you can do about it. We will also describe other addictions, including substances, gambling, food, and even your work. Our goal is to help you rid your marriage of harmful addictions before they harm your marriage.

Understanding Addiction

When someone is addicted, he or she has lost control. The thing the person is addicted to, whether it's alcohol, drugs, or even a computer, becomes all-absorbing. At an extreme, when someone is addicted, he or she loses all interest in anything that does not include the addiction. For instance, someone who is severely addicted to food will think about eating all day long. The person will wake up and think about what he or she will eat that day. Right after eating, the person will think about when he or she will eat again. At breakfast, he or she thinks about lunch, and at lunch, he or she thinks about an afternoon snack and dinner. Food totally controls his or her thoughts.

Think Twice
Don't think that you can be addicted to something and still have a good marriage. An addiction has no place in a healthy relationship. If you think that you might be addicted to something, do yourself and your marriage a favor by getting help.

A true addiction is so consuming that it makes it virtually impossible to have a healthy relationship with someone. The addiction comes before everything else, even the marriage. Addictions usually start out slowly and become worse over time. As you become more and more addicted, eventually you will fail to fulfill obligations at work, school, or home. It's much easier to stop an addiction before it has reached such an extreme. Unfortunately, it's also easier to deny that you have a problem in the early stages of an addiction.

Alcoholism

Alcohol is by far the most common addiction in the Western world. As many as one in ten adults in the United States may have problems with alcohol dependency. Alcohol is legal, relatively inexpensive, and easily available. People who are dependent on alcohol include men and women of all ages and backgrounds. At first, the person who is addicted to alcohol can function reasonably well. But, over time, the alcohol dependence can take over his or her entire life.

"On the Rocks"

Tony started drinking his senior year of high school, along with many of his classmates. He really enjoyed himself at parties, and drinking helped him to loosen up. During high school and college, he studied hard during the week and partied hard during the week-end. On Saturday nights, he often drank until he passed out and couldn't remember much in the morning.

After Tony graduated from college, his drinking patterns changed. He drank less on the weekends, but he started drinking most evenings after work to unwind. Able to hold his liquor well, Tony was successful at his job and had many friends. During this time, he met Laura, whom he dated for several years and eventually married. Laura had no idea that Tony had any problems with alcohol.

After five years of marriage, Laura came to see us for depression at the urging of her sister. When we asked her what was going on in her life, she burst into tears. She was pregnant and terrified to tell Tony. "I'm so afraid he'll just go crazy on me." She explained that Tony had been under a lot of pressure from work over the last year. His boss felt that he had been underperforming, so Tony had been working overtime to do a better job. He had been coming home stressed and was drinking three or four drinks every night. Laura said that when she mentioned anything to Tony about his drinking he would shut her up and tell her that she didn't understand the stress he was under.

At this point, Laura was sobbing hysterically. When she calmed down some, she told us that last week Tony had hit her the night she was going to tell him that she was pregnant. She just didn't know what to do. She felt that she couldn't talk to Tony, her parents, or any of her friends; she was embarrassed and was worried that Tony would become angry.

It was clear that Tony had a severe problem with alcohol. When Laura married Tony, some of the signs were there, but he was able to hide them from her (and himself) pretty well. Now the problem was out of control and threatening to ruin Tony's life, his marriage, and his relationship with his unborn child. We asked Laura if Tony would come in with her to see us. Laura said she would ask him, but she doubted he would say yes.

Laura missed her next appointment. When we reached her on the telephone, she said everything was fine. We were very concerned and strongly encouraged her to come back to see us or attend Al-Anon. She didn't return to see us. Hopefully, she and Tony received help elsewhere, though it's likely they didn't. Recognizing alcoholism and getting help are very difficult steps to take.

How Much Is Too Much?

Don't let what happened to Tony and Laura happen to you! Find out if you have an alcoholic tendency before it gets out of hand. Circle your answers to the following questions on a scale ranging from 1 (never) to 5 (always); they will help you (or your spouse) evaluate whether you have a problem with alcohol.

Alcoholism Quiz

1. How often do you feel that you just "need" a drink?

    1   2   3   4   5

2. Do you drink alone?

    1   2   3   4   5

3. Do you drink to increase your self-confidence?

    1   2   3   4   5

4. Have you made unsuccessful attempts to cut down the amount that you drink?

    1   2   3   4   5

5. Do you ever sneak a drink or lie about your drinking?

    1   2   3   4   5

6. Do you get in arguments with your spouse about your drinking?

    1   2   3   4   5

7. Do you drink in the morning to steady yourself?

    1   2   3   4   5

8. Do you have a drink before going to a party where you know liquor will be served?

    1   2   3   4   5

9. Have you had any legal problems as a result of your drinking (such as Driving Under the Influence)?

    1   2   3   4   5

10. Do you continue to drink even though it's creating problems in your life (including work, school, financial, or family)?

    1   2   3   4   5

10	This is an ideal score. If you answered "Never" to all of the questions, you don't even have a tendency toward alcoholism.
11–20	Watch out. Any question that you cannot answer "Never" to is a warning signal. Admitting that you have a problem now will prevent a lot of heartache down the road. Most people don't even realize that anything is wrong at this stage. But you can be one step ahead of them by getting help.
21–30	You have an addiction to alcohol. It probably has not yet totally consumed your life, but you are headed to that point if you don't get help. At this stage, you are probably able to work and carry on socially. But that will change over time if you don't get help now.
31–50	You are extremely addicted—alcohol is controlling your life. Get help immediately. Do it for yourself and your family. Don't wait until it's too late.

OH!

Bet You Didn't Know

Q: My father is an alcoholic. Does that mean I will be an alcoholic?

A: There is a strong genetic component to alcoholism. If you have family members (parents, grandparents, brothers, sisters, aunts, uncles, or cousins) who use alcohol to excess, pay extra attention to your drinking habits. You have a higher chance of becoming alcohol-dependent if you have relatives who are alcohol-dependent.

Getting Help

People have so many excuses for not getting help with their alcohol addiction. The excuse we hear over and over again is: "I don't need help. I can stop drinking at any time." This is not true. *When you are addicted, you have lost control. You cannot stop at any time. If you could, you would not be addicted.* Make that first step and get help.

Alcoholics Anonymous

A very effective treatment for alcoholism is Alcoholics Anonymous (AA). Two alcohol-dependent men founded it in 1935: a stockbroker and a surgeon. There are meetings all over the United States and all over the world; these meetings happen every day, and in bigger cities, many times a day. All types of people attend AA meetings, including physicians, lawyers, teachers, bank tellers, janitors, the independently wealthy, and the unemployed. There is an oath of confidentiality that members take seriously. Each Alcoholics Anonymous is a self-run group supported by donations. AA is free—anyone who wants to is welcome to attend a meeting. Alcoholics Anonymous is listed in the phone book, and you can call for meeting locations and times.

Soul Mates

If your spouse is ambivalent about attending an Alcoholics Anonymous meeting, offer to go with him or her. You will be welcome there, and your show of support will help your spouse. You will also learn what happens at a meeting.

Alcoholics Anonymous meetings are filled with people who are, or have been, addicted to alcohol. Guests who have never used alcohol are also welcome. Often people who have been sober for many years continue to attend meetings on a regular basis. AA gives alcoholics and ex-alcoholics a steady system of support. Initially, people often start by going to meetings several times a day, every day. When they stop drinking, the structure that AA meetings provide is invaluable. AA helps you realize that you don't have control over your drinking and believes that abstinence is the only way to control your drinking.

Al-Anon

Al-Anon is a contraction of the words "Alcoholics Anonymous." It's designed for the spouses of people with alcohol addiction. It works like Alcoholics Anonymous. It's a self-run group, it's listed in the phone book, and it's free. The goal of Al-Anon is to help spouses of alcoholics deal with the issues that they face. Al-Anon helps you restore your self-esteem, which is often undermined by an alcoholic spouse. It helps you break the cycle of feeling responsible for your spouse's drinking. And if your spouse (hopefully) is going through recovery, Al-Anon can help you set up a new, healthy, alcohol-free life.

OH!

Bet You Didn't Know

Q: My spouse is an alcoholic. Can I do anything to help?

A: A spouse often is an "enabler" of the alcoholic's drinking behavior. You might do things you don't even realize, such as covering up for his or her drinking or being extra nice when he or she is drunk. You will increase your spouse's chance for recovery if you attend Al-Anon meetings. If you identify and stop "enabling" behaviors, you will be doing the best thing for your spouse and your marriage.

Therapy

Thereare several different types of therapy to help someone with alcoholism. Because we will discuss different types of counseling and ways to get it in Chapter 25, we will limit this to a brief discussion. Individual therapy can help you understand why you need to be intoxicated and why you might be frightened to be sober. For instance, you might feel insecure socially or hate your job and not know how to get out of it. Or you might use alcohol to avoid problems in your relationship.

Couples therapy can be extremely helpful for many reasons. It can give both of you the support you need, help you to understand behavior patterns that occur because of the drinking, and help you restart your life without alcohol. Behavior therapy can teach you alternatives to drinking, including relaxation training and assertiveness training.

OH!

Bet You Didn't Know

Q: If my spouse and I are in couples therapy and also go to AA and Al-Anon meetings, are we spreading ourselves too thin?

A: The more ways you get help for your alcohol addiction, the better. Different treatments reinforce each other. For instance, many people in therapy receive a lot of benefit from attending Alcoholics Anonymous as well. Or a spouse of an alcoholic who attends Al-Anon also goes to couples therapy with his or her partner. Everything you do to help you get and stay sober is useful.

Medications

In addition to groups and therapy, medications can also be effective in treating alcoholism. Antabuse (Disulfiram) is a prescription medication that is taken every day. Drinking even one drink will make you feel quite sick. It can be very useful as a deterrent to drinking and can help motivated people resist impulse drinking.

Antidepressant medication can also be useful in helping someone with alcoholism. Some people use alcohol as self-medication. They are clinically depressed and use alcohol to cover up their bad feelings. When their depression is controlled by an antidepressant, they have less of a need to drink alcohol. There is also evidence that some antidepressants reduce cravings for alcohol. It's worthwhile to have a full evaluation by an internist, family practice doctor, or psychiatrist.

Drug Abuse

Although alcohol is the most common substance addiction, there are countless other substances you can become addicted to. Drugs that are illegal, such as cocaine, marijuana, and heroin, tend to be much more expensive than alcohol. With these substances, it's easy to get into financial trouble. A person who is addicted to a drug becomes consumed by it, just as an alcoholic does. As the addiction progresses, his or her life will revolve more and more around the drug.

There are also many legal prescription drugs that you can become addicted to. You may have originally taken them for an illness. These are usually medications that relax you, such as Valium or Xanax, or that relieve pain, such as morphine or codeine. Beware! You can become just as addicted to these prescription medications as you can to alcohol or crack cocaine.

Narcotics Anonymous exists for people who abuse other drugs besides or in addition to alcohol. It works the same way as Alcoholics Anonymous; there are self-run meetings that are cost-free, and there is an oath of confidentiality. Some people attend both Narcotics Anonymous as well as Alcoholics Anonymous if they abuse both.

OH!

Bet You Didn't Know

Q: How do I know where to find an Alcoholics Anonymous or Narcotics Anonymous meeting?

A: Look up the phone number in your local white pages under "Alcoholics Anonymous" or "Narcotics Anonymous." Call the number and ask for the time and location of the next meeting. Most locations have a 24-hour hotline available as well.

Other Addictions

There are other types of addictions that can affect your life and marriage. They might seem harmless compared to being an alcoholic, but they can ruin your life just as easily. Remember, the difference between an addiction and a habit is not having control over the behavior. We will briefly discuss gambling, food, and work addictions. You can use these concepts to generalize other possible addictions as well.

Gambling

A compulsive gambler constantly wagers money. He or she might place bets on sports, spend weeks buried in a casino, or use the grocery money to invest in a financial "opportunity." As with other addictions, gambling takes over the person's thoughts. Every day he or she will be thinking about past gambles, current gambles, and future gambles. An addicted gambler will place wagers anywhere and everywhere and will bet money he or she doesn't necessary have. He or she might think, "I know, I lost five hundred dollars last week, but if I bet three double-or-nothings this week, I will make that up and then some. Then I'll stop and everything will be okay." But of course, that doesn't happen. Compulsive gamblers keep on betting, whether they win or lose.

Think Twice
Don't think that your spouse couldn't be a compulsive gambler just because you don't see him or her gambling. You might not know it because he or she gambles outside of the house. Look out for these signs in your spouse: always borrowing money, worried, not sleeping well, and having difficulties at work.

The following questions can help distinguish between someone who places bets for fun and a compulsive gambler:

➤ Do you spend more money gambling than you originally intended?

➤ Do you gamble with money that is already budgeted for something else?

➤ Have you called in sick to work to spend time gambling?

➤ Have you given up other activities because of gambling?

➤ Do you lie about your gambling?

➤ Have you made unsuccessful attempts to cut down on your gambling?

➤ Do you continue to gamble despite problems it creates, including financial difficulties, work conflicts, and family problems?

If you, your spouse, or someone you know is a compulsive gambler, the best place to turn for help is Gamblers Anonymous. It works much the same way as Alcoholics Anonymous and is also listed in your local phone book. Gambling addictions are as serious as addictions to drugs or alcohol. It's very easy to become bankrupt and develop huge debts. This can devastate your family. *Get help* if you think you might be a compulsive gambler.

Food

Compulsive eaters think about food all of the time. They eat when they are happy, they eat when they are sad, they eat when they are bored, and they eat when they are stressed. They eat at home, they eat at work, they eat in the car, and they eat in restaurants. People who are addicted to food have lost control. They don't just eat to live, they live to eat.

> OH!
>
> ### Bet You Didn't Know
>
> Q: Are there other food addictions besides compulsive eating?
>
> A: There are two very serious eating disorders—anorexia nervosa and bulimia. People who are anorectic don't eat enough because they feel they are overweight, when in reality they are not. Anorectics think about food constantly, but won't let themselves eat. Bulimics, like compulsive eaters, overeat in an uncontrolled way. Then, to keep themselves from gaining weight, they get rid of the food by vomiting or using laxatives.

If one of you is a compulsive eater, it will affect your marriage. People who overeat tend to be overweight, which can affect your social life. For example, the person who overeats might want to avoid going to a party that will have a lot of fattening foods, or might not want to see people until he or she has lost some weight. This can be frustrating to his or her spouse. It's also difficult to have a normal relationship with someone who is preoccupied with food.

It's particularly difficult to treat food compulsions because you cannot abstain from eating. You have to eat every day, which can trigger signals to want to keep eating and eating. Because there are so many people who have problems with food, there are many places to turn for help. There is an Overeaters Anonymous, which works like Alcoholics Anonymous and is listed in the phone book. Groups that deal with problems with food can be reached through colleges, hospitals, and religious organizations. And therapy can be useful to understand your issues surrounding food as well as the emotional reasons you might overeat.

Work

There is a fine line between being extremely dedicated to your work and being a workaholic. A workaholic doesn't just work long hours. A workaholic is not someone working two jobs to bring money into the house. A workaholic is someone whose entire life is structured around his or her work. When at home, he or she is thinking about work. These days, with faxes and e-mail, he or she can easily be doing work all the time from anywhere. A workaholic tends to bring his or her work on vacation—calling into work every day, bringing along the portable computer, and sending e-mails to colleagues. Workaholics often have trouble relaxing and enjoying themselves.

Workaholics often have bad marriages. They talk about work over dinner (if they're home for dinner) and spend many weekends working. Sometimes people become workaholics to avoid dealing with problems in their relationships. Sometimes problems develop in their marriage because of the excessive working. If one of you focuses too much on work, it can undermine your relationship.

If you tend to work long hours, answer the following questions to see if you might be a workaholic:

1. Do you feel guilty about how much time you spend at work?

2. Does your spouse get annoyed at your working habits?

3. Have you given up fun activities because of your work?

4. Do you bring work with you on vacations?

5. Do most of your conversations with your spouse revolve around your work?

6. Are most of your friends from your work?

7. Do you talk about work when you are with your friends?

8. Do you often think about your work when you are watching a movie?

If one or both of you has workaholic tendencies, we can almost guarantee that it's interfering with your marriage. You might be trying to escape something painful or feel the need to prove yourself. Discuss these issues with your spouse and try to figure out why you are working so much. Do things to round out your life, such as getting involved with a hobby or developing friendships outside of work. Therapy might also help you understand your issues around work. Work can be a very important part of life to some people, but it shouldn't be to the exclusion of everything else.

Keep Your Marriage Addiction-Free

Any kind of addiction will interfere with and possibly completely ruin your marriage. If there is any chance that either of you is addicted to anything, from alcohol to the Internet, get help right away! Addictions generally get worse over time, so the sooner you get help, the easier it will be to get over your addiction. Don't be in denial if you might have an addiction! You owe it to yourself and your marriage to keep addictions out of your life.

The Least You Need to Know

➤ Addictions are all-consuming and interfere with a healthy marriage. What you are addicted to becomes more important than your relationship.

➤ Alcoholism is very common. Don't deny your excessive drinking. It can ruin your life and your marriage.

➤ Alcoholics Anonymous is an important resource when you need help with your drinking.

➤ You can become addicted to street drugs, such as heroin, as well as prescription drugs, such as morphine or codeine.

➤ There are many other types of addictions, including addictions to gambling, food, and work. Get help before the addiction ruins your marriage!

Infidelity

Everyone has seen movies or read books about the husband who has a mistress or the wife who has a lover. But you never think it's going to happen to you. Unfortunately, infidelity occurs more often than it should. In this chapter, we will help you examine your marriage and give you suggestions on how to deal with infidelity in a relationship.

Infidelity as a Symptom

Infidelity is usually a symptom of a troubled marriage. It's easy to point to the infidelity and say, "That's the problem." But most of the time, there is an underlying problem in the relationship. If you or your spouse has turned to someone else, it means that something big is missing from your marriage. And it was probably missing *before* the affair started.

One of the biggest mistakes couples make after an affair is ignoring it. They try to sweep all of their emotions under the carpet. Most important, they don't address the issues that are troubling their marriage in the first place.

Think Twice

Don't assume that your relationship will be fine as soon as an outside affair ends, even if your spouse never discovers it. Problems with your relationship will not go away without hard work.

An affair should not be treated lightly. A simple discussion or argument will not change the qualities in your marriage that need to be changed. You need to work hard and put in the time and energy necessary to repair your marriage.

Troubled Times

Christopher and Brenda had been married for 16 years. They had two children who were now teenagers. Over the last several years, they had become more distant from each other. They didn't spend much time talking about each other's work, and they only went out together about once a month. Each of them spent more and more time with outside friends. Christopher and Brenda were slowly drifting apart. It's not that they were fighting constantly or miserable with each other. But they were not making the same efforts to spend time together that they had in the first years of their marriage.

Christopher was spending more and more time with a female colleague at work who was eight years younger than he was. At first, they had a friendship, but over time they realized they were attracted to each other. They started having an affair. At first, Christopher felt very guilty. But then he rationalized that he wasn't that attracted to Brenda anymore, and Brenda wouldn't find out anyway.

Over the next six months, Christopher carried on a passionate affair with his coworker. He had rationalized to himself that it didn't matter, but it did. He started fighting with Brenda more and became defensive about everything. Brenda knew something was happening, but she didn't think Christopher would ever have an affair.

One afternoon Christopher called Brenda to tell her he would be working late that evening. Brenda sarcastically said, "If I didn't know better, I'd think that you were having an affair. You've been home late a lot recently." Christopher mumbled something and hung up. He was convinced Brenda knew.

Christopher's affair was a loud and clear signal that there was something missing from his marriage. Christopher ended the affair after realizing his colleague would never leave her husband for him. Brenda never knew about it. By ending the affair, Christopher had an opportunity to start repairing his marriage. But he didn't do anything.

After more than a year, nothing has changed. Christopher and Brenda are still distant from each other. This is sad because the two of them have a long history together, much of it very happy and fulfilling. Their marriage could be strong again, if they would both put in the effort to make it work. Ending an affair will not automatically improve a relationship. It's only the first step.

OH!

Bet You Didn't Know

Q: I think my spouse might be having an affair. What should I do?

A: The most important thing you can do is work on your marriage. Even if your spouse is *not* having an affair, the fact that you are worried means there are problems in your relationship. Start by identifying issues that are troubling you and working toward resolving them. Also, make sure you are spending fun time with your spouse on a regular basis.

Is It Over?

If you or your spouse has had an affair, it's very likely that your relationship is in big trouble. The two of you might even be on your way to divorce. An affair is a loud and clear signal that your relationship needs serious reexamining. But, don't assume your marriage is definitely over. In the majority of cases, it's possible, with determination and outside help, to salvage your relationship.

Your Spouse Cheated on You

If you found out that your spouse was having an affair, it would probably be one of the worst moments in your life. Some people feel there is no way they could ever forgive their spouse if he or she cheated on them. It's certainly justifiable to feel that way. But remember, if you cannot eventually forgive your spouse, you will never be able to repair your relationship.

If your spouse cheated on you, ask yourself the following questions:

1. Did you suspect that something was wrong in your marriage?

2. Do you have any idea what it is?

3. Do you think it could be fixed with time and hard work?

4. Is there at least a small chance that you will be able to forgive your spouse?

5. If you feel there is no way that you could ever forgive your spouse, do you want to give up on your marriage?

Think Twice

Don't push away the hurt, pain, anger, and fury you feel if your spouse has cheated on you. If you bury your feelings, you will not be able to work through and get past them.

After their spouse has an affair, many people realize or can finally admit their marriage needs work. Look at your answers. If you can identify a problem and are willing to go to therapy and work on it, there is an excellent chance your marriage will improve greatly. But, you also need one more element—forgiveness. It will take time to forgive your spouse; that's okay. But the most important thing is that you need to be *open* to the idea of forgiving your spouse over time. If you feel you can *never* forgive your spouse, you're saying that you're giving up on your marriage.

You Cheated on Your Spouse

If you are cheating on your spouse, you need to end the affair completely. This might seem obvious, but it needs to be said directly. Some people think that once their affair is discovered, they might simply need to be more careful! This will only prolong the agony of the situation, both for you and your spouse. You must end your affair completely before you can have a successful relationship with your spouse.

If you cheated on your spouse, ask yourself the following questions:

1. Why did you cheat on your spouse?

2. Do you know what is wrong with your marriage?

3. Do you think that it could be fixed with time and hard work?

4. Are you willing to completely give up the affair?

5. By having an affair, are you saying that you want to give up on your marriage?

Many people have an affair as a way of expressing their frustration in their marriage. Look at your answers. Consider carefully why you had an affair. If you're willing to go to a therapist and work hard on repairing your marriage, there is an excellent chance you will be able to have a great relationship with your spouse. If you feel like giving up on your marriage and continuing your other relationship, we still strongly encourage you to seek counseling. The decision to stay with or leave your spouse might be the biggest one you ever make. You owe it to yourself and your spouse to think it through carefully and make the decision for the right reasons.

Bet You Didn't Know

Q: I love my spouse *and* my lover. Can't I have a good relationship with both of them?

A: Some people fool themselves into thinking they can have a good marriage and an outside affair as well. They think they can keep each relationship separate and rationalize that they get different things from each person. There is absolutely no way that you can have a successful marriage while having an affair. You may only see this many years later—when it's too late to repair the damage you have done.

Starting Over

You and your spouse absolutely must do three things for the two of you to get past the infidelity and continue your marriage:

➤ You both need to recognize that your relationship needs work and agree to work on it.

➤ The person who is having the affair needs to end it completely.

➤ The person whose spouse was unfaithful needs to forgive, over time, and move on.

Moving On

When someone has an affair, it creates a division in your relationship. Your marriage is now divided into the time before and the time after the affair. You might idealize the time before the affair as a wonderful part of your marriage. You might remember it as a time in which you trusted your spouse, you loved each other, and your relationship was good, even if these things were not true. The time after the affair, on the other hand, is now tainted. There has been a huge breach of trust and you are living the aftermath of that.

To give your relationship the best chance of survival, you need to consciously and actively do things to *redefine* your marriage. You cannot simply go back to where you were because you have crossed over a line. Don't fall back into the exact same patterns you had before. What you need to do is start over.

Rebuilding Trust

The hardest thing you will need to do is rebuild trust in your relationship. Whoever was unfaithful, you or your spouse, did major damage to the trust in your marriage. You can start to rebuild trust in your relationship by starting small and being consistent. Always be on time, do what you say you will do, and be honest. There will probably be many setbacks along the way, but keep being trustworthy. It will pay off eventually.

If you cheated on your spouse, it will take time to rebuild the trust that the two of you had. Make sure you do the following regularly and consistently:

Think Twice
Don't lie to your spouse, even about small things. If you find yourself starting to exaggerate or tell an outright lie, ask yourself why you are doing it. Are you generally an untrustworthy person? Are you afraid of how your spouse will react to the truth? Is it a bad habit? Answer honestly, and work on it.

Soul Mates
Making the decision to go to therapy and actually going is a big first step to repairing your marriage. When you go to couples therapy with your spouse, you are doing something together to work on your relationship.

➤ Never lie to your spouse.

➤ Communicate clearly at all times.

➤ Accept the fact that your spouse wants to know your schedule in great detail.

➤ Talk with your spouse every day from work or if one of you is out of town.

➤ Always be on time.

➤ Take the time to reassure your spouse if he or she feels insecure.

➤ Remember to do one nice thing each day for your spouse.

➤ Show your spouse affection on a regular basis.

➤ Do one fun activity every week alone with your spouse.

➤ Be especially patient with your spouse.

Get Help

We believe some situations make it mandatory to get outside help, and the crisis of infidelity is one of them. It would be very unusual for a couple to get past infidelity without the assistance of a trained therapist. A therapist is a neutral third party who will help you understand what went wrong in your relationship. Instead of allowing your discussions to dissolve into yelling and screaming sessions, a therapist will constructively focus you toward solving the problems in your relationship. In Chapter 25, we will discuss in detail how to find a therapist and what a therapist can do to help you.

Warning Signs

Many people are secretly concerned that their spouse will have an affair. There are usually warning signs that your relationship might be in trouble before either of you has an affair. If you are worried, it probably means you are concerned about your relationship in general. Instead of spending time worrying about whether your spouse is cheating on you, spend time working on your marriage.

Here are five warning signs that you're worried your spouse is being unfaithful:

1. You feel your spouse pays too much attention to members of the opposite sex.
2. You feel your spouse spends too much time with members of the opposite sex.
3. You feel your spouse often stares at people of the opposite sex.
4. You feel your spouse is not attracted to you.
5. You worry that your spouse might be having an affair.

Here are five warning signs that even a small part of you is straying from your marriage:

1. You arrange work meetings specifically to be alone with someone of the opposite sex.
2. You spend a lot of social time alone with members of the opposite sex.
3. You dress up for a specific person besides your spouse.
4. You constantly fantasize about someone of the opposite sex besides your spouse.
5. You think about having an affair.

How many warning signs do you recognize in yourself? Every single warning sign should demand your attention. A completely healthy marriage would have no warning signs. If you recognize three or more warning signs in yourself, you need to seriously reexamine your marriage. Work on your relationship right now before it's too late!

> **OH!**
>
> ### Bet You Didn't Know
>
> Q: I have some old friends of the opposite sex. How can I include them in my life and not threaten my marriage?
>
> A: Bring your spouse along when you get together with them. This will reinforce to your friends the fact that you are married and also give your spouse an opportunity to get to know people who are important to you. If you don't like the idea of including your spouse, consider why not. It may mean that you have a romantic interest in a person, even if you have no intention of acting on it. Remember that all of your romantic energy should be channeled into your marriage, not into friends of the opposite sex!

Keeping Infidelity Out of Your Marriage

If your marriage is strong and healthy, you will not need to worry about infidelity intruding in your relationship. Everything that you and your spouse need will be right at home.

Soul Mates
The best way to prevent infidelity in your marriage is to always put time and effort into making your marriage the best it can possibly be.

People are unfaithful when they are not getting their needs met in their marriage. One of the best ways to keep infidelity out of your marriage is to make sure you set aside time every week to have fun with your spouse. If the two of you enjoy each other's company on a regular basis, it's unlikely that either of you will feel the need to turn elsewhere. Make sure your marriage is the center of your attention and give it the time and energy it deserves. These are the best ways to keep your marriage infidelity-free.

The Least You Need to Know

➤ Infidelity is usually a symptom of a troubled marriage. You need to work hard on your relationship to rebuild it.

➤ If your spouse cheated on you, you need to forgive your spouse before you can work on your marriage. If you cheated on your spouse, you absolutely must end the affair before you can work on your marriage.

➤ If you or your spouse has had an affair, it's very difficult to work on your relation-ship without the help of a therapist.

➤ It's possible to rebuild a marriage after someone has an affair if both of you are willing to work hard at repairing it.

➤ The best way to prevent infidelity is to be aware of problems in your relationship and work on them.

Help! We Need Somebody

In This Chapter

➤ Admitting you need outside help

➤ What happens in a therapist's office?

➤ Developing empathy for each other

➤ Finding therapy resources

➤ Organizing your goals

You've tried everything and nothing seems to work. You feel like you've hit a brick wall. You and your spouse are fighting more than you would like. Maybe you're even finding it impossible to enjoy each other's company anymore. It would be best to get help from the outside. If you and your spouse are at an impasse, the perspective from an objective outsider can often be invaluable. This chapter will help you decide when seeing a therapist would be useful. We will talk about myths that people have about therapy. We will help you find a therapist who would best suit your needs. We will also suggest alternatives to seeing a therapist, which you might find useful. By the end of this chapter, you will finally know, once and for all, whether you should see a therapist, and if so, how to find the best one for you!

When Is Therapy Useful?

There are many situations in which seeing a therapist would be helpful. If you and your spouse keep getting in the same argument over and over again, or find yourself in a situation you can't get beyond, therapy can be extremely useful.

Think Twice
Don't think you have failed because you turn to a therapist for help. You have been *successful* by recognizing you need help and going out and getting it.

A therapist can help you uncover issues you have that might be interfering with your relationship.

All of the issues we discuss in this book—money, sex, housework, extended family, parenting, work, relocation, aging parents, second marriages, illness, addiction, and infidelity—can lead to conflicts that a therapist can help you resolve. Throughout the book we've described situations where therapy has been useful. The biggest challenge in therapy is getting over the hurdle of admitting you need help.

Ten Common Myths People Have About Therapy

Many people don't seek help from a therapist because they have concerns about therapists and therapy. They have preconceived notions about who sees a therapist or what a therapist can or can't do. The following are some common myths that people have about therapy and therapists.

Myth #1: Only Crazy People See Therapists

Reality: A wide range of people see therapists. Many people who are in therapy are healthy, balanced, highly successful, have responsible jobs, and make a good living. They are seeing a therapist to work through a specific problem or to figure out why they are not happier with their success. Other common reasons for people to see a therapist are to get help with depression or anxiety.

Myth #2: Someone Who Doesn't Know Me Can't Help Me

Reality: The fact that a therapist doesn't know you is exactly why he or she can help you! The therapy process depends on the therapist being unbiased. Therapy is a special situation where an impartial, neutral person helps you sort through your issues so you can go on to be more productive and happy in your daily life.

Myth #3: Therapists Can Read People's Minds

Reality: Therapists can't read people's minds. Therapists are professionally trained to listen carefully and pay special attention to people's emotions.

Myth #4: A Therapist Can Solve All of Your Problems

Reality: A therapist won't solve your problems. Rather, a therapist will help *you* solve your problems. If you want to grow from therapy, it will take a lot of work on your part.

Myth #5: A Couples Therapist Will Take Sides

Reality: This is not true. A good couples therapist will remain neutral and help the two of you resolve your differences. At the end of each session, each of you should feel your point of view was heard and understood.

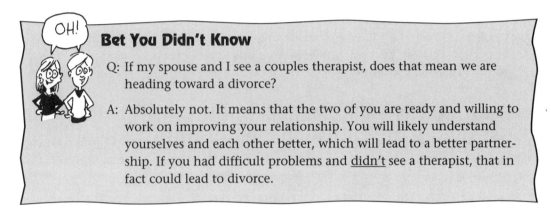

OH!

Bet You Didn't Know

Q: If my spouse and I see a couples therapist, does that mean we are heading toward a divorce?

A: Absolutely not. It means that the two of you are ready and willing to work on improving your relationship. You will likely understand yourselves and each other better, which will lead to a better partnership. If you had difficult problems and <u>didn't</u> see a therapist, that in fact could lead to divorce.

Myth #6: Therapists Never Say Anything

Reality: Most therapists, especially those who work with couples, are very interactive. They will listen carefully, ask you questions, and talk with you during all of your sessions.

Myth #7: Therapy Takes Forever

Reality: Short-term therapy, which can be extremely useful for couples, generally lasts between eight and twenty sessions, one session each week. It tends to be goal-directed and focuses on specific issues and problems. On the other hand, long-term therapy can last for one year or more. It tends to be psychodynamically oriented, which means it helps you understand your personal character development.

Myth #8: Everyone Will Know I'm Seeing a Therapist

Reality: A therapist will maintain your confidentiality and will not tell others what was discussed in your therapy sessions. The only people who will know you are seeing a therapist are the ones you tell. Often people who find therapy beneficial want to share this with others.

Think Twice
Don't forget the price of breaking up a marriage is costly, both emotionally and financially. Therapy is an investment that usually pays off in the long run.

Myth #9: Therapy Is Unaffordable

Reality: There is no question that therapy with a private therapist is expensive. However, many people overlook the fact that their medical insurance will cover a limited number of therapy sessions for "crisis intervention." Short-term couples therapy can be incredibly productive. There are also therapists-in-training and family service agencies who see patients on a sliding scale.

Myth #10: Only Weak People See Therapists

Reality: Actually, the opposite is true! It takes a *strong* person to go to a therapist. When you see a therapist, he or she will give you tools to become even stronger and more able to work through your issues.

Is Therapy for Me?

You may be wondering if couples therapy would be useful for you and your spouse. The following questions will help clarify this issue. On a scale ranging from 1 (never) to 5 (always), circle your answer to each question below.

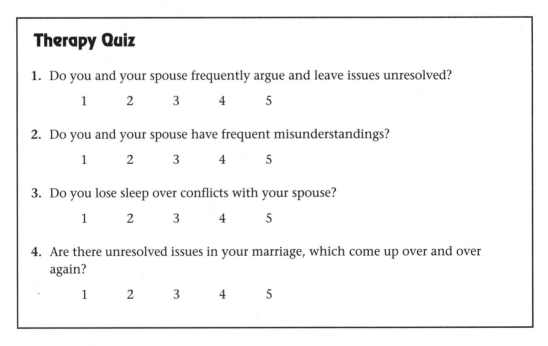

Therapy Quiz

1. Do you and your spouse frequently argue and leave issues unresolved?

    1   2   3   4   5

2. Do you and your spouse have frequent misunderstandings?

    1   2   3   4   5

3. Do you lose sleep over conflicts with your spouse?

    1   2   3   4   5

4. Are there unresolved issues in your marriage, which come up over and over again?

    1   2   3   4   5

5. Do you spend time being angry with your spouse even when you are apart from each other?

       1   2   3   4   5

6. Do you feel that responsibilities are unfairly divided in your marriage?

       1   2   3   4   5

7. Are you generally unhappy with your marriage?

       1   2   3   4   5

8. Do you often think of leaving your spouse?

       1   2   3   4   5

9. Do you ever feel you would benefit from an outside opinion on your life or your marriage?

       1   2   3   4   5

10. Do you think about seeing a therapist?

       1   2   3   4   5

If you answered several of the questions with a "4" or a "5," there is conflict in your marriage. Couples therapy might help you and your spouse resolve a specific issue together. It can also help you with conflict resolution in general.

If you answered all of the questions with a "1" or a "2," you probably don't have issues to work on in therapy. If you answered the questions somewhere in between, consider therapy as a way to help you understand and resolve specific issues.

Soul Mates
The first step to being happy—with yourself or in your marriage—is to figure out what is making you unhappy. The therapy process can help you understand why you aren't happy.

Finding a Therapist

The best way to find a good therapist is through a personal recommendation. If someone tells you that a particular therapist helped save his or her marriage, then that therapist is likely to be very good. Also consider asking your religious leader. He or she has probably referred couples to therapy in the past and would be happy to help you find a good therapist.

Another good resource is your primary care doctor. Many physicians refer patients to therapy and can recommend a good therapist to you. If you are using your medical insurance to pay for the therapy visits, you might be limited to a specific list of therapists. Bring along the list of therapists' names and show it to your doctor. He or she might know one or more therapists on the list.

The following are some initials you will need to know when finding a therapist who is right for your situation:

➤ M.D.—Medical Doctor (psychiatrist)

➤ Ph.D.—Doctorate (in psychology or social work)

➤ L.C.S.W.—Licensed Clinical Social Worker

➤ M.F.C.C.—Marriage and Family Counselor

Be Goal-Directed

If you are considering seeing a therapist with your spouse, it's useful to have specific goals for your therapy. This will make the best use of your time in therapy. Having specific goals is especially useful in short-term therapy because you want to make the most out of every session.

Soul Mates

Couples therapy can help you understand what your spouse is feeling. This is called *empathy*. You will feel closer to each other as you see what the other person has experienced in the past and what issues might be troubling him or her that you hadn't realized before.

You might have different types of goals for therapy. Perhaps you want help resolving a specific issue, such as dividing your child care responsibilities fairly. Therapy can be useful when you need to make a big decision, like whether to move. You might want to understand why you always argue about a particular issue. A goal in therapy can also be more general, such as improving communication with your spouse.

There are many issues a therapist can help you with, including:

➤ Communicating with your spouse

➤ Resolving an issue

➤ Time scheduling

➤ Making a big decision

➤ Understanding emotional issues about money

➤ Sex

➤ Dealing with your extended family

➤ Parenting

➤ Work-related problems

➤ Illness

➤ Addiction

➤ Infidelity

Other Resources

If therapy is not possible for you and your spouse, there are other resources that can offer you help. Here are just a few:

➤ *Religious leaders.* Many religious leaders are excellent resources if you are having conflict with your spouse. Some have special training in counseling, and all have dealt with people in crisis situations. If they can't help you directly, they can often find a therapist for you. Don't forget this resource!

➤ *Support groups.* There are many types of groups that can be useful to you and your spouse. Some groups focus on specific problems, such as parenting or illness. Others are designed for couples to work on their marriage. Groups tend to be less expensive than therapists and are a good way to get help without spending a lot of money. It can also be useful to hear how other people deal with issues similar to yours.

➤ *Anonymous groups.* In Chapter 23, we discussed some of the different anonymous groups. If one of you is addicted to something, anonymous groups can be an invaluable resource. Alcohol, gambling, and overeating are some of the addictions they deal with. Al-Anon groups can help you deal with your enabling behaviors and with issues that are common when your spouse has an addiction problem.

➤ *Encounter groups.* These groups often have weekend retreats to work on your relationship, with follow-up meetings. They can be secular or through a religious organization.

➤ *Classes.* Relationship courses and workshops are offered through colleges, extension courses, and health care centers.

Taking Control of Your Life

The single biggest factor in the success of your therapy is you! You need to work hard in therapy, be honest, and really use the information you learn about yourself and your relationships. Remember that going to therapy is not a passive but an active process. You will get the most from the time and money you spend on therapy by putting your best efforts into it both inside and outside the therapist's office.

The Least You Need to Know

➤ Therapy can be very useful if you and your spouse can't resolve an issue by yourselves or if you are having trouble making a big decision.

➤ Therapists are unbiased, will listen carefully, and will help you work through your issues.

➤ Couples therapy can help you and your spouse work on your marriage. It can also help you and your spouse better understand each other.

➤ The best way to find a therapist is through a personal recommendation from a friend, physician, or religious leader.

➤ There are many alternatives to therapy, including support groups, religious leaders, and anonymous groups.

➤ Remember that the most important factor in the success of your therapy is you!

Part 7
Planning Your Future Together

You'll have a lot of fun in this final part. We'll show you and your spouse how to reach your goals and make your dreams happen. We'll also review the qualities of a GREAT marriage—good communication, real partnership, effort, adaptability, and total commitment. And we'll show you how to treasure your past, cherish your day-to-day life, and look forward to your future together!

Chapter 26

We Have a Dream

In This Chapter

➤ Determining family goals

➤ Planning community goals

➤ Establishing personal goals

➤ Using a goal planner

➤ Prioritizing your goals

Planning for the future with your spouse is very important. Thinking about where you would like to be several years down the road will not only help you achieve your dreams, it will help you work together as a team to get there! In this chapter, we will help you think about your goals and show you ways to take steps to achieve them. We will also show you how to use a goal planner. By the end of this chapter, you will have stopped worrying about the future and already started planning for it!

Creating a Vision Together

It's easy to get so caught up in the day-to-day grind that you lose sight of your goals. Most people have hopes for their future, but they don't do anything to reach them. You need to plan ahead to have any chance of reaching your goals. Your life and your marriage will be enriched if you strive toward things that are important to you. By planning ahead and working hard, you will be able to reach your goals!

Soul Mates
Make sure you set aside special time to talk with each other about the dreams and desires you have for the future. If you have always wanted to travel to an exotic place, make sure you discuss it so that you can reach the goal together.

Family Goals

Setting family goals might seem unnecessary if you are regularly spending time with them. But, it's so easy for weeks, months, or years to go by and not do what you had intended. You might want certain things to be different in your family, but you haven't done the things you need to do to reach that goal. Planning ahead will allow you to work steadily toward achieving your family goals.

Marriage Goals

After reading this book, you probably have many goals for yourself and your spouse. You know that one of the most important things in your relationship is to spend time together on a regular basis.

Some of your goals will take time to reach. For instance, you might be working on communicating better or forgiving more easily. You might be committed to being more dependable. Or you might be trying to be more efficient at work so you have more time for your spouse. Be patient and keep working toward your goal.

Soul Mates
Planning for a large, special goal many years away takes teamwork. While you are sacrificing for it now, think about the wonderful experience you have to look forward to!

You might have other sorts of goals for your marriage, such as planning for your dreams. You might have certain dreams that are completely out of your reach. For instance, you might want to quit working and live in a villa in France. But there are plenty of smaller, more realistic dreams you might have that you can realize, *if you plan for them*. You might want to take a trip to Europe with your spouse but never have enough money in your budget. If you plan that trip for five years from now and are careful to save regularly toward it, you will be able to go!

Children

Spending time with your children is central to your relationship with them. If you have children at home, set aside time to spend with them, both in the week and on the weekends. You will never regret spending time with your children on a regular basis, but in later years you will probably regret *not* spending enough time with them. If your children are already grown, keep in regular contact with them.

Specific goals are also useful in your relationship with children. With younger children, you might commit to reading a bedtime story every night. If you have school-age children, you might consider coaching their soccer team or volunteering in their classroom. As your children get older, you might work on a hobby together. Your children will remember and appreciate this time together.

Extended Family

Your relationship with your extended family is important. You might have goals such as getting along better with in-laws or making amends with your parents. You might also have a goal such as spending quality time with your siblings.

Contributing to Your Community

Even if you are incredibly busy, you should take some time every month to contribute to your community. It will help you grow as a person and give you a feeling of satisfaction. There are many ways you can be extremely valuable to others:

➤ Volunteer to tutor students at your local school.

➤ Become a Big Brother or Sister.

➤ Get involved with a local shelter.

➤ Give money to charity.

Whatever you can do to help will be a benefit to your community and make you a better person.

Personal Goals

When you are married and have a family, it's still important to keep in mind personal goals. Your goals might be small, such as reading a new book every month, or your goals might be larger, such as

Think Twice
Ten years from now, don't look back and wish you'd done things differently. Think about your goals now and act accordingly. The clearer you are about where you want to be, the greater your chances of getting there!

developing a new hobby or learning a new skill. Personal goals will help you grow as a person and will enrich your life and your marriage.

> ### Bet You Didn't Know
>
> Q: Now that I'm married, is it still okay for me to have individual goals?
>
> A: Yes. It's healthy for you and important to your marriage to have individual goals. When you grow as a person, your relationship will grow too.

The more realistic your expectations are about the future, the more likely it is that you will meet your goals. But, there is a very fine line between reaching so high that you are always disappointed and not reaching high enough to maximize your potential.

Expanding Your Mind

It's very common for people to look back and say they can't believe they have not read a book in several years or learned anything new. This is not healthy. Human beings are naturally curious and need to have their minds nourished. Setting goals for yourself will ensure that you actually do expose yourself to new ideas. Take a class to learn about a new subject, or join a movie club to discuss films. Subscribe to a news magazine and read it regularly to learn more about the world around you.

One way to make sure you'll read a book a month is to join a book club that meets regularly. It's very fulfilling to read a book and talk about it with other people when you are finished. If you can't find a book club to join, start one! You'll be surprised at how many people are interested.

Hobbies

Developing a hobby is useful for many reasons. It can help relieve you of the stresses of modern life. It can be a skill that you develop and enjoy after you retire. And it's also a way to meet other people who share similar interests. Many hobbies are project-oriented and give you a sense of accomplishment when you finish them.

If you don't already have a hobby, think about finding one that you really like in the next year. Start by taking a class, perhaps in one of the following areas:

➤ Gardening

➤ Painting

➤ Photography

➤ Playing a musical instrument

➤ Crocheting or knitting

➤ Woodworking

➤ Model building

➤ Sewing and needlework

➤ Sculpting

➤ Dancing

➤ Fixing up old automobiles

The Spice Rack
One way to grow and spend time together is for you and your spouse to take a class to-gether. It can be something fun, such as ballroom dancing or painting, or more serious, such as financial planning. You can alternate choosing a class to take.

Once you find a hobby you like, set goals for your-self. For instance, if you like to garden, commit to learning about two new plants each year. You might even have the long-term goal of entering your flowers into a contest.

Taking Care of Your Health

Getting regular medical and dental care is important, but many people forget to schedule regular check-ups. Eating a healthy diet is another useful health goal. And exercising is an important part of a well-balanced, healthy life. For exercise, consider walking, running, or bicycling. If you are sports-oriented, play tennis, squash, or racquetball regularly, or join a basketball or soccer team. Remember that the healthier you are, the better you'll feel and the more you'll be able to reach your other goals.

Goal Planner

Thinking about your goals five years in the future will help you make decisions about how you spend your time and energy now. It's much easier to reach big goals when you are able to work slowly and steadily toward them. Answer the following questions:

1. What are three things you would like to improve in your marriage in five years?

2. Is there somewhere you would like to travel, or something expensive you would like to purchase, within five years?

3. If you have children, describe how you would like your relationship with them to be in five years.

4. How would you like your relationship with your in-laws to be in five years?

5. What could you improve in the way you deal with your parents and siblings?

6. Looking back five years from now, how would you like to have contributed to your community?

7. What are some books you would like to have read five years from now?

8. Are there any hobbies you would like to develop within five years?

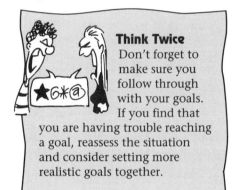

Think Twice
Don't forget to make sure you follow through with your goals. If you find that you are having trouble reaching a goal, reassess the situation and consider setting more realistic goals together.

9. Is there an area you would like to develop with your spouse? For instance, spiritually, artistically, a specific skill, or practical knowledge?

10. What could you do to improve your health?

Take the answer to each question and write down the following:

1. One thing you can start doing now to reach the goal.

2. How much time per month it will take.

3. How much money per month it will cost.

Prioritizing What You Want

If you have $1,000 to spend on a vacation, you need to decide whether you want to spend it on an extravagant weekend away with your spouse, a one-week car trip throughout the state, or a one-month camping excursion. All three options might sound good to you, but you only have a certain amount of time and a fixed amount of money. You need to decide on the vacation you want and set aside the proper amount of money for it.

Think Twice
Don't set yourself up to reach two incompatible goals. You'll frustrate yourself and possibly ruin your chances of reaching either of them. Instead, prioritize clearly and work on one as your primary goal and one as your secondary goal.

It's usually easy to see why you need to prioritize your budget, but it can be more difficult to prioritize other things. For instance, your goal might be to reach a certain level at your work. But another goal might be to spend more time with your children at home. Those two goals might be incompatible. If you try to reach both of them, you'll probably be disappointed and exhausted. At an extreme, you might even ruin your chances for reaching either goal.

Prioritizing Your Goals

List your top three goals from the earlier questions, along with the starting point and the amount of time and money needed for each one:

Goal #1

First step: _____

Time needed per month: _____

Money needed per month: _____

Goal #2

First step: _____

Time needed per month: _____

Money needed per month: _____

Goal #3

First step: _____

Time needed per month: _____

Money needed per month: _____

Once you decide to put in the effort, time and money are usually the biggest limitations toward reaching all of your goals. Can you realistically make enough time to do all of the things you need to do to reach these three goals? If not, readjust the amount of time you will spend on each one.

The Least You Need to Know

➤ It's useful to think about what sort of relationship you want with your children in the future. Then you can think about things you might do now to reach that goal, such as spending more time with them.

➤ It's important to define your personal goals and put time and effort into them. You will have a fuller, richer marriage if you keep growing as a person.

➤ Think about your goals for five years from now and determine what you should start doing to reach them. Consider how much time and money they will require, and figure out what you can do right away to accomplish your future goals.

Chapter 27

Soul Mates

In This Chapter

➤ Making your marriage GREAT

➤ Treasuring your past

➤ Cherishing every moment

➤ Looking forward to tomorrow

Congratulations, you made it through this book! In this chapter, we will review the five essential qualities of a great marriage. We will remind you how to appreciate your past together, how to make the most of your daily life together, and how to work toward an extraordinary future together! You married your partner full of hope, enthusiasm, and love. In order to nurture your relationship fully, you need to make use of the tools in this book. Give your soul mate love, care, and attention and your marriage will thrive and grow.

Having a GREAT Marriage

As we discussed at the beginning of the book, there are certain qualities that are part of every great marriage. The first letters of these five qualities spell the word "GREAT." Let's review these qualities.

"G" Is for Good Communication

Communicating well with your spouse is absolutely crucial to having a great marriage. Communication is the way you let your spouse know what you are feeling and what you need from him or her. When you listen carefully, you are showing your spouse how important he or she is to you. When you talk with each other, make sure you give each other your undivided attention, make eye contact, and use good timing. If you and your spouse communicate well, you will be in the best position to fully appreciate each other and solve your differences.

"R" Is for Real Partnership

A marriage is a partnership and takes teamwork. When you are part of a team, the success of the team is always more important than your individual success. Make sure you support each other and avoid blaming each other when things go wrong. Take time to work out your differences together. Remember that it's more important to develop a solution than to prove a point or to win an argument. Your partnership is your first priority.

"E" Is for Effort

Effort is what makes a relationship work. You cannot have a good marriage without putting in the time and energy to make it work. Many people think a good marriage should not take a lot of energy. Nothing is further from the truth! A great relationship is great because both people put in their complete effort to make it work. Make sure to give your marriage the time and energy that it deserves. Investing regularly and consistently in your marriage will be the best investment you will make in your entire life!

"A" Is for Adaptability

Soul Mates
When things are not going as planned, sit down with your spouse and try to work out a new solution. You will feel closer to each other by trying to make the best of a difficult situation.

Being flexible is so important in a marriage. You know by now that things do not always turn out as you planned. The fuller your life is, the more things can go wrong! Perhaps the restaurant that you had your heart set on going to Saturday night is booked. Or maybe your spouse has no interest in saving money for the car of your dreams. If you figure out ways to make the best of a situation, then you will be a happier, more satisfied person, and you will have a better marriage too!

"T" Is for Total Commitment

Remember that you need to stay committed to your relationship through good times as well as bad. When you are one hundred percent committed to your marriage, it will be much easier to be there for your spouse. If you feel like walking out of your marriage whenever things get tough, you will be undermining your relationship. But if you always stand by your spouse through thick and thin, you will be making it clear that you are completely committed to him or her. When both of you are committed to each other, you will give each other a wonderful sense of security.

Treasuring Your Past

You are creating a past from the moment your relationship starts. The memories you create between the two of you are yours and yours alone. When you are going through a difficult time with your spouse, think about some wonderful memories that the two of you share. Your past can also be your best teacher. You can use the past to learn from your mistakes and do things differently now and in the future.

Relive Fun Times

One of the best ways to relive fun times is to do things that help you remember them. The following are some ideas to bring back your wonderful memories:

➤ Look through your photo album together.

➤ Listen to music you danced to when you were first dating.

➤ Visit old friends you have not seen in a while.

➤ Have dinner at the restaurant you went to on your first date.

➤ Go back to a special vacation spot.

➤ Rent a movie you enjoyed together when you were first married.

➤ Take a second honeymoon and stay in the same room in the same hotel, if possible.

➤ Visit the place where the two of you met.

The Spice Rack
On a cold winter night, make a fire, pop some popcorn, and watch family videos together. You'll have a great time, and it'll make you feel like the soul mates you are.

Remembering the Hard Times Too

Think Twice
Don't forget all of the difficult things you and your spouse went through together. They will be reminders that you can make it through hard times.

Many people try to forget the difficult times in their lives. For instance, they might not want to remember an illness they suffered or a huge disagreement they had with their spouse. It feels painful, and people think it's best to push it aside. Actually, it can be a source of strength and give you a feeling of triumph to know that you successfully overcame a difficult challenge.

Cherishing Every Moment

Think Twice
Don't take each other for granted. Make sure you show your appreciation for each other on a daily basis.

Your marriage will be stronger if you take the time to enjoy the intimate things in your daily lives. Make sure that you have fun together, do nice things for each other, and treat each other with kindness. If you do, you will enjoy yourselves more and create good memories in the process.

Have Fun Together

Having fun together is one of the most important parts of your marriage. Your adult life as a married couple is filled with responsibility. The two of you deserve to have fun together. Every single week you and your spouse should spend fun time together. Schedule it on your calendar, along with all of your other appointments.

Make Each Day Count

It's so important to make each day count with your spouse. Most people let days, weeks, or even months go by without letting their partner know how important he or she is to them. That won't happen to you if you make a point of doing one nice thing a day for your spouse. Whether it's something small, such as preparing a special meal, or something large, such as planning a surprise vacation together, you will be acknowledging the importance of your relationship on a regular basis. Even a small thing such as calling from work and saying, "I love you," can make his or her day special.

Don't Take Each Other for Granted

Many people take their spouse for granted. Because they know that their partner will always be there for them, they don't always take the time or make the effort to be as kind and thoughtful as they could be. But you can make your marriage better than that! If you treat your spouse with kindness all of the time, your relationship will be better than you ever dreamed!

Looking Forward to Tomorrow

When you are married, you have the special opportunity to look toward the future with anticipation. Sometimes that involves making day-to-day plans, and other times it involves planning something really wonderful for two years from now.

Take time to do the following:

> ➤ Plan ahead.

> ➤ Discuss your goals.

> ➤ Anticipate together.

When you share your life with somebody, there are many things that require you to think ahead. You need to schedule fun activities together, make a budget, anticipate potential difficulties, and decide where to go on vacation. Make sure you set aside time every month for planning these things.

Think Twice
Don't forget to plan ahead for your big goals, such as taking a special vacation or buying a car or a house. Working together toward a particular goal can be extremely satisfying.

You and your spouse have family, personal, and financial goals that you should discuss with each other. It's worthwhile to talk about your goals once or twice a year to make sure that you are doing things today to help you reach your goals. Talking with each other about your goals can help you clarify what they are.

There are so many things that you and your spouse have to look forward to, from celebrating your anniversary to enjoying each other's company during the leisure of your retirement. If you have children, you can also look forward to getting pleasure from their accomplishments. Talk about the events and experiences that you are looking forward to with your spouse. Remember that anticipation is half the fun!

Counting Your Blessings

Your marriage has the potential to be the absolutely best part of your life. If you have begun to implement the ideas from this book, you probably feel closer to your spouse already! Just remember to always communicate with your spouse, be real partners in life, put time and energy into your relationship, be flexible, and commit one hundred percent to your marriage.

Being married is truly a wonderful blessing. You have memories to enjoy and help you through difficult times. You have the chance to enjoy your relationship every day. And you also have the chance to look forward to fun things in the future. Always remember to count your blessings and make the effort to maintain a stable, healthy relationship. Then you will always be able to look over at your spouse and say, "I am the luckiest person in the world to have you in my life!"

The Least You Need to Know

➤ There are five necessary qualities to every great marriage: good communication, real partnership, effort, adaptability, and total commitment. Make sure you contribute all five of them to your marriage.

➤ Shared memories are an important part of a marriage. Also, your memories of difficult times can serve as a source of strength.

➤ Make the most out of your day-to-day life with your spouse. Do nice things for each other, and treat each other with kindness.

➤ You have your whole future together to look forward to. Make the most of it by planning ahead and setting goals for yourselves.

➤ Having a fulfilling marriage is one of the most wonderful blessings in the world!

Case Studies

As you read the following case studies, you'll be surprised at how much you've learned from reading this book. Each of the topics covered here is discussed in detail in the book.

As you read through the problems that these couples face, try to answer the questions for each couple and think about what advice you might give them. The exercise of analyzing a problem and coming up with viable solutions is just the practice you need for your own marriage!

Case 1: Judy and Glenn

The Problem

Judy and Glenn have been married for one year. Their courtship was intense and romantic. After the honeymoon was over and the reality of being married set in, Judy and Glenn fought constantly. They fought about the phone bill, they fought about chores, and they fought about what movie to see. Even with all that fighting, they never resolved anything. Their marriage was one battle after another. After an angry bout, they would often not speak to each other for days. They acted like two children who walked off in a tiff if they didn't get their way.

The tension kept mounting until Glenn, in a fit of anger, accidentally knocked over Judy's crystal lamp. He was sorry the moment it fell to the ground, but Judy flew into a rage. She left for her sister's house, where she sat contemplating divorce.

The Questions

- ➤ What's going on here?
- ➤ Are both Glenn and Judy at fault?
- ➤ How is Glenn at fault?
- ➤ How is Judy at fault?
- ➤ What can they do to improve their marriage?

The Issues

Conflict Resolution

It isn't the issues in their marriage that are causing Judy and Glenn so much grief, but their inability to handle them. Judy and Glenn need to learn about tools that can solve their issues. They don't have any idea how to resolve conflicts.

For instance, they need to set aside time to have constructive conversations with ground rules such as not walking out of the room in the middle of an argument. They should also plan how they intend to handle specific conflicts. For example, if a disagreement comes up about the phone bill, they could agree to pay for extravagant calls out of their personal spending money. To solve household chore conflicts, they should create a chore chart and stick to it. With time and effort, most conflicts can be resolved in a way that makes sense and makes for a workable relationship.

Forgiveness

Glenn didn't mean to break Judy's lamp. It may have been thoughtless or careless on his part, but Judy has to realize he feels badly about it. If she stays at her sister's house, she'll probably work herself into a frenzy. This certainly won't nurture her marriage. Judy is angry because the lamp is broken and because of her husband's behavior. The more time that passes between an incident and its resolution, the more anger and resentment can build. But, if Judy can find it in her heart to forgive Glenn, he will probably make a sincere apology. Forgiveness in a marriage makes it strong and helps a couple rebound from the same daily mistakes we all make.

The Conclusion

Judy and Glenn are newlyweds and have a lot to learn about being married. Many divorces occur during the first year of marriage simply because the couple has not learned how to be married! Judy and Glenn could be put on the right track very easily just by studying many of the techniques in this book. A little bit of knowledge will go a long way toward turning their relationship around.

The more effort you put into learning how to get along, the better you will!

Case 2: Stacy and Brian

The Problem

Stacy and Brian have been married for eight years and have two children, ages three and five. Stacy recently switched from part-time to full-time work because they weren't meeting their monthly budget. After her switch, they were always exhausted, they fought more often, and they had less energy for their children.

Stacy and Brian began to let their children stay up until 9:30 or 10:00 P.M. to spend time with them. As a result, the children were exhausted in the morning and had trouble waking up. Stacy and Brian still felt they weren't spending enough time with their children, so they stopped going out every Saturday night like they had been doing since they got married. They figured they would have more time with the children and save baby-sitter money. But the new plan wasn't working well.

The children felt the additional stress in the house and acted up more than ever. Their family life soon became very unpleasant.

The Questions

> ➤ What is going on?

> ➤ What are Stacy and Brian doing wrong?

> ➤ What should they be discussing?

> ➤ What are they forgetting?

> ➤ What are some other choices they have?

The Issues

Finances

Sometimes the *easy* solutions end up taking the most effort. Working full-time seems like the easiest way to have more money, but Stacy and Brian should have examined other alternatives. Tightening their budget might have made it possible for Stacy to avoid working full-time. As they found out, there are always hidden expenses to working more hours, both financial and emotional. Their child care expenses went up, as did their stress levels, which is not good for them or for their children. While many financial decisions are made out of necessity, it's still important to analyze every option before you make decisions that will affect your entire family.

Time Together

In their desire to provide well for their family, Stacy and Brian forgot one of the most important factors in keeping their family strong: spending time alone together. Their intent was good—to spend more time with their children—but they forgot the single most important factor to raising healthy, happy children: healthy, happy parents. Nurturing their own relationship would give Stacy and Brian the strength and joy to nurture the whole family. Spending time alone—just the two of you—keeps your relationship healthy and stable. Children respond to happy, stable parents by feeling secure.

Family Consistency

Children need to have things they can depend on. Whether Stacy decides to continue to work full-time or not, Stacy and Brian should start some routines. They should get the children to sleep at the same time every night. They could go to the library one evening every week. They could even start a family tradition of having a Sunday brunch that they could all cook together. The point is that when the household feels hectic, these types of simple routines help children feel stable.

The Conclusion

Stacy and Brian realized the current situation was not working. They went through their budget carefully and thought about what expenses they could decrease or eliminate. They picked out a few things, but concluded they still needed the extra income from Stacy working full-time. They decided instead to see how they might rework their schedule to build consistency and calm into their lives.

They changed their children's bedtime to 8:00 P.M. From 7:00 to 8:00 every night they gave the children their complete attention. They helped them get in their pajamas, brush their teeth, and then they took turns reading the kids a bedtime story. As a result, Brian and Stacy had over two hours to themselves every evening. They were thrilled to have the time to unwind from the day and talk with each other.

At first the children hated going to bed so early, but after a few days, they began to look forward to the new routine. In the mornings, they woke up by themselves and didn't need to be dragged out of bed. The morning also became much more pleasant. The kids were in a good mood, instead of grouchy and exhausted. They seemed happier about going to child care as well.

Stacy and Brian also resumed their routine of going out on the weekends. Every other week, Brian's mother watched the children; the other week, they hired a baby-sitter. To save money, one week they would do something for free, such as take a long walk or browse at a music store. The next week they would see a movie or have dinner out. They were able to relax and have fun within a small entertainment budget.

Every problem has a solution, you just have to take the time and effort to find it!

Case 3: Melissa and Randy

The Problem

Melissa and Randy have been married for three years. Randy was offered a promotion in another city and was very excited about taking it. When he told Melissa about it, he described it as the "best opportunity of my life." He asked Melissa what she thought, and she said, "That sounds great." Randy felt wonderful and talked about his new job all the time. The new job was starting in two months.

Melissa, however, began feeling worse and worse. Every time Randy brought up the move, she said something negative about it. The more she thought about it, the more she realized that she didn't want to move. She had lived in the same place her entire life, and most of her friends and family were nearby. She didn't want to say anything to Randy because she knew how excited he was about the move. Instead, Melissa became resentful and angry with Randy because it was his fault they were moving. When they were one month away from the move, Melissa became more and more distressed. She was not sleeping well at night and was exhausted and irritable during the day. Melissa still didn't discuss her concerns with Randy.

She was slowly withdrawing from the relationship. A week before Randy and Melissa were supposed to move, Randy asked her to do some errands for their move. Melissa exploded. She screamed, "You're the one who wants to move! I didn't ask to leave my job. I didn't ask to leave my family. You're so hot on leaving town, why don't you do them yourself!" Melissa stormed out of the house, leaving Randy dumbfounded.

The Questions

- ➤ What is going on here?
- ➤ Do you think both Melissa and Randy are at fault?
- ➤ How is Randy at fault?
- ➤ How is Melissa at fault?
- ➤ What should they do?

The Issues

Communication

Good communication involves knowing your needs and expressing them. Melissa kept her needs to herself because she didn't want to interfere with Randy's excitement. Over time, she became angry and resentful. It's so important, especially in times of major life changes, to communicate as much and as clearly as possible. Melissa should have voiced her concerns before they became a major problem. Randy, on the other hand, should have made a special effort to ask Melissa to share her thoughts and emotions about moving.

Randy was so sure he wanted this job that his excitement made it difficult for Melissa to say otherwise. He assumed her silence meant that everything was okay. She didn't know how to talk about it, and initially didn't even realize she was upset. Good communication involves taking the time and effort to discuss issues before they have a chance to fester.

Managing the Stress of Moving

Making the decision to relocate to a new place is a major one. It's very important to think through many issues, not only one person's job. Both people need to discuss the pros and cons of all the factors.

The Conclusion

Melissa and Randy finally had the discussion they should have had in the beginning. Melissa told Randy all of her concerns about moving. As Randy was listening, he felt overwhelmed with emotion. He knew Melissa was upset, but he didn't have any idea how difficult this whole issue had been for her. He admitted that he had been so excited about the move that he hadn't given Melissa any opportunity to express her concerns.

Randy apologized and suggested they consider the move temporary. They would return within two years if Melissa was unhappy. Melissa agreed and was quite relieved. She still wasn't thrilled about moving, but when she thought about it being for only two years, she could tolerate the idea. She started sleeping better and overall felt less anxious and worried.

As it turned out, Randy was the one who wanted to move back to their old city. He was unhappy in his new job and was offered a position at his old company. Melissa had been pleasantly surprised at how easily she had made friends. It was a good experience for her and increased her self-confidence. When they did move back, it was Randy who was thrilled to return and Melissa who was sad about leaving her new friends.

Take the time and effort to communicate before little problems become big ones!

Case 4: Angela and Barry

The Problem

Angela and Barry had been married for five years and had bought a house. Barry had been married before and had started his current marriage with significant credit-card debt. Their finances had become extremely tight when Barry could no longer work full-time. He had reinjured his back while doing some home repairs. Angela was very angry because she had warned him not to attempt the home repairs by himself, but he hadn't listened.

Paying the mortgage, alimony to his ex-wife, and his old credit-card debt became impossible—they declared bankruptcy and had to move out of their house. Angela was furious. She blamed Barry for the fact that they lost their house. In a fit of anger she yelled, "Our life is falling apart and it's all your fault! You never listen to me when I tell you anything. I warned you not to try to fix the plumbing yourself! You're so careful to save money on a plumber, but half our money goes out in alimony and your debt. You're such a loser!"

The Questions

➤ What is going on?

➤ Who is at fault?

➤ What should they do?

The Issues

Dealing with Illness

Barry didn't accept his limitations. He tried to repair the kitchen plumbing even though he knew he had a bad back. If he had acknowledged to himself that he had a physical problem, he wouldn't have attempted to perform the activities that caused the injuries that caused him to decrease his work hours. But, once he did reinjure his back, it was destructive for Angela to blame him for his injury. Even though she was angry with her husband for not listening to her, yelling at him was not constructive. Rather, she should help him take better care of himself in the future.

Second Marriages

Angela needs to accept that alimony is part of their budget. She married Barry knowing full well that he had been married before and had monthly alimony payments. To bring up this unpleasant fact in the middle of an argument is unproductive and will cause resentment.

Conflict Resolution

One-liners such as "You're a loser" stop an argument. The only thing they accomplish is to make the other person feel bad. Long after the argument is forgotten, that one-liner will be remembered. Don't take cheap shots at your spouse. You certainly don't want your spouse to take them at you.

Finances

A reduction in income is very stressful. It's particularly important to go through your budget, think through all of your options, and reorganize your lives accordingly. You need to look for solutions, not blame each other for the problems.

The Conclusion

Barry didn't know how to respond to Angela. He was hurt and furious. Barry already felt like a loser, and Angela's comment just made him feel worse. Angela remained furious and would not apologize for her comments.

Barry and Angela have reached a crisis point in their marriage and are unwilling to take responsibility for their roles in the difficulties in their marriage. They are under financial stress and don't have the tools to make important decisions together. They went to a course of couples therapy to help them through their difficult times.

Be careful what you say in times of crisis—your comments will be remembered!

Case 5: Denise and Chuck

The Problem

Denise and Chuck have been married for 17 years and have two teenage children. On the surface, their relationship seems okay—they rarely argue, all of the chores and errands get divided up fairly, and they generally keep their expenses within their budget. Their children are reasonably content and, so far, have done well in school and are involved in after-school activities.

But Denise has been unhappy for many years. She feels her life and her marriage are absolutely empty. Many nights she cries herself to sleep. Denise feels she works hard to be a good wife and mother, but her efforts go unnoticed. She feels there is no passion left in her marriage. Denise would like her marriage to be better, but she has no idea what to do. She assumes that her husband Chuck is reasonably content with their life.

Denise and Chuck had a great marriage for the first several years. When they had their second child, Denise stayed home with their children while Chuck became more involved with his work. Rather than partners, they started living parallel lives. Over time, they stopped talking about what happened in each of their days. Denise assumed that Chuck wasn't interested in the details of her day with the kids, and Chuck assumed that Denise wasn't interested in his day at work.

They spent most of their leisure time with the children. Although they did go out by themselves on most weekends, they usually went to a movie and didn't spend time talking with each other. They went on vacations with their children and had not been away overnight together in many years. Denise and Chuck have drifted apart over the years.

The Questions

> ➤ What is going on here?

> ➤ Is anybody at fault?

> ➤ What can Denise and Chuck do to improve their marriage?

The Issues

Communication

Denise has many strong feelings that she is not sharing with her husband: she wants the passion back, she wants the excitement back, and she wants to have something to look forward to. But before her marriage will improve, Denise needs to make her needs clear to both her husband and herself. Sitting around feeling sorry for herself is not going to solve anything.

Lack of Effort

Chuck and Denise have put very little effort into their marriage for many years. They are assuming that it should just run on its own, but they have barely had an intimate conversation with each other for years! They have forgotten how to discuss their innermost feelings, their needs, and their dreams. Rather than always going to a movie, they should start taking walks together or go out to dinner so that they have a chance to talk.

Children Affect Your Marriage

Chuck and Denise's marriage changed dramatically when they had their second child. Somehow they each stopped caring about what the other person did all day. That lack of concern causes staleness in a marriage. It's a bad habit that's easy to change. Chuck and Denise should set aside time every day to greet each other warmly and ask about each other's day. They should go away overnight at least once a year without the kids. Spending time away from home with each other will invigorate their marriage. If Denise and Chuck don't put effort into their marriage, no one else will!

The Conclusion

In trying to sort out their marital problems, Denise realized that she was fixated on the fact that her children would soon be moving out of the house. She knew she would be devastated. Denise began talking about this all of the time with Chuck. He suggested she see a therapist, and Denise reluctantly agreed.

In therapy, it became clear that Denise received the majority of her self-esteem from her children. As they were growing up and needed her less, she felt a sense of emptiness. The therapist worked with her about ways she could grow as a person. The therapist also suggested that she bring in her husband so that they could work directly on marital issues in couples therapy.

Therapy helped Denise and Chuck understand the issues that were interfering with their marriage. Over time, they began to put more effort into their marriage. They spent time talking, went out of their way to do nice things for each other, and planned their first vacation in many years. Denise went back to work and developed hobbies that she enjoyed. Over time, Denise began to feel complete as an individual, as well as part of a married couple.

Marriage can be wonderful, but you *have to make it happen!*

Quizzes

Over time, you'll notice that your ability to use the tools you have learned in this book will grow. It will become easier for you to communicate, easier for you to understand what your relationship obstacles are, and easier for you to handle difficult situations. To reinforce the ideas you have learned, we have chosen several quizzes that will be valuable for you to take again and again. These quizzes are also valuable for your spouse to take, both as a learning tool and as a way to begin discussions on some difficult topics. It's also helpful for you to review your answers to these quizzes, as your answers may change over time. You can monitor your own growth as well as see areas for potential growth in your relationship.

These extra quizzes have been taken from the following chapters:

➤ **Think Positive! Quiz**—Chapter 2, "Obstacles to a Perfect Marriage"

➤ **Rate Your Date**—Chapter 4, "Keeping the Passion Alive"

➤ **Expectations Quiz**—Chapter 10, "…For Richer, For Poorer"

➤ **Intimacy Quiz, Intimacy Quiz (For Women Only), Intimacy Quiz (For Men Only)**—Chapter 12, "My Pillow Is Your Pillow"

➤ **Priority Quiz**—Chapter 18, "Employed, Unemployed, Reemployed"

Think Positive! Quiz

1. List your spouse's three greatest qualities.

   a) _____

   b) _____

   c) _____

2. What most attracted you to your spouse when you first met him or her?

   _____

   _____

   _____

3. What do you like most about your spouse's sense of humor?

   _____

   _____

   _____

4. Write down a description of the most romantic evening you ever spent with your spouse.

   _____

   _____

   _____

5. What are some positive things people say about your spouse?

   _____

   _____

   _____

Rate Your Date

1. How often do you and your spouse go out alone?

    1   2   3   4   5

2. Do you do things that are fun for both of you?

    1   2   3   4   5

3. Do you spend time getting ready to go out for the date?

    1   2   3   4   5

4. Do you ever plan ahead for your dates?

    1   2   3   4   5

5. If so, do you look forward to them?

    1   2   3   4   5

6. Do you focus on your spouse's good qualities when you're out together?

    1   2   3   4   5

7. Do you leave your grudges at home before you go out with your spouse?

    1   2   3   4   5

8. Do you feel you can have a good time with your spouse without spending a lot of money?

    1   2   3   4   5

Expectations Quiz

1. Are you living the lifestyle, more or less, that you envisioned you would?

       1   2   3   4   5

2. Do you feel you make enough money?

       1   2   3   4   5

3. Do you feel your spouse makes enough money?

       1   2   3   4   5

4. Most of the time, are you able to afford the things you want to buy?

       1   2   3   4   5

5. Do you and your spouse tend to agree about money issues?

       1   2   3   4   5

6. Do you have enough money to feel secure?

       1   2   3   4   5

7. Do you save a reasonable amount of money every year?

       1   2   3   4   5

8. Are you able to spend a reasonable amount of money on yourself?

       1   2   3   4   5

9. Do you try not to blame your spouse for not making enough money?

       1   2   3   4   5

10. Do you and your spouse have a workable household budget?

       1   2   3   4   5

Intimacy Quiz

1. Do you find it hard to make the transition from being a responsible adult to being relaxed enough to enjoy sex?

   Yes   or   No

2. Is sex a relatively low priority in your relationship with your spouse?

   Yes   or   No

3. Do you feel distracted much of the time when you have sex with your spouse?

   Yes   or   No

4. Has your general sex drive diminished since you have been married?

   Yes   or   No

5. Are you often exhausted when you have sex with your spouse?

   Yes   or   No

6. If you have children, do they interfere with your privacy?

   Yes   or   No

Intimacy Quiz (For Women Only)

1. How often do you accept your husband's advances?

      1   2   3   4   5

2. Do you feel relaxed with your husband in the bedroom?

      1   2   3   4   5

3. Are you clear with your husband about when you want to have sex?

      1   2   3   4   5

4. Does your husband try to please you?

      1   2   3   4   5

5. Do you communicate to your husband what you like?

      1   2   3   4   5

Intimacy Quiz (For Men Only)

1. How often do you accept your wife's advances?

         1   2   3   4   5

2. Do you think about your wife's sexual needs?

         1   2   3   4   5

3. Do you create a romantic atmosphere if you are interested in sex?

         1   2   3   4   5

4. Does your wife try to please you?

         1   2   3   4   5

5. Do you communicate to your wife what you like?

         1   2   3   4   5

Priority Quiz

1. I try to be in a good mood at work.

   True or False

2. I try to look my best at work.

   True or False

3. I generally give my undivided attention to my work.

   True or False

4. I put my best foot forward at work.

   True or False

5. I would never be late for work.

   True or False

6. I give 100 percent effort to my work.

   True or False

7. I try to be flexible at work.

   True or False

8. I am reliable at work.

   True or False

9. I am committed to my work.

   True or False

10. I am loyal to my work.

    True or False

11. I try to be in a good mood for my spouse.

    True or False

continues

continued

12. I try to look my best for my spouse.

    True   or   False

13. I generally give my undivided attention to my spouse.

    True   or   False

14. I put my best foot forward for my spouse.

    True   or   False

15. I would never be late for my spouse.

    True   or   False

16. I give 100 percent effort in my relationship with my spouse.

    True   or   False

17. I try to be flexible with my spouse.

    True   or   False

18. I am reliable for my spouse.

    True   or   False

19. I am committed to my spouse.

    True   or   False

20. I am loyal to my spouse.

    True   or   False

Index

D

U-V

W-Z